CHILDREN OF MAO

Also by Anita Chan

CHEN VILLAGE: The Recent History of a Peasant Community
in Mao's China
(*with R. Madsen and J. Unger*)

ON SOCIALIST DEMOCRACY AND
THE CHINESE LEGAL SYSTEM
(*co-edited with S. Rosen and J. Unger*)

CHILDREN OF MAO

*Personality Development and Political Activism
in the Red Guard Generation*

Anita Chan

University of Washington Press
Seattle

Printed in Hong Kong

Library of Congress Cataloging in Publication Data

Chan, Anita.
  Children of Mao.

  Bibliography: p.
  Includes index.
  1. Youth—China—Political activity. 2. Political
socialization—China. 3. China—History—Cultural
Revolution, 1966–1969. I. Title.
HQ799.C5C47 1985   305.2′3′0951   84–21944
ISBN 0–295–96212–7

For my parents, Chan Chok-hon
and Ko Kwan-ying

Contents

Acknowledgements

The writing of this book has been a valuable experience, not only in wrestling with sociological concepts but also in sensitizing me to the tone of life in modern China. In Hong Kong, I am indebted to all of those who allowed me to interview them and who shared with me some of their deeper feelings. My appreciation goes also to the dozen and more young emigrants from China, including several of the interviewees, who became lasting friends and who, during long informal discussions, provided repeated insights about Chinese society. In particular, Huang Wangchao has contributed a number of crucial ideas and formulations to the study.

Above all, heartfelt gratitude goes to Professor Ronald Dore, my doctoral supervisor, who provided stimulating guidance and encouragement from the initial conception of the project onward. I am indebted also to my husband Jonathan Unger for sharing his extensive interview notes with me, for the many hours of discussion we have had and for reading and providing suggestions on the manuscript. So too, Stanley Rosen, Rudolf Wagner, Paul Levine and Richard Kirby are owed thanks for reading and commenting critically on sections of the original manuscript. My friend Ng Chung-yin, another reader, helped introduce me to a deeper understanding of politics in general and Chinese politics in particular.

The fieldwork was conducted in office-space provided by the Universities Service Centre in Hong Kong, whose staff are owed appreciation for their helpfulness. The University of Kansas and its Centre for East Asian Studies graciously provided office-space and typing facilities. My thanks go also to Maureen Dickson, Nancy Kaul and Sandee Kennedy for typing the successive drafts.

1 Introduction

I constantly had been studying Mao's works. So I often gave other people the first choice of a good place to sleep and carried them water to drink – showed my good heart. It was so natural. I'd been a Study Mao's Thought Counsellor for so many years and had studied revolutionary models like Lei Feng, Wang Jie, Norman Bethune and Zhang Side; I had absorbed it from them. I followed their example and let Mao's thought influence my behaviour. I was studying and using Mao's thought in a lively manner.

Scepticism is aroused when one comes upon such proclamations in the Chinese mass media of the 1960s and 1970s. The fervor seems affected, overblown and unbelievable, and might easily be dismissed as clumsily contrived propaganda.

Yet this quotation is not taken from any official Chinese publication. It is from a taped conversation in 1975 with a young woman in Hong Kong – recounting, ironically, her behaviour while in a Chinese prison. Her political commitment to Maoist teachings had been shared, in the course of growing up, by most of my interviewees, all of them emigrants of the Red Guard generation.

The acting out of this devotion is known in China as 'political activism'. This book will examine how and why some of China's urban young people became fervent political activists, why so many became zealous Red Guards in the Cultural Revolution, and why they divided into rival factions that battled each other in defence of Chairman Mao.

The study will also be delving into the social psychology of this first generation brought up under socialism: with findings some readers may find controversial. In the course of my research, I gradually but ineluctably have been drawn to the conclusion that young interviewees of very different dispositions had shared in what the Frankfurt School of social scientists has called the 'authoritarian personality'.

It shall be observed, moreover, that the authoritarian beliefs and emotional needs that these young people held in common were not so

1

much a product of their parents' influence but rather a product of their political socialization[1] at school. And it shall be seen that those young people who strove hardest to live up to the Maoist credo, and who therefore were officially recognized as political activists, tended to develop more highly authoritarian personality traits than their less devoted or less politically successful schoolmates.

I am not suggesting, however, that the school authorities or the Communist Party leadership had consciously tried to instill in the children the extreme form of authoritarian traits that surfaced in the fanaticism of the Cultural Revolution. Party educators had been bent merely on encouraging highly moralistic and disciplined behaviour that was in keeping with the teachings of Mao. But we shall see that the very system by which these teachings were promoted created competitive aspirations to prove personal devotion, instilled exaggerated needs to conform to political orthodoxy, and encouraged strong prejudices against outcaste groups. In the urban high schools of the 1960s, I shall show, the 'authoritarian personality' became the dominant social character of these children of Mao – with devastating results in the Cultural Revolution.

It shall also be seen that personality traits, once formed, are not necessarily permanently fixed. In the emotionally shattering aftermath of the Cultural Revolution fighting, the same young adults became politically 'desocialized'. With peer-group constraints disintegrating and their ideological beliefs thrown sharply into doubt, their conformity to the authoritarian social character tended to fade.

I do not want to dwell long here on the themes of the authoritarian personality and its erosion, before laying out my evidence about the effects of political socialization on the Red Guard generation. The book's concluding chapter will attempt to put the empirical data in theoretical perspective, and at that point readers will be able to judge for themselves whether my conclusions are convincing.

METHODOLOGY AND SAMPLE

I was drawn to this study of Chinese youths after several brief encounters in Hong Kong in 1971 with a small group of young people who had just come from China. Cantonese myself, brought up in a British colony perched on China's coast, it was astonishing to me to encounter the vast difference between these former Red Guards from Canton and us Hong Kong young people. The accent of Cantonese that they spoke was not in the slightest different from ours, but that very fact served to accentuate the other aspects of their speech which sounded odd to our ears. It was the different vocabulary they employed, and the meanings and connotations behind that vocabulary, and the experience and worldview behind that, which set them off from us. I was intrigued by the differences.

In 1974, I returned to Hong Kong to conduct my doctoral field-research. Through the former Red Guards I had met three years before, I established contacts first with their friends and then with friends of friends. Because these acquaintances were made by personal introduction, there was an atmosphere of trust when we first met. They had some idea of who I was, what my area of research covered, why I wanted to meet them; and I, too, had a general idea of who they were, what their backgrounds were, what their activities had been during the Cultural Revolution, and their current situation. I began to see them frequently, sometimes individually, sometimes in groups. Gradually, most of them informally began to study English with me, some individually and some in twos or threes. I have tutored in this way eleven out of the fourteen people whom I have interviewed in depth.[2] I liked this arrangement because it allowed me, in good conscience, to request formal lengthy interviews with them without putting any of them in the embarrassing position of being a 'paid informant'. On their part, they enjoyed having one more friend to confide in; and some did have an urge to tell an outsider about their own life experiences and about what they know best – China. By the time the interviewing ended in 1976, I had come to count several of them among my best friends.

With each of the fourteen I used a lengthy questionnaire of mainly open-ended questions. Interviewees were encouraged to digress into anecdotes and topics of their own. Each session lasted two to three hours and, on average, eight to ten such sessions were conducted with each interviewee. All of these were taped, translated *verbatim* from Cantonese into English, and transcribed.

Many more hours were spent together in restaurants and at their homes and mine, chatting, gossiping, discussing. As a result, though there were moments of hesitation and distinct embarrassment when they had to reveal inner feelings during interviews, our mutual familiarity lessened the difficulties. The rationalizations they sometimes offered were not so hard to detect once I had come to know them well personally, and, indeed, the awareness that they felt defensive or embarrassed over particular incidents provided additional food for analysis.

Most of these young people happened to share two things in common. First, the majority of them had a similar officially-designated class label (*jieji chengfen*). These labels referred to the occupational status of the head of one's family at the time of Liberation in 1949. They were kept in government dossiers and were inheritable in the male line. In China, it was officially argued that people of 'good' class labels (people who at the time of Liberation were workers or poor peasants or members of the Communist Party) would normally hold to more revolutionary attitudes, and that those of 'bad' class background (the families of the former capitalists, landlords, rich peasants and Guomindang [Kuomintang] officials) would generally still hold to suspect political attitudes. These attitudes, it was believed, tended to be transmitted, at least to some degree, from parent to child.

The class labels of my interviewees affected their lives enormously. The new government's perception of them – what became their ascriptive political status – went a long way in determining their standing in school and their chances for upward mobility, and became reflected in the youths' views of themselves.

Most of them had been classified as members of the petty-bourgeoisie, the 'middling' (*yiban*) category, which ranged from families of the old pre-revolution literati to families of pre-revolution street peddlars. Within this broad range, most of my interviewees had been subclassified as of 'intelligentsia family' origins, which meant their parents before Liberation had belonged to a social grouping equivalent to Western society's 'white-collar workers', covering the spectrum from professionals to teachers to office clerks.

These families have had an ambiguous political status. Mao's famous 'Analysis of the Classes in Chinese Society', written in 1926, had portrayed the petty-bourgeoisie in terms of their revolutionary potential, as comprising a right wing, a middle and a left wing:

> In normal times these three sections of the petty-bourgeoisie differ in their attitude to the revolution. But in time of war, that is, when the tide of the revolution runs high and the dawn of victory is in sight, not only will the left-wing of the petty-bourgeoisie join the revolution, but the middle section too may join, and even the right wingers, swept forward by the great revolutionary tide of the proletariat and of the left-wing of the petty-bourgeoisie, will have to go along with the revolution.[3]

On this basis, the petty-bourgeoisie was closely watched after the revolution, to distinguish the genuine supporters of the revolution from those of the hidden right wing who had shifted only momentarily to the proletarian camp. Thus the petty-bourgeoisie were trapped, from the 1950s onward, in the awkward position of being at once trusted and distrusted. Their children at school had to learn at times to walk the same tightrope.

In reality, the parents of most of my interviewees fell within the ranks of the middle and left-wing petty-bourgeoisie. Most of them in the 1940s had supported the Communists over the inefficient and spectacularly corrupt Guomindang government. They were also patriotic; in fact, not a few of the parents had *chosen* to remain in China, though they could freely have left Canton for Hong Kong in the days immediately after Liberation. Seeing the country in a shambles after decades of war, they were prepared to offer their services to building up the nation and, more specifically, to constructing socialism. They believed that China had great need for their professional skills and education. These perspectives shall be seen in the following chapters to have influenced their children's attitudes in quite specific ways.

While the first common denominator of my interviews lies in their middle-class backgrounds, their second shared attribute regards the role they played in the Cultural Revolution. Most of them had thrown themselves wholeheartedly into the upheaval. Two of them, indeed, rose to be the two top leaders of the secondary-school Rebel Red Guards in Canton, and several others were leaders in their own schools or work units. It was precisely their activities and attitudes as Red Guards which first drew me to focus on the relationship between political activism and the authoritarian personality.

To what extent can we base a study of politically active Chinese youths on this handful of respondents? To what degree can we generalize? That the interviewees are no longer residents of the People's Republic of China certainly suggests a possible bias. There is the normal worry that 'refugees' from socialist countries tend to see things through right-wing anti-Communist spectacles. That was not, however, the case here; the political critiques of China on the part of my interviewees only rarely were politically conservative. But even such a comment is beside the point. Their current attitudes towards China are not what we are concerned with in this study. Our interest is in certain aspects of growing up in China, and as teenagers these young people had been firm believers. Readers will soon discover for themselves how devoted they had, in fact, once been to the party credo. Indeed, it was the intensity of this devotion, their righteous intolerance of any deviant beliefs, that constitutes the major subjects of this study.

My interview sample still does have a strong bias – it focuses, we have seen, on young people from one type of inherited class status. But as long as this is taken into account in the analysis, the bias does not invalidate the study or its conclusions. Through the collective recollections of the interviewees, it is possible to gain a perspective on the situation of young people of the urban middle stratum; and by way of that group's circumstances, I believe, we can formulate some generalizations about Chinese society as a whole. Kenneth Keniston's *Young Radicals – Notes on Committed Youths* reveals, in juxtaposition to its main topic, something about the *non*-committed young Americans of the 1960s; Oscar Lewis's *Children of Sanchez* focuses on Mexican slum life but in the process tells us something more general about both poverty and Mexico. In the same way, but with more modest aims, this study can also provide a deeper understanding of other types of young people in China.

POLITICAL ACTIVISM

This is a study of young 'political activists' – that is, those who were actively committed. But the words 'political activist' (*jijifenzi*) must be comprehended in the context of China's political system.

Genuine political activists were, first and foremost, supposed to be total believers in party teachings. The ethical and utopian character of these teachings was supposed to provide them with an anchor, an ultimate meaning. A central part of their belief was that, through widespread commitment on the part of the masses, China could be remade into a prosperous and politically pure society. The activists, through their enthusiasm, were to serve as catalysts for mobilizing the masses: the vital link between the Truth held at the top and the ability to implement that truth at the grassroots. They were not only to help launch and organize a mass upsurge of participation during campaigns, but also, at ordinary times, to 'cultivate' the masses' enthusiasm.

In line with Leninist beliefs, only disciplined organizations could move history forward; only through active membership would one's own contributions become truly efficacious. Activists were supposed to strive to join the elite Communist Party or, if younger, the Communist Youth League. In exchange for the chance to be an integral part of the 'revolutionary vanguard', they were supposed to submit themselves willingly to the needs of their organization. They were supposed to find emotional security and satisfaction in this: to be bound into a fellowship that reinforced their commitment.

Former activists, when asked about activism or about activist organizations, often turned to the word 'glorious' (*guangrong*), connoting both spiritual achievement and personal prestige. That was the nub of a major dilemma. Activism could bring status and local fame – and sometimes, in addition, opportunities for personal aggrandizement and even material gain. These latter were, to be sure, the very rewards that a genuinely committed activist was not supposed deliberately to seek. They were supposed to steel themselves, constantly, repeatedly, against the allures of self-interest. They were to do so in order to preserve their own righteous integrity and commitment and in order to serve as a proper model for the 'masses'.

The problem was that the various rewards for successful activism provided a strong temptation for ambitious young people with ulterior motives to perform in an energetically, devotedly, ostentatiously activist fashion. People who, in this manner, performed the activist role without possessing genuinely activist convictions were known as 'phoney activists' (*jia jiji*); and some Chinese suspected that most of the activists whom they knew were, in fact, insincere opportunists. There evolved a saying: 'In front, one set [of behaviour]; behind, another set [of beliefs].' Given the potential rewards, those who were genuinely activist (*zhen jiji*) always faced a major difficulty in proving that their public conformity to the activist norms was motivated by a genuine inner adherence to the values.

Of my fourteen interviewees, eleven claimed to have been genuinely committed to the activist course at certain periods in their lives. But most of them – eight of the eleven – never succeeded in obtaining any rewards or power. Such interviewees shall be classified in this book as 'unrecognized activists'. In contradistinction, activists who were deemed suitable to serve as leaders among their peers and were, therefore, vested with the power to carry out a leadership role shall be called 'official activists'. In primary schools, such activists were the student cadres, in secondary schools the Communist Youth League members and, as adults, the party members. Three of my interviewees, as teenagers, had climbed into positions of official activism.

To be sure, the various people who sought the activist path were not of one kind; they were driven by different needs, and their proclivities as activists differed accordingly. Bearing this in mind, from my eleven interviewees with activist inclinations I have chosen four for special description here. I have selected these four precisely because they diverged so sharply from one another as personalities and in their particular modes of activism. Of special importance, each of these four activists was very differently oriented towards authority. This particular dimension is significant because activism, after all, fundamentally involves positive responses to the demands of authority. Since we shall be exploring the links between activism and authoritarianism later, we shall, in particular, want to view how the attitudes of young people who were differently oriented towards authority were influenced by the activist roles they played.

The four chosen interviewees – Ao, Bai, Chang and Deng – were so distinctly inclined towards different types of activism that at times they almost seem to fall neatly into stereotyped images. For heuristic purposes I will be taking the liberty, hence, of affixing to each of them a descriptive label. Ao was a *conforming activist*. She was committed to the values, but her predominant concern was to conform diligently to the proper behavioural norms. She was invariably on the side of authority, uncritical and a faithful follower. Bai, the *purist activist*, also conformed to the norms expected of an activist, but held on to the values so religiously and with such compelling passion that he could not tolerate the human failings of ordinary activists. He strove for the absolute, allowing no compromise for anything less than the ideal. Under the dictates of a higher truth, he had no qualms in criticizing mere authority figures when he was convinced that they had misinterpreted the values. Chang, our *rebellious activist*, internalized the values but rebelled against authority and generally rejected the norms it imposed. He refused to recognize conformity to official norms as a fair measure of activism. Deng, our *pragmatic activist*, conformed to the norms and adopted the values, but with considerably less emotional attachment than Ao, Bai or Chang. When observing the norms, he was by far the most careful of the four in ensuring that his efforts did not go against his self-interests.

My depiction of this activist quartet by no means provides an exhaustive taxonomic classification of the types of possible activism. Moreover, at one time or another in the course of growing up, none of these young people fit consistently the thumbnail sketches of them that have been presented here. It is only in the summation of their adherence to values and behavioural patterns that we can assign them to these different modes of activist behaviour.

The attributes which we have noted for these four different young activists can be presented diagrammatically, as shown in Figure 1.

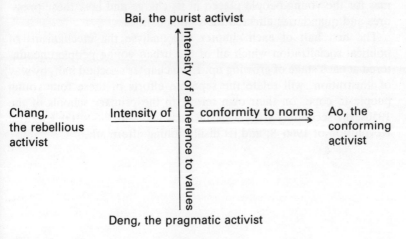

Bai, the purist activist

Chang, the rebellious activist

Intensity of conformity to norms

Intensity of adherence to values

Ao, the conforming activist

Deng, the pragmatic activist

FIGURE 1

Of these two dimensions of genuine activism, as noted earlier, only the activist's conformity to the activist norms could be judged by outside observers; one's inner convictions could never readily be measured. It is not at all surprising, thus, that the enthusiastically conforming activist, Ao, was selected as an official activist at an early age; nor was it surprising that the rebellious activist, Chang, remained among the unrecognized activists. By happenstance, another in our sample, Deng, was accepted into the Communist Youth League only in his last month of senior high school. For most of his student years, he endured the same unrecognized status as Chang; while Bai, like Ao, rose in high school to become a cadre in the Communist Youth League. By selecting Ao, Bai, Chang and Deng as our four case studies, then, we will be able to study, through paired examples, the different roles and circumstances of official and unrecognized activists. These differences will be important to explore; as shall be seen, belonging to one or the other status influenced behaviour quite differently.

I shall be interested here not directly in the attributes and activities of mature activists, but rather in the question of how four children of very different dispositions became activists of different types. The four case studies will accordingly provide us with an opportunity to view in some detail, and from different angles, how the system of political socialization was structured. Their stories will illustrate how the system's demands created certain important tensions and dilemmas for the young people placed in its charge and how these pressures and quandaries affected their personalities.

The first half of each chapter will analyse the mechanisms of political socialization which all of the urban young people encountered at each stage of growing up. Each chapter's second half, by way of illustration, will relate the separate efforts of these four young people to cope, on their own terms, in the primary schools of the 1950s, the secondary schools of the early and mid-1960s, the Cultural Revolution of 1966–8, and its disillusioning aftermath.

2 Political Education and Character Formation in Primary School

I joined the Young Pioneers on June 1, 1956. I can remember the date well. We went to the fire brigade building for the ceremony. My heart was jumping. It was a grand ceremony, very solemn. All the Pioneers of the school were there. A band composed of Young Pioneers was beating drums. With all the drumming, the Young Pioneers anthem, and the older Young Pioneers putting the red scarf on for us, it was the most emotional experience I'd ever had. I thought of it as the beginning of my political life. There was an oath to take. The most serious parts were 'to be prepared every second' and 'to struggle all our lives'. These few sentences were a must to memorize. But at that time it was already chiselled into our minds to struggle for Communism, though to tell the truth we didn't yet quite know what Communism was.

Interviewee Bai, Hong Kong, 1976

Primary school teaching staffs were supposed to devote much of their energy to instilling the type of emotional attachment to party teachings that Bai expresses here. The successes achieved in this regard during the 1950s were remarkable considering the difficulties facing the school system's administrators. At the time of urban China's 'Liberation' in 1949, the vast majority of the teachers had not necessarily shared the party's goals in education; quite the contrary, they had been trained (if they had been trained at all) in 'petty-bourgeois' teachers' institutes. Party educators not only needed to reshape what went on in these teachers' classrooms. At the same time, they needed to train a vast new army of teachers to accomplish the party's promise of a mass system of elementary education. The scope of that mission can be seen in the following numbers: in 1950 China counted 29 million elementary school pupils; by the end of the

11

decade, in 1959, the primary school population had expanded to 90 million.[1]

In this massive effort to triple the primary-school population in so short a period, the government found it could not hope to supervise rigorously the education offered by rural teachers. But, in what effectively became a bifurcation of China's education system, the state mounted a very concerted drive to transform the thinking and practices of urban teachers. This effort was reflected in the contents of the education journals of the 1950s, which were filled with articles demanding that teachers adopt a new conception of children.[2] It is worth our while to consider briefly what the party educators were propounding.

THE PARTY'S PEDAGOGIC TEACHINGS AND DEWEYISM

The 'new socialist men' whom the school system was supposed to mould were pictured as possessing two contradictory sets of attributes: on the one side, consciously self-abnegating and submissive to the collective; and on the other, self-motivated, purposive and creative. The teacher's job was to help shape the children's beliefs in such a way that they would encounter no conflicts in trying to accommodate the two contrasting demands.

In line with Russian views in the field of child psychology, Chinese journals emphasized that a child was a unique personality to be respected and 'nurtured'. Physical punishment and scolding, which were liberally employed in traditional Chinese pedagogy, were absolutely forbidden. Physical punishment, it was pointed out, only stifled creativity and encouraged resentment and unreasonableness in a child. Any passive submissiveness exhibited by children out of fear of punishment were to be considered as merely superficial displays of conformity.[3]

The new pedagogic tracts devoted repeated attention to the Marxist principle of uniting theory with practice, arguing that learning should originate from a child's observations of the environment and from the child's acting upon the environment.[4] On the premise that man's nature is malleable, all children were to be viewed as full of potentials awaiting the correct stimulation to help them develop.[5]

However, the authorities' views on childhood creativity were not quite what they might seem at first glance – as can be seen by the government's concerted efforts to root out the influence of Deweyite theories.[6] Even though popular thinking in China still adhered to Confucian notions about education, it was John Dewey, the famous liberal American educator, whose philosophy was popular among China's non-Marxist progressives,[7] who most frequently was targeted for verbal onslaught in the education journals of the 1950s.[8]

What was it in Dewey's educational theory about which the Chinese Communists felt so antagonistic? It would appear, after all, that many of the pedagogic principles professed by the Chinese (and their mentors, the Soviet educators) were in considerable agreement with Dewey's educational philosophy. Both Dewey's and the Chinese party educators' pedagogic writings, for example, were directed towards radically overturning traditional educational practices that stifled the individual development of children.[9] The child ought to be given, according to Dewey, the responsibility and opportunities for self-initiative: learning was to be an active process rather than a passive receptive experience. Rote memorization was declared anathema to the learning process. Dewey believed that children learned through their own motor activities and should therefore be encouraged to engage in *doing* things. It was an idea somewhat similar to the Marxist precept of uniting theory and practice.

With Dewey also, voluntary adherence to values was regarded as essential, in contradistinction to overt conformity through fear of authority. Like China's Marxists, Dewey believed, too, that education should be geared to the promotion of personal development, with a social end.[10] Both Dewey and the party educators advocated, moreover, that education should repudiate as a goal the ranking and sorting of children in terms of their intellectual abilities. However, despite these broad areas of similarities between his teachings and the Communists' (similarities which Dewey himself had recognized on his trip to Russia in 1928),[11] a fundamental difference in ideas remained. Though the two schools of pedagogy converged in their concern for the nurturant development of children's potentials, Dewey's teachings clashed with that second half of the party's conception of the 'new socialist man': a consciously self-abnegating person responsive to collective needs.

For precisely this reason, the Chinese attacks against Dewey focused on his idea of 'learning by doing'. Dewey's theory of practice argued for allowing a child maximum initiative in acquiring knowledge from his or her own surroundings, with only limited direction from adults.[12] Children were encouraged to move freely in the classroom, each learning at his or her own fashion and pace. The child was to be encouraged to discover its own natural inclinations and its own natural course of development. Dewey believed that by doing things independently, using induction with very little overt interference from adults, children, from their own unconscious right feelings and right actions, would be able to develop a conscious understanding of the consequences of their actions and of the general moral principles involved.[13]

This pedagogic theory was anathema to Chinese educational authorities. When they talked of 'practice' for children, they meant activities that the children were to think of as efficacious in behalf of the greater cause:[14] such as helping the school to earn money through assembly-line labour.[15] Moreover, party educators decried the Deweyite ideal of children moving freely about in a classroom, each learning in an individual way, as intolerably chaotic. They were convinced that adult authority had the crucial role in the systematic transmission of knowledge, most importantly in moral and political values. They strongly believed that children had to start from an acceptance of authoritatively given 'right principles', to which they had to learn to conform. This training had to begin early; children in nursery schools were to learn to restrain themselves firmly from giving way to their whims and desires.[16] Primary school pupils were taught how to *fanxing* (a Confucian term meaning to reflect retrospectively) on how well they had controlled and channelled their behaviour each day. Dewey's ideas were viewed as subversive to the development of this requisite self-discipline.

Creativity was to be encouraged – but only within designated bounds. This can be illustrated by the educational authorities' views on children's art classes. In 1952 two books on primary school art education were severely criticized for allowing children too much spontaneity and freedom in their drawings, which was said to undermine the guiding role of the teacher.[17] Instead, children in primary school art classes were to be taught, as in traditional China, to copy their teachers' drawings. Art classes are conducted in this manner up to the present day.

In short, there was to be little encouragement for spontaneous expression. The colourful children's artwork which modern Western primary schools proudly display on classroom walls as spontaneous projections of the inner worlds and individuality of children was not to be found in Chinese classrooms.[18] Not only was art as an expression of the self not recognized in China; this lack of colourful displays probably also reflects the fact that to Chinese educators learning was conceived as duty more than fun. The serious purposiveness of education could be seen in the most heavily decorated corner of a classroom – the bulletin board – on which were pinned model essays written in the conventional moralizing style, a couple of carefully copied drawings, and special exhibits pertaining to whatever political campaign the schools at the time were pushing.

Chinese educational practices sharply differed from Deweyism, moreover, in the techniques used for motivating children. Dewey had been opposed to using competition among children as a spur to learning.[19] Contrarily, under the Chinese system children were prodded to compete fiercely with each other, not just in the academic sphere, but even more so in a display of political morality. Above all, they were to aspire to join the Leninist vanguard; and that meant competing to be among the select minority who could serve as Young Pioneer officers and Communist Youth League members, the most activist of the activist.

THE ORGANIZATION OF POLITICAL EDUCATION

This demand that children compete to show that they adhered to the proper values started early. All of the reading primers were heavily laden with morality tales,[20] and as the children learned to read, the teachers were supposed to teach them to abide by the moral/political messages. To make these political lessons more concrete to the pupils, the schools promoted a wide range of highly organized activities, and it was based on their enthusiastic participation in these activities that the children's political activism was to be judged.

Each week, at least one two-hour period was set aside for Young Pioneer activities, be it hobby clubs, voluntary labour for the school or song-and-dance peformances. To train the children to be socially conscious, they were organized to do token housework at old people's homes and to plant trees for the nation. They made rounds of the neighbourhoods in squads during holidays to pay their respects to the families of armymen, as the representatives of one glorious organization to another. They stood vigil to make sure people did not spit on the streets.

To make participation in these Young Pioneer activities appear a privilege rather than a chore, Young Pioneers was portrayed as a politically elite organization. In keeping with this image, when children became eligible to join, in the third grade, enrolment was

restricted to the best behaved, most enthusiastic and most academically diligent children. Then successive new crops of well-behaved
children were invited to join. By the end of the fourth grade, it was
made embarrassing to be left out, with a scarfless collar marking a
child as a naughty reject. To press home the message, in the final
years of primary school the decision on entry had been placed in the
hands of all the classmates who were members, through majority
vote. The school system was turning explicitly to peer-group pressures
to reward conformity and to impose sanctions against misbehaviour.

To enhance the concept of discipline, activities were usually played
out in tightly organized units. Each classroom was a 'company'
(*zhongdui*) headed by a student 'commander' and 'deputy commander'. Within the Pioneer company, each classroom row became a
Pioneer squad (*xiaodui*).

The most important of the squad's functions was to provide a
forum for children to learn how to behave in 'small group' political
discussions, which often took place following a school-wide Pioneer
assembly on the school's political topic of the week. In these small
groups of a dozen or so children, each pupil was to express his or her
opinion in turn, which often amounted to no more than mouthing
what had been announced earlier. Children were to learn through
this what their formal opinions and attitudes *ought* to be, and how
these had best be phrased; if, by error, they presented unorthodox
opinions they had acquired from home, the other children in the
small group were to criticize them.

Teachers could use these small group sessions to hint at an unruly
child's acts of misconduct (normally not naming the child openly, to
avoid humiliating the child too much). The better-behaved pupils,
getting the cue, each in turn would make comments like 'Chairman
Mao says we should help classmates. Why is it that one of us here
does just the opposite?' In primary school, the young activists were
still learning their paces. They were generally hesitant to criticize
classmates when not in the presence and under the gentle prodding of
the teacher. But by senior high school, such sessions rarely had to
include the teacher. The more activist students had almost entirely
taken over the teacher's role in pressuring their more backward peers
into conformity with prescribed behaviour.

In primary school classrooms, more than one kind of student
organization was established and these functioned together like the
several fingers of a single glove. They provided multiple means by
which the peer group could perform as agents and supervisors of their

own political socialization. For example, overlapping the Young Pioneer leadership was the class committee, composed of six to seven class cadres (*ban ganbu*) who divided among themselves the duties of overseeing the children's labour activities, academic study, entertainment, etc. Under this committee, each front-to-back row of seats in the classroom had a row-head who took charge of the daily activities of the students in that row, from lining up in the morning to leading study-group meetings. In all, about a third of the children in each classroom held responsibilities as an organizer or leader of one sort or another. This way, children learned early how to play two sets of roles: as leaders and as followers. They were learning in complex ways both how to work in a chain of command and how to take orders.

This system of intensely organized activity proved effective. A great many children were adopting the views and patterns of behaviour that were desired of them. But the school system's very successes posed a dilemma for educators. Chinese theory upheld the development of creativity and self-motivation, but the education system gave precedence to iron discipline and competitive submission to the collective and to higher authority.[21] Aware of this contradiction in their programme, party educators decided that at least a handful of China's youngest generation should be provided with opportunities to receive special training in creativity and independence, 'without the restrictions of classroom teaching'.[22] For this, they looked to a small number of specially contrived Children's Palaces on the Russian model. In confiscated mansions which had been converted for the purpose, selected children would be able to participate during their after-school hours in diverse kinds of stimulating hobbies and group projects, in line with their own inclinations. It was here that 'Deweyism' was to be applied in practice.

An article on the youth palaces was candid in sketching out the goals:

If we rely simply on classroom teaching . . . the children's thirst for knowledge . . . cannot be satisfied. Children's Palace, on the other hand, can supplement the schools to satisfy the children's needs . . . From the feeling that they themselves are today the masters of the Children's Palace, they can develop the idea that they have the capacities to take charge of our national society; from the ability independently and creatively to initiate all sorts of activities, they can develop the ability to seek out knowledge, to

better understand the world and be able to solve problems
independently.[23]

The programme became caught in a paradox. The several children
who were selected by each school to participate – children who had
become leaders in the Young Pioneers and were regarded as devout
child activists – tended almost by definition to be obedient in their
behaviour and conformist in attitude. The directors of the Children's
Palaces discovered to their own dismay that these selected children
were not enthusiastic either about initiating their own projects or
joining the group activities that aimed at stimulating creativity.
Conversely, a small group of children who had not been recommended by their schools, but who had applied to Children's Palaces
of their own accord, proved far more interested in, and far better
able to handle, the projects.[24]

What the school authorities had considered the cream of the
younger generation had not been eminently suited to take up the
challenge of self-expression and independent initiative. Herein lay a
major contradiction in the 'Leninist' pedagogy of China – the contradictory demand by the school system for children simultaneously to
conform and submit to authority and yet retain a sense of creativity
and initiative. In so far as the system was structured to reward
conformity, creativity was stifled. All of my interviewees had
struggled with this contradiction to a certain degree, some more
consciously, some less so. The four case studies will be illustrative of
this dilemma.

THE CONFORMING ACTIVIST AS A CHILD

Ao is now in her mid-thirties, a good-looking woman, intelligent but
not an intellectual. Her junior high school education and then ten
years of peasant life in the countryside as an 'educated youth'[25] had
not provided her with the same kind of intellectually stimulating
experiences that most of my other interviewees had acquired on city
streets during the turbulent days of the Cultural Revolution. Her
interest in and grasp of Marxist–Leninist political theory were minimal. Yet she was the 'reddest' of all my interviewees in the fullest
sense of the word. She had had an awesome capacity for accepting,
internalizing, memorizing by heart and reproducing word for word
the political messages and slogans of Maoist China. As a grassroots

cadre in the countryside, where it was her duty to transmit these slogans to the peasants, she had developed her skills to the point that the rhetoric still came naturally to her. It had become her *own* vocabulary.

As an interviewee she is marvellous: her narration is the least tarnished by her current interpretations and feelings. In recounting her story she can bring incidents vividly back to life, not because she is particularly good at story-telling – there are others better than she is at this. Rather, it is her unconscious way of extricating herself from the present and living momentarily in the past, as if she were reworking emotions which she had not completely expended. For instance, at times in telling her story she got so carried away in her excitement that her voice broke into the same cadence as Peking radio: the same high-pitched, urgent, imposing, strong, 'gung-ho' tone of voice. I have become convinced that she was able to do this so naturally only because she had internalized with the deepest conviction the same values propagated by the radio broadcasts.

She was also unusual in the extreme openness of her discourse about herself. She told of her embarrassing schemes, her quest for power and her failings with an honesty that at times was startling. This willingness to be self-critical was, it seems, a habit she had cultivated as a good Communist Youth League member. Through her, it is possible to gain an unusual feel for the inner frame of mind of a young person successfully weaned to the politically activist role.

Ao is the eldest of six children born into a middle-class family. Her official family class background label is 'intelligentsia', since her father was a doctor. Politically, he was a patriot, and intellectually a traditionalist. It was father who made them recite T'ang poetry and the formulae of traditional Chinese medicine, and who, even before they started schooling, daily had them practise Chinese calligraphy and Chinese painting. 'We recited and recited. He always told us how good in their studies our cousins were in Hong Kong, and that we must do the same. We must get our Master's degrees, become professors or engineers – that type of high-class job – so that we could contribute to the country. My parents felt that education would be the key to doing things in life. You would be better at things, and hence would help others and help yourself.' Influenced by such parental expectations, Ao adopted at an early age notions of the 'glory' of academic achievement: 'Even as a little girl, I wanted to be on top, educated, to be the *first*.'

These desires for educational achievement continued to pervade her thinking all through her years in school and even into adulthood. Despite great financial difficulties in Hong Kong, Ao tried to struggle through a degree at a junior college during the day and attended Chinese medicine classes in the evening. Her case is not unique. All but one of my fourteen interviewees grew up in this kind of achievement-oriented family environment, and in Hong Kong almost all of them, though in their early thirties, hoped, finances permitting, to take up some form of higher education: not necessarily to gain a career, but to fulfil their unrealized dreams of so many years.

Ao's father was no Marxist–Leninist, but Ao says of him, 'He likes the idea of socialism. He doesn't like Hong Kong.' When Ao finally decided in the mid-1970s to leave China, he was against it, not because it was dangerous but because he thought 'that type of society [Hong Kong] is useless. People eat people. I came back to China in the days after Liberation just because I did not like that society.'

At the age of seven, Ao entered primary school. It was located in the huge surburban factory compound where they lived and where her father worked as a doctor. She knew that, compared with the nearby primary schools for peasant children, it was a good school, but that some of the schools in the city were considerably better. Even in first grade, she was eager to do well so as to get into a good junior high school later.

In the 1950s, unlike the period just after the Cultural Revolution, the Chinese school system reinforced these aspirations. It was the policy and in the interest of the primary schools to encourage students to study hard in order to perform well later in the junior high school entrance examinations: for the sake of the students' future and to bolster the prestige of the school (and thus of the staff). So too did both family and school similarly encourage obedience, respect for teachers and authority, honesty, frugality, concern for others, humbleness, self-discipline, cleanliness, tolerance of hardship – and intense patriotism.

What her family did not teach, but what her teachers stressed, were ideas like 'loving Chairman Mao', 'loyalty to the party' or 'emulating martyred revolutionary heroes'. Despite this, middle-class parents who themselves had no emotional attachment to the party saw no reason why they should discredit such teachings in front of their children. They realized that their children were born into a political system very unlike what they themselves had been raised in and that it would be best for their children to be at home with the new political values. The families of two of my interviewees had positively

sought to strengthen these values in their children. In fact, in numerous cases, even when the parents unfairly got into political trouble
with party authorities during the Anti-Rightist Campaign in 1957,
they did not breathe a word of their discontent in front of their
children. Only one interviewee, of 'petty capitalist' origin, had
adopted a negative attitude towards the national order from over-
hearing his family's adult conversation, so much so that he was
caught one day in class jokingly injecting a negative into all the
positive statements about the party and revolution that the class was
repeating in unison after the teacher.

School lessons were in keeping with the 'class line', a government
policy of deliberately raising the social, political and economic status
of the workers and peasants and downgrading that of the former elite
classes. Eulogies of the workers and peasants filled the school primers. The children were taught that 'Old Uncle Peasant and Young
Uncle Worker create the world'. They were to learn from the
hardiness and valuable contributions of the workers and peasants and
empathize with the inhuman sufferings they had borne before Liberation in 1949.

But when the children went to the countryside on school outings
they were struck by the peasants' 'backwardness' and dirtiness. One
interviewee says that when writing essays she would include, almost
as a matter of course, sentences like: 'When I grow up I will be a
worker or peasant.' But she observes that 'I never thought about
whether or not I *really* wanted to be a worker or a peasant'; her
actual aspiration was to become a dancer. The praise given the
workers and peasants did not in the least diminish her respect for her
parents' profession of secondary school teacher; indeed, even in
school she was taught that 'teachers are the engineers of the human
soul'. Similarly, Ao wanted to become a doctor, a literary critic or a
writer one day. In fact, all of my fourteen interviewees had dreamt of
becoming nothing less than professionals, if not great scientists.
Teachers encouraged them to work towards these goals, though with
the qualification that the ultimate motive should be to serve the
people.

Thus, all the while that the workers and peasants were extolled,
middle-class parents did not feel their own status threatened, nor the
career hopes they held for their children. Family socialization and
state socialization generally upheld the same values in the 1950s – and
indeed were mutually reinforcing. Children growing up in a middle-
stratum family environment knew of only one value system in their

formative years. There were no opposing values that deterred them from becoming attracted to political activism.

Activism was necessarily associated with a measure of ambition and self-assertiveness, which drew, in turn, upon a self-confidence built up from childhood. Almost every one of my interviewees who became a political activist had been able to take pride, as children, in either outstanding academic grades or superior intelligence or, among boys, for being superior athletes or, among girls, for being pretty. So it was with Ao. Shortly after entering first grade, Ao had already distinguished herself as the best student in the class:

> My level was much higher than the other students in class. Too bad I wasn't able to jump a grade. I can remember the teachers were lazy. They often asked me to instruct the other classmates and even let me mark all their homework. I was proud, and this made things very difficult for me later. I was spoilt and had a feeling of superiority.

She was more than just excellent academically; she had an all-round capability:

> I was king. I was famous . . . Usually students good in studies were bookworms, sissy girls, inevitably poor in sports. Not me. I was good in everything, like a monkey, good in sports, in singing, arithmetic, everything. My work was always pinned up on the notice board.

She had also the advantage of being an appealing little girl. (Ao was not the only activist who referred to her childish appeal; several others, even boys, have mentioned that with some pride.) For that, she was doted on by adults and enjoyed the envy of her peers.

She was the teachers' pet. Within a few years, she was selected by the teachers to be in the school-wide Young Pioneer Committee. Even more highly honoured, she was often the one child chosen, again by the teachers, as school representative for city-wide Young Pioneer activities. She claims that within the factory compound she was famous. When reprimanding their children, mothers singled her out as the perfect example of a bright and diligent daughter. 'See how clever Dr Ao's daughter is! How stupid you are!' There was, however, one element which sapped some of her self-confidence. No other interviewee was more aware of social status than Ao.

Ao's sensitivity about her social standing at such an early age had its circumstantial roots. Her classmates were children of the same factory's employees, all of whom worked and lived in the same huge compound. Most were blue-collar workers' children. Some, like herself, were from the middle ranks of the industrial hierarchy, and a handful of children had fathers who occupied the managerial party posts. Living in an enclosed compound where the residential and work unit was combined, where, so to speak, everyone knew others' and their own place, where the relationship between living standards and the occupational status of one's parents was so obvious, children could easily rank the different families' status. As Ao observed:

> The workers' living quarters were small and dirty, the managers' and party cadres' were spacious, at least in comparison, and while my own family's quarters were somewhat cramped compared with to the managers' and cadres', the home was kept spotless. The workers' children were poorly dressed, dirty, had to go home to light the fire and cook rice right after school and were poor in their studies. The managers' children dressed much better, had a wider social circle. They were more conceited. They felt superior to the other children, and the teachers were more polite towards them. They played among themselves. They became the royalty in the class.

How about Ao? 'I was in the middle. My case was a bit special; my family put a lot of stress on culture and education. It was a special case.' Sandwiched between two groups of very obviously different status, she had developed a feeling of superiority towards her working-class classmates ('We looked down on the workers' kids') and a sense of her parents' inferiority *vis-à-vis* the managers and party cadres. Had it not been for her superior academic performance, she feels she might have been snubbed by the cadres' children. The fact that her academic record enabled her to draw abreast of the socially superior cadres' children served to provide an even greater incentive for her to tower through her own efforts above all others.

Each of her personal successes served as a reinforcement to her ego, fuelling her aspirations for prestige and recognition and reinforcing her positive identification with the teachers and her eagerness to please them. She was acquiring the aura of a model student.

To become a model student, Ao had to be more than a good pupil. She also needed to succeed as a political activist. As a good pupil, she had worked at her studies diligently, had been obedient, quiet and respectful to teachers, had observed school regulations, and had performed duties such as cleaning the floor or wiping the blackboards when her turn came. An activist had to take the initiative to do more. When asked how children could become activists, Ao took herself as an example:

> Organize something for the class. Take, for instance, what I did. I was good in my studies, and unlike those who cared nothing about the grades of the backward students in class, I helped the poor ones in their work. Then in my study group,[26] the grades of backward students showed improvement. In labour sessions I did my utmost, ignoring the filth involved in vegetable gardening. Whenever I noticed any problems among the children in class, I pointed them out to the teacher. When things were broken in class I helped to repair them. Once I saw every teacher had to use their hands when pointing at the blackboard, so I went home, got some sticks and made pointers for *all* the teachers in school. I was really ambitious.

Ao's activist performance did succeed in attracting her teachers' attention. She was selected for a variety of classroom cadre posts, positions which pushed her more than ever to live up to the image she had earned. Ao became an official activist at an early age.[27]

Official activists were to act as a 'bridge' between teachers and students. Two or three times a week, the Young Pioneer and class cadres discussed with the teacher the activities for the week, topics for class discussion, problems that had arisen in the class, even individual students. The student cadres were supposed to 'reflect the situation of the class' to the teacher. This naturally gave the official activists a very special status. Direct communication with figures of authority gave them the status of lesser authority figures in the eyes of the student body.

But their posts inevitably demanded that student cadres act in a patronizing manner towards fellow students, and this aroused the resentment of the other children. The cadres' dual roles, as a classmate and as a cadre with special links to authority, came into conflict. Two 'factions' tended to develop among the students: the official activists comprising one social grouping, and the majority of the ordinary students the other. One interviewee, asked how he felt about the Young Pioneer cadres, replied:

Oh we felt they were arrogant. They ordered you in class to put your hands behind your back, etc.

Q: But that was their duty.

A: As children we did not care. It was none of their business.

In some cases, the ordinary students brought social sanctions to bear against anyone who showed the slightest attachment to the student cadres.

A student cadre was supposed to solve this problem and bridge the gap by balancing delicately the twin loyalties to authority and peer group. But this balancing act was difficult to achieve. A wide gulf almost always existed between cadres and fellow students in Chinese classrooms.

Ao, striving to conform *in toto* to the formal requirements of her posts, reported dutifully and unstintingly to her teacher about the peccadillos of classmates. Temperamentally unable to sustain a delicate sense of balance, she swung wholesale towards her role as teacher's little helper. Gradually, the teachers' and school principal's praise became more important to her than popularity among her peers. It is only now, on reflection, that she laments that she had few friends. Those she associated with were 'children of the upper stratum; those with good grades went together', but even among these she could not count one close friend.

Another interviewee, like Ao a school-level Young Pioneer cadre, swung more the other way and was careful never to snitch on classmates and never to order his classmates to keep quiet in the teacher's absence, except when they got truly out of hand. 'No matter what, I didn't want to have a bad relationship with the other kids. Usually cadres were rejected by the students . . . Not me. I was a cadre yet I got along with the rest.' None the less, the demands on an official activist to serve as a model of good behaviour placed an uncomfortable strain on him. It prevented him from acting as a child. 'Since at school I had to present myself as a model for other children, the moment I got home I became terribly naughty. I let loose.' How naughty were you? 'I messed around with the neighbourhood kids, playing hide-and-seek, marbles and chess.' If that was considered 'naughty', one can appreciate how tight were the demands placed on student activists to behave at school with all the rectitude and seriousness of adults.

Yet another respondent, an easy-going, unambitious boy, got

elected as class-head only because the incumbent student cadres were too disliked to be ratified by classmates. To his consternation, he found that, after his election, his friends were drifting away from him. 'It happened naturally. You had to keep them at a distance, and they were careful to keep you at a distance.' He preferred to revert to the status of an ordinary student, 'because in holding a post you had the responsibility not to do what your classmates wanted'. Unlike Ao, these two boys valued peer-group solidarity more than the rewards of activist conformity.

The role of the young official activist was riddled with 'contradictions'. To perform as good cadres, child activists were instructed to try humbly and altruistically to be concerned with the problems of their classmates. But at the same time the workings of the system required that the activists be given the limelight, be commended publicly as models for emulation, 'be held up to heaven high'. All this served only to feed on the vanity of activists like Ao, to spur their desire for individual self-advancement and to encourage arrogance, quite contrary to the altruism that was aimed for. Incessantly, Ao's supercilious attitude towards classmates and her ambition to be 'the best' worked against her effectiveness as a Young Pioneer officer. She could not easily bring herself to be friendly and caring towards her classmates as a genuine activist should. She all but invited their enmity. For all the years of her youth Ao was acutely conscious that she should rid herself of her hubris, but despite persistent efforts, she could not shake it off. 'So I was not very consistent; sometimes I succeeded in being extremely good to people, and sometimes I treated them badly.'

Her need to preserve her position as a model activist had, in fact, driven Ao to cling to her power and prestige even by means which did not befit a genuine activist. Because of her unpopularity, class elections had become for her a source of great anxiety. The seven class cadres in each class were supposed to be democratically chosen by the students. In practice, however, the teacher almost always 'guided' the students to choose her favourites.[28] Often the teacher initiated the nominations and the students showed their compliant support with a show of hands. In rare cases, however, students might reject the teacher's choice and insist on someone more to their own liking.

Ao recalls that when 'the children voted in such an election and they raised their hands, I watched carefully to see who did not vote for me. I hated them, ha, ha.' To maintain her power she resorted to faction-building. When she had a quarrel with her group of friends of the 'upper stratum', she sought suddenly to befriend the workers' children:

> I was in the minority, but I used all my strength to oppose them [her former friends]. That made them mad. They wanted to win everybody to their side. But I wouldn't let them and kept several over on my side. I think we had four. Three of them were workers' children. It worked like this: people bullied them, so they came over to my side, and I gave them advantages such as helping them in their studies and behaving as if we were good friends. We built up a faction. I was good in my studies, had prestige, so I could recruit several children to my side.

Though still young, she quite obviously perceived herself as above her fellow classmates, in much the same way as some adult cadres probably come to perceive people under them as objects that can be manipulated.

In the fifth and sixth grades, despite her own and her teachers' efforts, her classmates adamantly refused to confirm her nomination as classhead. Yet she continued to be an important school-wide Young Pioneer cadre, since the selection for this post was in the hands of the teachers.

Ao was, officially, a very red activist: for conforming so well to the norms and publicly identifying so faithfully with the school official-dom. But to speak of her need to conform without reference to her beliefs would be to lump her together with the phoney activists. She certainly was not one. Her conformity was accompanied by strong emotional support for the official values. I say strong *emotional* support because children's first conceptions of political authority seem to possess more affective than cognitive content. Findings in the West have suggested that even with the mild form of political sociali-zation taught in Western elementary schools, children 'learn to like the government before [they] really know what it is'.[29] It is not surprising that the Chinese version of political socialization, so much more forceful than in the West, was able to arouse a more intense positive response, except in the rare cases where family political socialization was very much at odds with that of the state.

When asked about their childhood attitudes towards the political values and symbols taught them in primary school, all my interview-ees, though less so the one of 'petty capitalist background', affirmed that even though they had not quite known what the party was, they had loved it. They hated the Guomindang, Chiang Kai-shek and the Americans. They hated the capitalists and the landlords, but admit now that they had done so only in a vague and detached sense, because most of them had never actually encountered those 'horrible ugly class enemies'. They adored the People's Liberation Army and longed to emulate the storybook war heroes one day. They understood that they would have a part to play in building up socialism when they grew up and vaguely understood that they should sacrifice their own personal goals to the state and the collective. They all claim that during the Great Leap Forward they participated enthusiastically and genuinely believed in the value of their efforts.

As children, they could not have felt otherwise unless a completely different set of ideas was deliberately thrust upon them. Our task, therefore, is to examine the intensity with which different children adhered to these values and beliefs, and to see whether a young activist like Ao internalized the official values of childhood more than others.

So much glory, myth, symbolism had been built into the red scarf worn by Young Pioneers that the children's range of attitudes towards the scarf can provide a reliable indicator for sorting out the serious and the conscientious from the couldn't-care-less. When asked whether the red scarf of a Young Pioneer symbolized something important, Ao replied breathlessly, with almost childish earnestness:

It is a corner of the red flag. It's dyed red by the blood of the revolutionary martyrs. That was why we cherished it so much. If you dirtied it, they scolded you. You couldn't reverse the underside when putting it on. If you lost it you would be criticized dozens of times. Once I lost mine; the teacher asked me again and again, but I refused to tell how. I was stubborn. I said to myself: 'I lost my red scarf and so what. What's your business to keep on asking me about it. I lost it and I feel such a big burden on my conscience already, and you still keep on harping on it.' The teacher punished me by making me stand. I stood for a long time. For several weeks I was not allowed to put on a new red scarf. Oh, the teacher was so furious. She punished me for so long. I was such a good student and had become this bad! I cried and cried in front of the school office. At last they gave me another one, in a big and impressive ceremony.

Ao held the red scarf as sacred. For it, she was prepared to defy authority for the first and only time while in primary school, out of a strong conviction that she had already justly atoned for her sin through feelings of contrition.

By the upper years of primary school, not all pupils – especially boys – took the red scarf so seriously. It was allowed to stay dirty, was crumpled up and stuffed inside pockets. By the fifth and sixth grades, when almost all the children were Young Pioneers, belonging no longer seemed to hold any great value. In one school, as a sign of seniority, it became a fad to let the scarf get as old and stained as possible. Many boys took the red scarf as an unwanted symbol of conformity to adult authority, no longer as a glorious cloth dyed red by the blood of martyrs. Several interviewees recall that they had begun refusing altogether to put on the scarf. In one interviewee's class, the peer-group pressure not to wear the scarf became so strong that few boys wore it despite persistent harassment from teachers and student cadres. It was not uncommon in upper primary school to have student cadres stationed at a school's main gate to intercept any students without scarves, jot down their names and report them to the teachers. Despite this harassment, nothing could make some of the boys conform, lest they be teased as sissies like the girls, who always wore theirs. One interviewee observed that it was only in the sixth grade, when good comments from teachers were necessary for entering a good junior high school, that he and his friends became less openly defiant.

Not all children, in short, took the Young Pioneers as much to heart as Ao did. She believed in it with an almost religious fervour:

> The Young Pioneers was a very good organization, which is why everyone loved it with their whole heart. Wow, those enrolment ceremonies were so impressive. I can't even describe them to you properly. I once participated in the Young Pioneers Representative Convention. It left an impression on you for the rest of your life. The adult leaders talked intimately to the Young Pioneers . . . Those were the days when things were so good. All the organizations – the party, the League and the Young Pioneers – were very good. All of them had a strong sense of responsibility, a great militant strength.

One could argue that it was her position as a Young Pioneer cadre and the formal prestige she enjoyed that led her to hold the Young

Pioneers in such high esteem. But from her tone of voice, even today, it is clear that, more than that, she had deeply absorbed the official values and beliefs; her trust in authority and the organizations was unswerving. Her position and her beliefs reinforced each other, leading her to conform more than other children normally would.

By the final two years of primary school, Ao encountered two new problems. One was that her intellectual abilities were lagging behind some of the brighter children in class. Academically she still stood top of her class and could still afford to look down on most of her classmates. But her grades were maintained only with much hard work and 'dead' rote learning; 'dead' is an appropriate Chinese term for the type of undigested memorization so many children engaged in. She admits that the boys who were her runners-up attained high grades without much effort, and that if they had invested more time they could have done better than her. They learned new arithmetic far faster than her 'because they were boys', or so it seemed to her. Ao was handicapped by an uninquisitive mind, which not unlikely was part and parcel of her 'conformist' tendencies. Caught on a treadmill of ever lengthening rote effort, she began sacrificing her Saturdays to stay at home to study.

The second of Ao's gnawing concerns was her lacklustre class label. As she grew older, her sense of inferiority on this score intensified. She envied the glory bestowed on good-class labels. Even in primary school, she made sure that when filling in official forms she included the names of two pairs of uncles and aunts who were cadres and party members. She was ashamed of her parents' non-red status. She literally resented her family in the final month of sixth grade when she thought her family background was the reason for her failure to be selected, as the best student in her year, to be sent to a good junior high school without having to take an entrance examination. (It turned out later she was wrong; that year this special privilege for best students was universally withdrawn.) She began to speak less to her parents, despising them for their political backwardness:

> I looked down on them because, compared with the revolutionary cadres and workers, their thinking was very traditional. Whenever he bought things, my father bargained and I hated that. In Primary Five I also noticed he sometimes acted obsequiously to his superiors. I didn't go out with my father anymore in junior high school, and after I went down to the countryside [after graduating from junior high school] I seldom talked to him at all.

Of the three most important agents of socialization – family, peer group and school/state – Ao was effectively cutting herself off from her family and the peer group, one-sidedly leaning towards the school and state authorities.

THE PURIST ACTIVIST AS A CHILD

Bai is the second of our official activists. Born in 1941, he is the oldest of all the interviewees. He is also the only one who affects the appearance of a country bumpkin. When I first met him he already had been in Hong Kong for four months, but he was still wearing a pair of baggy pants, a suit two sizes too large for him, and black Chinese cloth shoes – the type of motley attire none of the other interviewees dared venture out in into the Hong Kong streets. He is the constant object of ridicule among his group of friends from China, as parochial, clumsy, unable to catch up with the times. Yet his indifference to physical appearance reflects a tradition of 'proletarianism' and Communist puritanism which in attire and gestures flouts all things materialistic and temporal. He continues to walk with the ungainly splay-legged gait of a Chinese peasant – a walk he had cultivated in China.

Bai's uncouth mannerisms belie his background. He is the only one of the interviewees with a university education. He has a sharp intellect, and is well read and well versed in Marxism. His wide experiences, geographically and socially, endow Bai with an ability to link theory with national policies and grassroot politics to an extent lacking in my other interviewees.

His interest in politics has not been extinguished since leaving China. He continues to be actively involved, organizing study groups, analysing current Chinese political developments, writing articles for Hong Kong magazines, and later even editing one himself. Unlike Ao, he does not idolize formal education – after all, he had been to one of the most prestigious universities in China – but he continues to talk of studying and disciplining himself, for fear of backsliding: 'Yes, you must make yourself a schedule, make yourself read a certain amount every day within a certain amount of time. Otherwise you'll become lazy and will never be able to do anything.'

Bai's life history is the most interesting of all my fourteen interviewees, almost novelistic in the variety of adventures he has experienced. To top that, he is a superb story-teller, setting the atmosphere for every scene, filling in the minutest details, replete with names and dates drawn from an incredible memory which outdoes even Ao's. He is, however, not so good in describing either himself or his inner feelings. The reasons for this we shall come back to later, since they are, I think, characteristic of his kind of activism.

Bai's native village lay in a North Chinese district where the Communist Party, the Guomindang and Japanese were all contending for control. Bai was the fourth in the family, with three older sisters and one younger brother. His father, being more patriot than ideologue, had run errands against the Japanese for both the Communists and the Guomindang. He owned some land, and, according to Bai, the family should have been classified during the land reform as somewhere between rich peasant and upper middle peasant. During the interview, without my asking, Bai was eager to let me know that his family had not exploited anyone, that they had only one hired labourer who was given several plots of land all to himself, and that his parents and older sisters worked the land with their own hands. In this need to defend his family's 'cleanliness', it is clear that he continued to hold to the values of his childhood, even though he is now in a completely different sociopolitical system where family wealth is held a source of pride, not a cause of shame.

When the tide of the land reform reached their village, the lineage that was rival to the Bais gained control of the land reform workteam (several members of that rival lineage had earlier joined the party) and made use of the land reform to destroy the extensive Bai lineage. Bai's family managed to flee south. By the time the Communist Party won the civil war the Bais were penniless, hungry destitutes in Canton. They had to seek help from a state relief agency, which gave the father some money to start a small stall and which put the two youngest children in an orphanage. This is why Bai's family today carries a 'small street-seller' class-origin label and why he himself, not an orphan, grew up in an orphanage. But all the time he was a child, Bai had only disjointed impressions of that same family history which he can tell today as a coherent gripping account. He could remember himself as a toddler being his grandfather's favourite grandson; of the Bai lineage's sudden fall, his adult cousins badly beaten and carried back stark naked with faeces dripping down their buttocks; the family on the run; the rumour that his grandfather was hanged, with his abdomen slit open; and scenes of himself begging in the streets with his sister. These kaleidoscopic impressions were not put together for him by his parents, not, that is, until he was in high school, when he was required to give an account of his family history. Bai's father for many years avoided implanting anti-Communist feelings in the children.

While in the orphanage, Bai saw his parents only rarely, once every several months, which is to say that starting from the age of eight, for six years Bai grew up in a very closed environment, almost exclusively socialized by a state institution. What kind of influence had Bai received from the family prior to that? Not very different to what Ao received from hers, even though Bai's father had had only several years of formal education. He comes across from Bai's description as a capable, self-taught man, reasonable, down to earth, hard working, with brains for business, a righteous man abiding by Confucian ethical principles.

Bai, like Ao, was the favourite child. His father focused his attention on him, because Bai was a bright child and, more important still, was the eldest son: to the father, daughters did not count. He was strict with his children, demanding from them good manners and high moral and academic standards. By the age of five, Bai already knew how to write and do multiplication and division on an abacus. When he entered the orphanage, he felt confident of his school abilities and was already armed with some notions of social ethics.

The orphanage provided its own programme of primary schooling. It differed from ordinary schools in that it was run on a half-study half-work basis, so that the orphans could partially support their own upkeep. They laboured daily for three hours and had three hours of classes. The political teachings were no different from those of the school Ao attended. But we shall see how, as a very secluded environment, the orphanage attracted Bai to a different kind of activism than Ao's factory compound had helped instill in her.

The six years Bai remained in the orphanage were divided into a three-year stretch of chaos and confrontation between teachers and students, and another three of reform and harmony. The orphanage had been run by the Guomindang before Liberation, and when Bai arrived, shortly after Liberation, life was harsh. His description is Dickensian. The food was meagre. The teachers, carried over from the Guomindang regime, felt no sympathy for the orphans. Beatings were the order of the day. The children, 90 per cent of them orphans, varied enormously in age and temperament, ranging from juvenile delinquents and beggars to 'well-bred' types like Bai. From Bai's memory:

When it was meal time everyone was present, but when it was time for lessons the kids climbed over the fence and went to play. The teachers were fierce. They slapped you right in the face. And you know, some of the students were accustomed to fending for themselves in the streets and were quite old. These kids were very obstinate and tough, so they often fought with the teachers.

Bai himself took part in none of this. 'I was never beaten. I was always very obedient in school because I'd been influenced by my family.' He was unassertive, well liked by the teachers, and academically always occupied the fifth or sixth position, though never the very top. His sympathy, unlikely Ao's, went to his schoolmates.
The students erupted in prolonged rioting one day:

These kids' resentment had been suppressed for too long, so once they had risen up, surrounding the school office, nothing could stop them. Suddenly someone yelled: 'Attack!' And the students picked up bricks and bamboo sticks, chairs and tables and flung them at the teachers.

Many of the teachers were hurt and the most hated one had some bones broken. Bai was too young to participate but sided completely with the students: first, because they only manhandled those teachers who liked beating students, and second, because at that age he already saw an inconsistency between the teachers' practices and the values they preached:

The books said people shouldn't beat others, so how come the teachers beat people? No matter what, I felt adults beating children was unreasonable. Because I myself had never been beaten by my father and mother. So when the students fought back, especially as they were my classmates and friends. I was on their side.

Such experiences did not lend themselves to any myth regarding the sacredness of authority figures of the sort that Ao had always held. 'It gave me a sense of righteousness. To the very end I always feel there are certain things which always should be opposed. It's a part of me; the influence of those years was great.' From his detailed recounting of a myriad of incidents from his youth, it does seem that for Bai there was always a truth, an absolute value, over and beyond authority: whereas to Ao, values and authority were one and the same. Bai would not defy authority for the sake of rebelliousness, but he was ready to reject it when it did not put into practice what it professed.

The plight of the students was not alleviated until a year after the riot, when two PLA officers were dispatched from upper levels temporarily to take over management of the orphanage. Bai recalls the patience which the two army cadres demonstrated in breaking down the initial suspicions of the orphans:

> The armymen came to play with us and went to attend classes with the students. And they sat on the ground and ate together with us. Ah, the teachers were surprised. During the night, the two toured the orphanage and adjusted blankets for the children. It was the most intimate demonstration of concern that the orphans felt they could expect from any adult. The two soldiers also generally improved the material well-being of the orphanage; food rations, for example, were increased. When the armymen finally left, a lot of students cried. They had become like their father and mother. I still have a clear picture of that day in my memory.

Both Ao and Bai had great esteem for cadres, but with a difference. Bai's enduring admiration for the PLA was based on concrete emotional experiences: his recollection of their workstyle, patience and compassion, qualities which had nothing to do with their official positions as cadres or as figures of authority. Ao's adoration for cadres was based on a romantic notion of the glorious and prestigious halo that hovered over someone with power.

Conditions in the orphanage improved remarkably during the following few years. Teachers showed more sympathy towards the students. The atmosphere was one of serious learning, with the children's manual work interspersed with organized recreation. But from Bai's description, the students were provided with much more freedom than in Ao's school. Bai developed skills in marbles and snake-catching and went swimming with friends, pursuits condemned and prohibited in regular schools. For instance, that boy cadre who attended an ordinary primary school had not dared to play marbles in school, and only did so 'naughtily' after school. In the orphanage, because the children did everything together – ate, slept, worked, studied, played – always in the presence of teachers, there was no double role to play.[30]

In both the orphanage and ordinary primary schools, manual labour was upheld as a virtue unto itself, essential for the full development of the child, not merely as an economic function. But whereas in the orphanage manual labour was part of everyday life, in Ao's and other interviewees' schools it was not – and the effects differed accordingly. From Bai's account, seeing the concrete rewards of their labour, harvesting and selling their own produce, able to observe its real economic contribution, made manual labour seem 'natural' and a personal accomplishment. Today Bai still speaks with conviction in support of an education policy coordinating study with work. His description serves to show the extent to which manual labour had become an integral part of his education and of the orphans' outlook:

> For example, the teacher gave us some problems to solve related to our labour. We grew our own vegetables and cut them ourselves. We calculated our own yields and sold them to our school canteen at half the market price. And when we collected manure, fed the pigs, etc., we were always dealing with statistics. Our maths and abacus work were so good because we had a lot of actual practice. And in our nature class, we had a peasant sent down from the general office. He taught us how to apply manure. This is sugar cane, now you should apply this manure, and apply so much. In the regular primary schools you taught the kids and they did not understand. We understood. Our syllabus was simplified. Things that we could learn out in the fields we learned in the fields.

At the regular urban day schools, in spite of all the official proclamations to the contrary, manual labour sessions were never apportioned an equal status to book learning. At the most, a class got a small strip of plot to tend, and sometimes there was so little space that the work was no more than token exercise. When taken to factories, children were asked to do only light errands. One of the interviewees recalls:

> We weren't very serious about labouring on our little vegetable patch. No one cared where the vegetables went afterwards. We didn't care about the application of fertilizer – only applied some when we felt like it. Every week the class spent two sessions with the teacher on the class's patch. We enjoyed working in the field. We wasted a lot of time there.

We have discussed how, in Ao's case, the social and economic difference separating the families of her classmates contributed to her sharp awareness of social inferiority and superiority. In Bai's orphanage, without families or separate homes, everyone felt equal in this respect. Children there held a similar social status in the eyes of their adult mentors.[31] But to say that the orphans were not aware of class differences among themselves does not mean they grew up without any class consciousness. By 'class consciousness', I mean, as the Chinese do, an awareness of belonging to a class which is or has been exploited. From their personal experience and, just as importantly, from what they had been taught repeatedly, the orphans viewed themselves as epitomizing the formerly oppressed classes; and Bai 'took on the feelings of my classmates'. The two armymen had addressed the orphans as 'flowers of the mother country', and they felt it to be true. Like Israeli children studied by Melford Spiro, who regard themselves as 'children of the kibbutz', Bai and the orphans came to regard themselves proudly as 'children of the state'. Like them, Bai learned to feel grateful to the state, to the party and to Chairman Mao for having delivered him from destitution and hunger. The Chinese notion of 'gratitude' (*en*) implies a blessing and favour to be repaid (as in Japanese culture). If need be, the orphans were expected to sacrifice their personal desires to repay this '*en*' to the state. Bai observed that most of the students in class hoped to go on to junior high school; but when, in the sixth grade, it was decided suddenly that they would have to begin working for a living, they took the decision without complaint. It was a means of demonstrating their *en* – whereas Ao and other bright and ambitious students at the regular schools were dissatisfied if they could not get admitted to a prestigious junior high. Bai uses the term 'docile thinking' approvingly to describe his classmates' mentality. In China, Bai kept up contact with his old friends, some of whom are now working in factories as shopfloor squad leaders or similar lower-ranking cadre positions. They are to him the real activists:

They were very docile. [Here he makes sure I do not lump 'docile' and 'red' together.] They are not running after anything. Not betraying other people. Not that kind. [This is Bai's current definition of 'red'.] They're just honest, making use of their skill and hard work. Their idea of gratitude, of repaying, is manifested to this very day. They haven't climbed very high, gaining at most the positions of blue-collar foremen, because they don't know how to be opportunistic, don't know how to be phoney activists.

In primary school, Bai had not yet taken on the role of an official activist. He did not feel any need to serve as a model for his classmates. Reading war novels behind one's desk during lessons was widespread, and Bai did so frequently in flagrant disregard for the teachers' authority. There were few impinging factors, either from home or from the school environment, encouraging Bai to strive for personal ambition and prestige in the manner of Ao. Indeed, Bai had always been one of the youngest children in a class of enormous age range. He occupied the place of a playful kid brother to be pampered: 'So I never had the situation of being in any leadership limelight, of coming out to order people around.' Ao's role from the very beginning had been that of a big sister, the class cadre and overseer of discipline.

However, Bai already held many of the values of an activist. His feelings of gratitude to the state far surpassed, from the state's point of view, Ao's merely positive orientations. And Bai had adopted the values of collective spirit and enthusiasm in manual labour with far less internal conflict than Ao, who always had to make a conscious and repeatedly unsuccessful effort to ward off the self-seeking streak in all her activities.

THE REBELLIOUS ACTIVIST AS A CHILD

When I embarked upon interviewing Chang, he had already been living in Hong Kong for four years. He was, in fact, the most articulate of the several ex-Red Guards I had earlier met in 1971 and who had made such a deep impression on me. At that time Chang had just left China; but he was already delving into Fromm and Freud in Chinese translations. By the time our interviews began in 1975, he was able to use Freudian concepts to describe his own early years, and I faced the problem that this intervening period of readings had led him to restructure in his own mind the recollections he held of his past.

Chang was, of all the interviewees, the most receptive to things 'Western' both in ideas and life-style. In many respects, he presented the image of a bright, Western-educated, rebellious university student of the Vietnam War era. His years of constant and varied reading and his participation in Hong Kong's New Left and then the colony's small Trotskyist movement had opened up for him a wide range of new ideas and modes of expression. At the time of these interviews, he was, in his own words, splitting away from 'dogmatic Marxist–Leninist groups' as he 'matured into a humanist Marxist'.

Yet Chang, as evidenced from the interviews and testified to by his friends, was basically the same Chang as ten years before, when he was one of the most famous of the high school Red Guard leaders in Canton. He still held to the same fervour; the same urge to rebel against the Establishment, any Establishment; the same instinctive headlong plunge into the vortex of a political maelstrom. Chang was a unique case among the thousands of young people from China in that, partly due to his personality and the type of activist he was in China, he still attempted vigorously to uphold the banner of 'international proletarian revolution' from outside socialist China – all the while recognizing that such efforts might be insignificant and futile. For Chang, active participation in politics remained central to his existence; his one grand aim in life was to 'continue the revolution'. He was engaged as a full-time 'professional revolutionary' and had no interest in taking up a permanent job. He had no wish to climb up in Hong Kong society, nor had he cared to do so in the socialist society he came from.

Chang eschewed self-discipline, whereas to Bai and Ao it remained an important virtue. In China, self-discipline had been deliberately 'cultivated' in the schools; activist youths were taught that they should restrain their feelings and individualistic indulgences, with the aim of more completely devoting themselves to the collective good, the state and the revolution. Chang continues to allow himself to be carried away by 'undesirable' whims, just as he used to as a child and youth. Today he pursues a self-indulgent, entirely unregulated lifestyle, a compulsive spendthrift and incessant money-borrower despite resolution after resolution to the contrary. He seems to rebel even against his better self.

As noted, because of Chang's acquaintance with Western social science, his interest in psychology and long-habituated absorption in his own pscyhe, the story Chang tells about himself comes replete with his own analysis, almost Freudian in its approach. Recapturing the mood of his childhood from his narration (which Ao is so good at) is not easy with Chang. The following quote is typical of the self-analysis he inserts into his reminiscences:

My mother was an ordinary working woman. But she was the type with the drive to work, an able woman – I mean able as a working woman. I think in a way I inherited some of her character. In ordinary cases a child so much suppressed by the father would tend to develop an unsociable character, but due to the nurturant influence of my mother, I still had some warmth, and as a result my character did not develop in an antisocial direction.

Of the thirteen interviewees whose formal education ended with secondary school, Chang is the most intellectual and widely read. He is the only one who had struggled through volumes of Marx and Lenin on his own. He, too, like Bai, can detach intellect from emotion when criticizing China. But unlike Bai, he is more interested in theory than in amalgamating theory with practice. Never a cadre and never much involved with the countryside, he does not possess that interest and concern on the personal level for the peasantry and the 'masses' which is so evident in both Ao and Bai. He does not speak of the Communist Youth League and party with the same enthusiasm. He had never been part of it. In Hong Kong he has participated in political demonstrations. But he has neither the interest nor the patience to do basic nuts-and-bolts organizational work. His undisciplined nature apart, he lacks the experience, never having held a cadre post in high school or as an adult. He is the first of our unrecognized activists.

Chang was born the year before Liberation came to Canton. His parents had been poor. His mother was illiterate and the father had barely any schooling. When his mother was pregnant with Chang she was fired from her job as a shop assistant. His parents had to turn desperately to street-peddling. 'That is why when talking about the old days my old man is still filled with hatred.' Frustration caused by financial difficulties turned into bitterness towards Chang as well. Father and son never got along.

When I was born, I was a drag on the family, getting sick, et cetera. My parents had to spend a lot of money on me. We were so poor. That was why he hated me when I was young . . . My father said that the Chang's son was useless, and therefore he beat me all the time, asked me to kneel for one whole day sometimes in front of the ancestral altar. He treated me poorly, beat me all the time. Perhaps because I developed comparatively earlier and because of my stubborn unbending character, even as a kid I had a lot of conflict with my father. He particularly hated me. But he was nice to my sister because she was born after Liberation. He thought the Chang son was no good but the daughter was good.

Chang, as seen, grew up a stubborn and independent child. His independence, however, was not entirely a result of his rebelliousness; it was also a product of his social class and neighbourhood environment. By official classification, Chang's family came under a 'middle-class' label, subcategorized 'office worker', since his father, just before Liberation, had secured a job as a warehousing clerk in a factory. But the household did not possess a middle-class gentility. His parents did not drive the children on with an ethic of achievement. The family had more of a working-class flavour. Both the parents worked (the mother sold cigarettes in the street), more absorbed in trying to support a growing family than in providing a 'proper' upbringing for the children. With minimal parental surveillance, Chang grew up in the streets, in a slum neighbourhood.[32]

But the absence of a nurturant environment was made up for by Chang's precociousness. Here is his memory of his early intelligence: 'In the first and second grades, my grade scores were extremely good. I could absorb things very fast. I myself could feel my speed was frightening when I was young.' In the fourth grade, his essay-writing was evaluated by teachers to have reached junior high school level. That year, his class mistress had suggested to his parents that he should enter junior high school directly, jumping two grades, but his parents declined.

Had it not been for his precociousness, Chang might conceivably have turned towards juvenile delinquency. Indeed, in primary school Chang 'messed' around with the prepubescent delinquents in his school and neighbourhood. But because he distinguished himself as exceptionally bright, beginning in kindergarten, 'the teachers were particularly nice to me, and this allowed me to gain pride in myself'. The absence of any encouragement for academic achievement from home was amply made up for by positive reinforcement from teachers in school. From his recollection, every term at least one teacher favoured him. The prestige he enjoyed in this respect equalled Ao's or even surpassed hers; both of them attained school-wide fame.

But the similarity ended here: Chang was an uncontrollable student. His outbursts of rebelliousness came in torrents. He got into slugging matches in school and gang fights in the streets. He stirred up chaos in the classroom, rarely listened to the lesson, had quarrels with teachers, swore at them and even attacked them. Chang talks of an inner urge that had nothing to do with his likes or dislikes for a teacher. 'With those teachers I did not like I was bound to be naughty . . But with those I liked I was just as naughty. There was even a strange psychology – I did not have to be naughty, but I chose to be naughty, naughty for no reason.' Yet he had internalized the school's values sufficiently to be aware that this kind of rebelliousness was wrong. Chang moved to the edge but not over. He merely hovered near forbidden zones. The same kind of rebelliousness and deliberate release of self-control, the same urge to play with fire, persisted through his adolescence and, as we have seen, to this very day.

He could afford to be defiant in school. Despite his commotions there were, after all, always teachers who appreciated his intelligence. His defiance was at once a cry for attention and an urge to show that he could be as bright or as naughty as he himself chose. Other interviewees preferred to attract teachers' attention by conforming, but Chang chose to do so through resistance. He won approval from some classmates for the turbulence he dared cause, while others respected him for his academic prowess. By the fifth or sixth grade, his academic achievement won respect even from his father. He began taking his son to his factory to play Chinese chess, so that young Chang could gain prestige in the factory for Chang the Elder by beating everyone: 'He needed that; you see, he was a nonentity in his work unit.'

Both Ao and Chang were arrogant towards their peer groups, and neither of them had close friends. But their arrogance was expressed in different forms. Ao alienated herself by identifying with authority, while Chang remained on the side of the peer group, at the same time standing aloof from it. Neither of them possessed that collective spirit and feeling of group solidarity which Bai found so gratifying. On the surface, Ao tried to *manifest* such a spirit because she was genuinely trying to conform to the norms demanded of her by the political teachings. But in reality, she was not *of* the group, always regarding herself above others. Chang on the other hand took no interest in conforming to the norms at all.

The dichotomies that posed dilemmas for Ao, such as selfishness–selflessness, arrogance–humility and individualism–collective spirit, did not disturb Chang. But he did embrace the broad political ideas that he was taught. During the Great Leap Forward, as a fourth-grade pupil affected by the excitement and bustle of the rush to create a utopian China, he felt uplifted. He excitedly began reading the newspaper daily, hungrily devouring all the reports on the country's miraculous achievements. But political knowledge was not normally counted as political activism. His concern for the progress of the country was translated outwardly only into further academic success. Having read the newspapers, he could answer any and all questions on current affairs.

No matter how rebellious and contemptuous his behaviour towards authority and the official norms, Chang, in his own way, had internalized some of the national values as deeply as Ao and Bai. And in the sense that Chang did not regard values and authority as one and the same, he and Bai were similar. But because Chang's positive orientation to the values was not manifested by conformity, it went unrecognized. For how did a child show himself to be 'a good student of Chairman Mao' except by externalizing it, by conforming actively to the school authorities' demands? In his 'political manifestations' (*biaoxian*) Chang appeared at best ordinary, at worst antisocial. He did not distinguish himself in manual labour, in organizational ability or concern for his classmates. He had no interest in outdoing his peer group in public displays. He was pleased that he had acquired a reputation for being the brightest and the naughtiest, but had no additional aspirations for the power and prestige that could be derived from official posts. In the fourth grade, for reasons unknown, aside from the almost predictable volatility of his character, he suddenly became very obedient, to the extent that thankful teachers rewarded him with a seat in the schoolwide Young Pioneers Committee. But he barely cherished such an honour. Within the year he had regressed to his old pattern of disobedience while still holding the post: 'I did not give a damn. I told them I didn't care. I was still stubborn.'

But again, that was simply a matter of unwillingness to conform to authority. When forced by economic circumstances to act against the essential values he had been taught, he faced an agonizing experience. This episode, during the calamitous economic depression which followed the Great Leap Forward, illustrates how intensely he had internalized the values:

> During the three years of terrible national economic difficulties, my family was in great hardship. So I took my picture books – I read a lot of them – and rented them out in the streets to make money for the family. I also sold food in the black market. For example, my mother would buy some eggs at 30 or 40 cents each, cook them and sell them at 50 cents each. A lot of people did that in those days. So I took my sister with me and stood in the streets with a bowl of several eggs. Sometimes we couldn't sell any for a whole day. The hunger was unbearable; I was growing at that time. Emotionally, I felt confused. On the one hand, I couldn't stop helping my family. Besides, my family was in real trouble. My mother could only make some 30 dollars a month and she had a

liver disease. But on the other hand, in our society this type of black marketing was condemned. I was criticized for it in school. When the school broadcast my name over the microphone: 'So-and-so was selling in the black market', I felt I had nowhere to hide myself. I was terribly ashamed. I was a Young Pioneer Committee member. I loved my country. I felt as if I had sinned against it. So when they criticized me my heart was torn. Very painful. But then I had to help my family. So one could say my childhood was very complicated. When I went black marketing I came into contact with the vagrants. What pained me was that kids from the petty-bourgeoisie or kids of professors could never understand this. They could never have experienced this.

At ordinary times he could defy authority, break the rules, ignore the norms, but when it came to the school authorities condemning him on a point that related to his inner integrity, he was deeply hurt.

In school, children were taught to adulate China's revolutionaries, look up to the archetypical worker and peasant and condemn the former exploiters and those who were indifferent to the revolution. Children growing up in protected environments, as in middle-class families or Bai's orphanage, tended to idolize the 'good guys' and shun the 'bad guys'. But growing up in a poor working-class environment, Chang had seen society's underside even as a young child and was able to take the social realities as natural facets of life. He was tolerant of others' indifference to politics and the revolution, or even to comments and actions which could be classed as 'counterrevolutionary'.

Chang's earliest memory of his 'father kneeling and worshipping in front of Mao Zedong's photo, thanking the Chairman for giving us such a good life' was the deepest experience of 'class feeling' contained in the early childhood memories of any of my interviewees. But Chang did not share Bai's sense of 'class consciousness', in that he did not feel strongly about having been once of an exploited class, nor that he himself therefore should be grateful to the party. For one thing, his father's attitude towards the revolution wavered with his economic situation. Looking around his own neighbourhood, Chang observed that 'actually a lot of workers were like that. That is, only when they got some benefits out of it would they say the Communists were good.' In the three years of economic difficulties, Chang's father cursed the party and repeated the rumours spreading among the less-educated stratum of society, that omens had appeared adumbrating the downfall of the Communists and the comeback of the Guomindang. Other interviewees, with more educated parents, rarely heard complaints during this period. Their parents had been careful to let their children accept the official explanations for the country's calamities – either to preserve the children's trust in the political system or from fear that the children might unintentionally get the entire family into political trouble by uttering taboo sentiments in public.

Chang's reaction to his father's 'counterrevolutionary' comments was one of forbearance:

> I didn't say anything. I was against it. I had always thought the Guomindang was terrible. But I didn't feel like opposing him. After all, he was my father. Besides, our family was really in difficulty. So I let him talk. I thought it was difficult to blame him for saying this kind of thing.

Chang had not wavered in his belief in the party and the chairman when presented with two opposing sets of ideas, but could be tolerant of his father's political 'backwardness'. Ao, by contrast, might well have condemned her father to his face as a 'counterrevolutionary'. As it was, she despised him even for his lack of a revolutionary image. Chang did not feel inferior nor was he embarrassed about coming from a family of low social and economic standing. He had never wished he had a father of higher social status. He had never rejected his family. 'No, I never blamed my old man. I pitied him. To the very end I would not despise him or hate him. I think this had something to do with the confidence I had in myself.' When he saw the material comforts his richer classmates enjoyed, he merely felt an uneasy incompatibility. Ao, on the other hand, admitted she had wished for better clothes and better shoes. But at the very same time, Chang could not idolize the proletariat in the manner of Ao, who took her images from schoolbooks and children's magazines. He never shared the same romanticism. Already, he was beginning to extract himself from his own social class, identifying himself more with the intelligentsia.

When it was time to apply to a junior high school, Chang chose a second-rate school five minutes from where he lived. He dared not apply to a better one for fear that the history of his bad conduct would affect his application. But equally, it was because he did not share Ao's driving ambition to attend a prestigious school. If he had, he would have behaved himself temporarily, as had several other interviewees, so as to win better recommendations from the sixth-grade teachers. But he would not readily surrender his wilful sense of independence, would not compliantly bend the knee to authority just to get ahead.

THE PRAGMATIC ACTIVIST AS A CHILD

When I was first introduced to Deng, the second unrecognized activist, he had been in Hong Kong for only a few months. It was evident that he was caught up in personal change, and during the months of interviewing his conversational interests shifted in step. Initially he was consumed with interest in recounting tales of political action. But, unlike Chang, he was soon toying with ideas on how to make good money. By the end of the year he had abandoned talk of politics altogether, to channel his energy into establishing himself in a business career in Hong Kong.

Ten years before, Deng had been as famous and prominent a Red Guard leader as Chang: the two of them led the high school Rebel Red Guards in Canton. For a while in Hong Kong, among his old 'comrades-in-arms', he still commanded a certain charisma and continued to view himself as a political leader of his peers. His eventual decision to relinquish that self-image was made only with hesitation and inner struggle, due partly to feelings of nostalgia and due partly to his own last claims to idealism. In one of his rare moments of self-pity he depicted his adaptation to the allures of Hong Kong materialism as, 'My end had come.' But the degree of idealism that Deng, a once pragmatic activist, had ever possessed is arguable; it will be one of the aspects of this kind of activism that we shall scrutinize.

Once having made the decision, Deng took the stereotyped mercenary image of human relationships in Hong Kong to its extreme, and seeing Hong Kong society in no other terms, he talked about the raw pursuit of money unashamedly. He had retained a strong sense of self-discipline, now concentrated on acquiring the necessary practical skills and knowledge for climbing the Hong Kong economic ladder. No other interviewee who learned English from me did so with as much avidity as Deng, for he realized that an ability to use English was the crucial first rung up the ladder of success. Unlike Ao, who chose the time-consuming formal academic route to fulfil her ambitions in the new society, Deng preferred the more expedient and direct road, which in Hong Kong meant starting one's own business, becoming a capitalist.

Interviewing Deng was difficult. He liked to be in control, always wanting to bend the interview sessions to suit his own moods, to demonstrate that he remained in command of the situation. Deng is intelligent and had read a fair amount, but he was eager to appear more knowledgeable than he actually was. He tended also to be guarded when asked sensitive questions; he did not like his inner thoughts to be probed. Just as frustrating to an interviewer, he liked to play up his present cynicism. People who knew him describe him as having been pragmatic, not cynical. The change in heart apparently came only after the Cultural Revolution.

Deng was born two years before Liberation. The three other interviewees had been exceptionally bright and mature for their age, but not Deng. Academically he was a failure in primary school. He matured late, a child with little intellectual inclination or much emotional attachment to the political values that he was taught. As a result, his memory of his affective and intellectual orientation to the socialization process is vague, and his answers to such questions curt. His most animated descriptions are of the series of fist fights he had in lower primary school, some of which he can recount in meticulous detail. His recollection of his childhood was that 'it did not have any brilliance to it, not a bit of beauty in it. I didn't know what I wanted. No ideals. Nothing. Very dull. No inclination towards anything.' Deng offhandedly blames it upon a lack of superior innate qualities, but the observer looking back at his history can see that the objective conditions in which he grew up were not conducive to early intellectual and emotional development. His childhood education passed through one kindergarten and five primary schools. Each change in study or living environment was accompanied by difficult adjustments, with little parental or parent-surrogate concern and encouragement.

Deng was the second of three sons. His parents had both received higher educations and were employed by the socialist government as 'cadres in technical matters', of some standing in their own work units. Their official class label, however, was 'middle': 'petty-bourgeois', subcategorized 'office worker'. In the days when a child's class background was not yet officially important, Deng sometimes filled in 'technical cadre', sometimes 'office worker'. Economically, the family was quite well off; the neighbourhood was one of well-to-do homes. From Deng's present analysis, his parents were 'expert', not 'red': 'What I could remember when young was that my father was an important cadre in his work place; but he did not even apply to join the party. My parents believed in moderation, in the golden mean. They were not activists. Activists were those who stepped on others to climb up.'

Deng's parents had great expectations for their children, but little time for them. They were tied down by their work and by the many afterwork meetings and political study sessions. There was no time to coach the children, no time to take them out, no time even to eat at home together, for, from what Deng could remember, he often had to eat in the mess-hall at his parents' work unit. There was, in short, no time for a family life. Deng was put in a boarding kindergarten.

> My parents didn't show much warmth. On Sundays they took me out sometimes and I loved that, but often they didn't come to fetch me because they were very busy in their units. I would get angry with them for not coming and hide away the next week they came. I pouted. I became so wild that I did not even want to go home on Sundays. On Sunday you could turn the place upside-down because there were so few people around . . . How could our relationship be close? There was so little chance to be together with them.

One cannot miss the tone of resentment in his voice. Another interviewee, also with parents who were 'technical cadres' with little time for the children, similarly had built up feelings of resentment. Deng became uncontrollably naughty in kindergarten. He was a bully among his peers. As far as he could remember, neither the children nor the teachers actually liked him. When his mischief was reported to his parents, he was scolded and given painful spankings, but, with an aggressive personality and no nurturance from either home or school, these had no effect on him.

In his primary school years he was sent twice, in rotation with his brothers, to live with his grandparents in North China. There he spent his first and second grades. Deng has only disjointed memories of this period – his fights in the streets and disinclination towards studying. The year after, he was back with his parents again. Immediately, he encountered the problems of dialect and a discontinuous school syllabus. In the first term he failed in all subjects. As a 'northerner' who now spoke Cantonese with a funny accent, he became the object of ridicule. At one point, fighting back against classmates, he engaged in two major 'battles' a week. From the way he describes it, fighting back had become a means of survival, a view of life that has stayed with him. Two other interviewees similarly had spent their primary school days shuttling between one region and another. They, too, testify to the strong regional prejudices among Chinese children. But they never encountered such extreme isolation. Deng observed how other out-of-province children submitted to the leadership of their Cantonese classmates and, by adopting a meek posture, were left alone. But he himself, though not at all rebellious, was stubborn. As a result he was repeatedly beaten up by groups of classmates. He complained to his parents:

> But their reasoning was that if you did not bully people, others would not bully you. So they would give me a good scolding. 'Don't be naughty ever again like you used to be when you were in kindergarten.' But actually I was already like a piece of wood by then. I was no longer naughty, no longer assertive like I had been in kindergarten.

He resented his parents' lack of sympathy. He began to play truant as a means of escape.

None of the political values taught in school seemed to have penetrated his thinking. 'What they told me I just listened to. That was all.' Nothing demonstrates better how alien the political values were to him than his attitude towards the Young Pioneers, which Ao took as near sacred. When most of his classmates joined the Young Pioneers in third grade, Deng was denied admission because of his frequent fights. He told himself that he did not care; he would not like to cherish the things cherished by people who bullied him.

In the fourth grade, he was told, finally, he would be allowed to enter. The enrolment ceremony, which several interviewees regarded as the most memorable day of their childhood, was to take place several days later, after school. But Deng forgot entirely and did not turn up. This was unheard of and, to his teachers, the greatest insult a child could express towards what the Young Pioneers stood for. His parents were immediately sent for, and Deng received a torrent of scoldings from both teachers and parents. Yet so little had been the influence of the school's political socialization – so little did he comprehend the 'glory' of entering the Young Pioneers – that he remained perplexed as to why the adults should make such a fuss over his forgetfulness.

School took a turn for the better when Deng's mother belatedly realized the problems her son was facing and found time to coach him in his studies. When, to his own surprise, he passed his year-end examinations, he began to gain confidence in his own abilities. In the fifth grade, he transferred to his fifth primary school. Fluent now in Cantonese, and left alone to pursue his own interests, he began reading on his own. He even began to gain teachers' commendations for his essays, in which he was studiously employing all the vocabulary newly acquired from his readings.

Even then he remained isolated, without close relationships with either students or teachers. In such circumstances the teachings about collective spirit meant little to him: those storybook morals about being nice to your classmates, helping others in difficulties, comradeship in meetings, striving your best in voluntary work. But like any normal child, he wanted to be accepted and respected. In the fifth grade, once his feuds with other children had abated, he grew envious of the Young Pioneer members – especially the Young Pioneer cadres: 'They had one stripe, two stripes, three stripes. I had none.' In the sixth grade, finally, he was admitted. This was uncommonly late. He felt relieved and proud for a few short weeks. But he remained oblivious to the sacred political values attached to Young Pioneer membership.

Soon after joining the Young Pioneers, I didn't want to put on the red scarf anymore. Although I was happy with being inside it at last, I also wanted to show that I didn't care anything about the red scarf. My parents made sure that I did. They'd say: 'You've thrown away the glory once, now how come you don't cherish it properly?'. . . So I would wear it when leaving home and when going back. My younger brother had joined the Young Pioneers when very young; and under my influence, every day after we stepped out of the house we tore off the red scarves and stuffed them in our pockets. I was caught once doing that by my father. But even after that I refused to keep it on.

By the close of his primary school education, Deng had achieved average grades. He was unsociable, but not antisocial. He had no romantic respect for the school authorities, did not hold them in awe, less still have any inclination to win their approval through activist efforts; but neither was he rebellious against authority in the manner of Chang. He had internalized little of the political values, but he was not averse to them. He had no sense of superiority or inferiority in terms of his socioeconomic background, in part because he had never taken the initiative to make any friends and therefore did not see himself as part of a group with more or less prestige than other groups. He felt an outsider for having been rejected for so long; but he assumed a sour-grapes attitude instead of deprecating himself. He had begun to harbour some ambition, and his ambitions were rising.

He was, morever, beginning to absorb some of the polity's moral values, but as he puts it, in an 'unorthodox way', by reading fiction on his own. The first long novel he read, *An Old Communist Youth Leaguer*, struck a chord in him. 'Its message was that people should devote themselves to the party and the revolution, and while reading it I felt it a highly admirable aspiration; I felt people should emulate that.' His was not a case of deviance. It was one of late maturation in political socialization. But it should also be borne in mind that he had not experienced any of the passion for the political values shared by Ao, Bai and Chang. These strong childhood feelings had formed the foundation for their own kinds of later activism, different from the 'pragmatic' activism that would be characteristic of Deng.

3 The Political Socialization of Adolescents

As young people rose through the three years of junior high school and the three of senior high school, they came under ever increasing pressures to perform in an activist fashion. It was partly that the students, as they grew older, recognized that a good political record would be helpful in securing admission to the higher levels of education. But more than that, the top party leadership's demands that students be activist were intensifying during the half decade from 1962 through 1966, precisely the period when this generation of students moved through adolescence.

The leadership's tightening demands upon the students were due, in part, to the split with Russia. Starting in 1963, secondary school students were required to study party Central Committee documents directed against the evils of Soviet 'revisionism'.[1] And in editorials, party leaders began addressing China's teenagers in urgent tones about the potential degeneration of their generation. Repeatedly, this worry was conveyed in the youth magazines as a dramatically crucial moral question:

> Enemies inside and outside China persistently try to take advantage of the lack of experience of young people in struggle and tempering and their weaknesses in class vigilance, to spread bourgeois poisons, gradually to erode away the youths' revolutionary will-power, to corrupt the youths' revolutionary souls. The notorious former American Secretary of State, Dulles, even at the moment of his death emphasized the use of the 'lifestyle of western civilizations' to corrupt the 'third generation' of the socialist countries, to make the 'third generation' degenerate so as to realize their vicious plot of 'peaceful evolution', from socialism regressing to capitalism.[2]

To stave off this danger, the schools, aided by the mass media, stepped up their programmes of political education. In an emotional throwback to the revolution's roots and in an appeal to the loyalty of China's good-class majority, 'class education' about the sufferings of the poor under the *ancien regime* was added to the syllabus of extracurricular activities. The cult of Mao assumed a steadily larger and more emotionally-charged role in party teachings, with Mao's thought, Mao's quotations and Mao's deified image increasingly tied to demands that young people prove themselves genuinely activist.

In this chapter we shall explore how Ao, Bai, Chang and Deng, each in a different way, accepted the political teachings, and the differing means they chose publicly to exhibit their dedication. We shall also observe the tensions and dilemmas that each of them faced. To understand these, however, we must first examine the mechanisms by which the school authorities encouraged and sustained activism.

THE SMALL GROUP

As in primary school, educators sought to shape the behaviour of teenagers through the careful organization of peer pressures and a tightly controlled social environment. Even more than in primary school, discussion 'small groups' were utilized for these purposes.[3]

In weekly criticism/self-criticism sessions, the dozen or so small group members[4] were supposed freely to exchange ideas, to bring up their own or others' particular problems, both political and personal in nature, to discuss each others' bad thoughts and backward performance, or praise each other for having performed good deeds. The aim was that, through the well-intentioned aid of their peers, the students would be channelled towards correct behaviour.

But the small group was not meant to be a solidarity group; it was the very opposite. This was to prevent the peer group's own informal norms from dominating the small group, and to ensure that friendship or embarrassment did not mute the criticisms and self-criticisms. The activist behaviour observed in a small group was usually the product of competition among members, under intense pressure from the group's activist leaders.

To promote this competition, the small groups were given the power to nominate members for the titles of 'labour activist' and '3-good student' (good in attitude, labour and studies). At the end of each academic year, these titles entered the winners' dossiers, and accordingly were helpful in the contest to get into university. This inducement, coupled with the watchdog role played by the student activists planted in every small group, all but guaranteed that only officially orthodox views had an airing in group discussions, to the exclusion of any utterances to the contrary.

To bring out the weight of conformity in the small group, it is best to quote at length the experience of one of the interviewees:

> Before we left for the countryside to help with harvesting for about two weeks, we held a session during which you had to take turns to express your resolutions. You'd say how you were determined to temper yourself this time, how you'd learn from the poor and lower-middle peasants.[5]
>
> Q: But didn't this mean the same things were repeated over and over again by everyone?
> A: Yes, every time before we went to the countryside it was the same.
> Q: So you only had to memorize the right expressions?
> A: Oh, we could spurt those out naturally.

But this did not imply rejection of the values, for he continued:

> At that time I was thinking of reforming my thoughts . . . The teachings up there tried to make all of us students do so. So everyone tried as hard as possible to look for their own faults. Everyone thought of going down to understand the countryside and to learn from the peasants of 'poor and lower-middle peasants' class category . . . At that time there was this tendency – everyone forcing himself to look at the peasants from the good side. But every time we came back from the countryside and thought it over, actually apart from the ability to withstand hardship, the peasants had seemed terribly selfish. Some of us happened to talk about it privately among ourselves, and we felt scared to see that the peasants were so selfish. If someone among us met a good peasant he'd boast about it because he had discovered the good side of the peasants through his own experience.

On returning from the countryside they had another meeting to report on what they had learned from labouring with the peasants:

> That meeting was very ritualistic. Everyone would say: 'Before, I was lazy, afraid to labour; but after this experience I feel . . . blah, blah, blah!'

Q: Everyone said the same thing?
A: Yes, everyone.
Q: No one said anything that should not be said?
A: Other kinds of things couldn't be said. Only rightists would.
Q: Anyone ever tried?
A: Never.

Two effects may be noted here. On the one side, the technique of repetitive role-playing did get the students to 'spurt out the right sentiments naturally', and peer-group pressures then induced them to act according to those sentiments. But on the debit side, it was at the expense of ritualization, hypocrisy and the deadening of free discourse.

CLASS EDUCATION

On the grounds that the young people had not personally experienced exploitation in the pre-Liberation days, they were required, beginning in 1962–3, to attend 'recall bitterness and contemplate [present] sweetness meetings' (*yiku sitian hui*). The schools invited peasants and workers who had suffered starvation and physical abuse before Liberation to come into the classrooms to relate the horrors of their previous lives. But many students had ambivalent feelings about the sessions. This was because peer pressures turned such an occasion into yet another opportunity for competitive shows of activism. As one interviewee who went to an all-girl school recalls:

> We'd sit around the old fellow telling the story and all wail. After he finished his story we'd eat a 'recall bitterness' meal of leaves, sawdust cakes, etc. We ate it all, red and swollen eyed. I was so moved! I cried and cried and cried!
> All the students cried when they heard the stories. The atmosphere was that if you didn't, others might think you didn't have class consciousness. There was this type of suppressiveness . . . and it became a show. Those girls didn't have to wail so loud; they really went ooh . . . ooh . . . ooh; they might be moved, but not to that extent. If they hadn't cried it actually would have meant they were genuine, but to cry like that was faked . . . But I was *really* moved.
> For about ten days after a recall bitterness meeting, most of the

students would become more activist: keeping quiet in the classroom, walking properly, and doing more good things in the dormitory, things like hanging up others' mosquito nets, making dormmates' beds . . . However, after that, they'd revert to their usual behaviour. Ha, that was really funny.

THE COMMUNIST YOUTH LEAGUE

The Communist Youth League provided a more far-reaching, far more effective instrument for eliciting sustained activism than either the small groups or these 'bitterness' sessions. But the league's influence was not fully felt until senior high. Since students could not apply for membership in the highly selective league until they turned fifteen, a second-year junior high school classroom generally contained only two or three members; and an entire school grade (comprising up to ten classrooms) normally contained only enough members to compose one league branch. With the league centred outside the classroom, it remained marginal to the affairs of the majority of the junior high school student body. Too old to participate any longer in the Young Pioneers, a junior high school class's formal leadership gravitated towards the elected class officers.

However, in the better junior high schools, where most of the students hoped to get into a good senior high school, attention shifted towards the league in the last year of junior high. The students there knew that senior high admissions policies gave special weight to league membership. An interviewee remarks,

In the final year of junior high, my classmates suddenly were very much concerned with becoming league members. You see, when you filled in application forms there was a column for 'political features': that is, whether one's a league member or just an ordinary member of the masses. But there was no column for 'class officer posts held'. Once the golden words 'league member' were inscribed on you, nothing could remove them. The party is the vanguard and the league member is an assistant to the party, right?

By the time students were in senior high school, a classroom would have contained enough league members to form its own league branch. The branch was given the power to recruit new members;

and through this discretionary power league members could influence their classmates' chances of entering a university. At most schools[6] the students flung themselves into an ostentatiously activist performance, eager to win the approval of the league members.

Candidates had to request one or two league members to be their 'league-entry introducers'. To impress on their political mentors their sincerity and devotion, they were supposed to lay bare their inner thoughts in 'heart-to-heart' talks. They were to ask for guidance on problems that were troubling them, be these their personal failings or their inability to understand certain party policies, or episodes of negligence, as in oversleeping or missing the morning calisthenics.

Beyond the heart-to-heart talks, the applicants were on show. They constantly had to appear enthusiastic, show their concern for classmates, take the initiative to do good turns, try to study well, work hard during labour sessions, speak up in meetings and criticize themselves without reservation. In addition, they had to 'lean close to the organization'.

Below is Bai's account, he himself having been a league member, of the considerations his league branch took into account when recruiting new members. In the final year of senior high school (1961), his league branch had just decided to enrol a student of capitalist background. (This was quite unusual, even though the class line was not yet strictly implemented.)

> Even that fellow was a bit phoney. In the application session, we league members, sitting in judgement of him, criticized him most for being hypocritical. That is, whenever he did a good deed, he had considered using it as an opportunity for being in the limelight, to prove himself. But in the main he was still good; at least in class he helped the others. He was vain in his heart and he was criticized most for this.
> Q: But shouldn't this be considered phoney activism?
> A: Phoney activism is 'in front of you one set of behaviour, behind you another set'. He still, after all, performed good deeds, both behind and in front of you. But when he did anything he always put the desire for glory in the first place. Ah, we criticized him until he was sweating. He was terribly scared we wouldn't let him through.

In the end, though knowing full well he had impure motives, the league branch allowed him to 'go through the gates' because he 'leaned close to

the organization'. What does leaning close to the organization mean?
Bai continues from his inside-the-league perspective:

> It means to come into contact more with the league members and
> hand in more reports on your political thought. By 'coming into
> contact', I mean talking to the league members more, going out
> with them more, frequently revealing [*fanying*] one's own thoughts
> and actions to the branch, and basically carrying out what the
> branch told you to do. Anyone who didn't pay attention to the
> league would be looked upon as having an attitude of animosity.
> The comments accompanying their university applications were
> bound to be bad because the comments were written by the teacher
> and the league branch together. First the teacher wrote the com-
> ments on everyone, then they were handed over to the league
> branch committee for evaluation.

It is interesting to note here how ulterior motives, a serious ideological failing which non-league members usually scorned as phoney
activism, could be overlooked by the league branch provided one
'leans close to the organization'. The latter criterion, of course,
guaranteed recruitment only of those who were willing to conform
unconditionally to the behavioural standards defined by the league –
the national league, in view of the centralized structure of the
organization. The league branch – and through it the national league
– became the final arbiter of all behaviour in the classroom.

If an applicant's self-proclaimed class origin was in doubt, the
league branch could apply to the school-level league branch for
authorization to look into his dossier, or could even go to the work
unit of the applicant's father to investigate the family history. In
China, this procedure is known as 'collecting material' and is a matter
of paramount importance to the individual concerned, since his
family label and history, which he himself may not be entirely aware
of, will strongly influence his life chances. Neither the individual
himself nor the class teacher had access to the dossiers. That is why,
as one interviewee who was not a league member notes, 'You had the
feeling that the league branch knows everything about you, and you
know nothing about them.' Bai, himself a member, jokingly but not
without some truth, once said of his league branch: 'Ah, we were like
secret agents.'

A teacher held no official power over the league's recruitment of
students unless he himself occupied a senior position in the league

hierarchy. He might put in a few words, though, for students he considered suitable for admission, but who had been ignored by the league branch. In one classroom in my sample, where a league branch composed mainly of good-class students was limiting recruitment to students only of similar class background, the teacher intervened, only to find himself in deadlocked confrontation with the league members.

A branch sometimes selected 'targets for cultivation' from among the students. In such cases, the branch members approached a student whom they thought suitable to join their ranks, instead of waiting for the student to approach the league. Such a student was normally from a family of sterling class background or had an exceptional record of activist performance but as yet had shown no overt interest in applying.

As the class line strengthened after 1963, those selected for league membership came increasingly from among the students of good-class origins, at the expense of the middle-class students. Unlike the students of capitalist or other bad-class origins, who had long ago grown accustomed to discrimination, the middle-class children, especially those from the professional classes, were used to enjoying prestige and social success at school. They felt aggrieved about their narrowing chance for league membership. But they believed wholeheartedly in the political system and wanted desperately to be in the vanguard, the league. They responded to the 'class line' in enrolments by stepping up their competitive efforts to seem activist. Quite differently, the young people of bad-class origins, who were almost entirely being squeezed out of the competition to join the league, were realistic about their chances and normally opted out of the activist contest.

In the 1965–6 school year, on the eve of the Cultural Revolution, the party leadership sought to alleviate the middle-class and bad-class students' feelings of discouragement. A new national policy was promulgated, succinctly embodied in the slogan, 'Don't talk just of the theory of class origins; the emphasis is on behaviour.' But this slogan was open to various interpretations. Students of different class backgrounds had different ideas on how to recognize genuine activism. The disagreements which erupted over this were later to assume a violent shape in the student fighting of the Cultural Revolution.

On the one hand the Communist Youth League had provided the political authorities with a potent means to promote activist ambitions among teenagers, but on the other hand the contest to enter the league had sown discord among the students; and when the class line was injected into this competition, the student body was pushed into potentially antagonistic class groups.

MODEL EMULATION

Even though many students were disturbed by the competition to get into the league and the class line, they were in no way politically disaffected. They wanted to behave in a genuinely committed fashion, and to encourage this, the government provided a pantheon of heroes upon whom they could pattern themselves, rather than let them have free rein to select randomly their own perhaps harmful role models. These official heroes were always presented as inhumanly perfect. The goal was to help teenagers form an idealistic projection of their own revolutionary potential. Young people trying to emulate their heroes were supposed to stretch their hopes and efforts to their outermost limits.[7]

From books and magazines, adolescents came into contact with a very considerable range of these exemplary heroes, both real and fictional. But two types, in particular, were pushed by the authorities. First were the war heroes and martyrs of violent revolution. This category of heroes had dominated the youth literature in the 1950s,[8] just as the country was emerging from the years of devastating war against Japan, the civil war and the Korean War. Memories of the recent Communist victory were still fresh; and the threat of foreign invasion had not yet disappeared. The party was seeking to consolidate patriotic sentiments and to place patriotism at the service of the revolution. Through the model war heroes, youngsters were to be introduced to a romanticized history of the new nation, with strong intimations that they should prove themselves worthy of the struggles and sacrifices of their revolutionary elders.

Second were the heroes of socialist construction. As China moved into the 1960s, the biographies of war martyrs increasingly were overshadowed by these newer heroes of a peacetime era of day-to-day work chores. Of them all, Lei Feng was given greatest publicity. His special stature as a model was signalled by a March 1963 double issue of *China Youth*, launching a Learn From Lei Feng campaign. The several characters 'Learn From Comrade Lei Feng', in Chairman Mao's own calligraphy, graced the front page. Precisely because the party leadership had specially selected Lei Feng as the foremost national model for emulation, we can presume that of all the models, Lei Feng best exemplified the personal attributes that the party wanted youngsters to acquire.

Lei Feng had grown up in hardship. Suffering the oppression of a landlord, the members of his family had died one after another from hunger and illness, culminating in his mother's suicide. At the age of six, Lei Feng was an orphan. Four years later his village was 'liberated'. Grateful for the changes brought to him by the party, he became an activist and eventually entered the People's Liberation Army and the party. He died an accidental death in 1962 at the age of twenty-two. His diary was discovered posthumously and excerpts were immediately published,[9] but never the complete diary.

Day after day, in page after page of the published selections, he recounted his gratitude towards Chairman Mao, the party and the masses. Lei Feng wrote of the party and the chairman as if he were engaged in a personal dialogue with them. He made resolution after resolution to devote himself entirely to the cause. Almost daily he entered this kind of sentiment in his diary:

> This morning when I got up I felt particularly happy. The reason was no other than that last night I dreamt of the great leader Chairman Mao . . . To the party today I have boundless words to say, boundless gratitude to express and boundless determination forever to struggle in its behalf.[10]

On the day he joined the party he wrote:

> Oh my excited heart! It hasn't calmed down for a second. Oh, the Great Party! Brilliant Chairman Mao! Only because of you did I have a new life. While I was facing imminent death struggling in a hell of fire, longing for the moment of life, you rescued me, provided me with food and clothes, even sent me to study in school . . . Under your continuous cultivation and education, from a poor child I grew up to become a Communist Party member with a certain degree of knowledge and consciousness.[11]

Lei Feng was perfectly altruistic, without the slightest self-interested calculations or self-doubts, righteousness incarnate. But even more importantly, he personified total gratitude, unflinching loyalty and unswerving, unquestioning belief.

As the cult of Mao began to build, Lei Feng's example taught

young people the precise manner in which Mao's teachings should be
studied. Lei Feng copied out in his diary long passages from Mao's
speeches and writings; and whenever in want of guidance to solve a
dilemma he would leaf through his diary for the appropriate quote to
'arm himself with Mao Zedong's thought'. A short story about Lei
Feng relates in meticulous detail the way the exemplary model
studied Mao's *Selected Works*:

> It was in this manner of night after night squeezing out time
> without being aware of fatigue that Lei Feng finished reading all
> the essays in the four volumes of *Mao's Selected Works*, as well as
> the articles by Chairman Mao which had appeared in the newspa-
> pers. And of these, he had read at least two or three times all the
> essays in Mao's *Selected Works*, Vol. 4, some of them more than
> six or seven times. Articles like 'In Memory of Norman Bethune',
> 'Serve the People', 'An Analysis of China's Social Classes', 'Carry
> the Revolution to the Very End', he had read countless numbers of
> times; and he had written several times on what he had gained
> from them.[12]

The message of Lei Feng was clear to students: in reading Mao's
works one does not question. Mao's words are to be taken as dogma.
Independent thinking has no place. The correct way to study Mao's
works is by repeated reading, better still by memorization, accepting
all of Mao's writings as axiomatically the Truth. This rote learning of
Truth was not new to China; it had been the major way to learn for
centuries. After Liberation the method of study had been basically
retained. But it was not until the 1960s that it became attached to
political dogma to such an extent or in this formalistic manner.

The campaign to learn from Lei Feng stressed, above all else,
'doing goods deeds' (*haoren haoshi*). In his diary Lei Feng described
the good deeds he consciously sought out as his means for serving the
people. When riding a train as a regular passenger, he would grab a
broomstick and begin sweeping floors or clean the carriage windows
or serve water to other passengers. Below is a typical account of how
he spent his Sundays while his colleagues all went off to see movies.

> Today is Sunday. I didn't go out. I washed five sets of sheets for the
> comrades in the platoon, mended one blanket for a comrade-in-
> arms, helped the kitchen staff wash 600 catties of cabbage, cleaned
> up the rooms and outside, and also did a lot of other odd jobs . . .

In all, today I've succeeded in doing what an orderly should volunteer to do. Though a bit tired, I feel very happy. The comrades in the platoon felt very surprised. Who washed the sheets so clean? Another comrade remarked with amazement: 'Who took my torn blanket away?' Actually he didn't know I have mended it for him! I felt that being an anonymous hero is the highest glory. From now on I should do even more, everyday minor things, and say fewer pretty things.[13] -

Lei Feng had not accomplished any great deed that rendered a historic contribution to the Chinese people. He did not even die an heroic death; a truck backed up on him, accidentally crushing him. His image was that of a man who had led an ordinary existence, but who tried his best. And it was precisely these good deeds, considered by some as trivial, which were upheld as essential for the revolution. He had never even *aspired* to become a leader or famous figure. He was content to lead a life anonymously adhering to the words of the party and the chairman. He contributed his share to the revolution by being a 'never-rusting screw', an everlasting cog in the wheel. Lei Feng wrote of the contribution made by a mere screw:[14]

A man's usefulness to the revolutionary cause is like a screw in a machine. It is only by the many many interconnected and fixed screws that the machine can move freely, increasing its enormous work power. Though a screw is small its use is beyond estimation. I am willing to be a screw.

In short, the kind of ideal socialist man the party and Mao had in mind for the younger generation was a completely self-abnegating individual quietly performing drudgery for the construction of socialism. The party had begun to push that theme hard in the 1960s at the very time that fewer good jobs were becoming available for the mounting numbers of students graduating from school. With upward mobility no longer a likely prospect for the majority of China's urban young people, the political authorities were employing the Lei Feng campaign to deflate expectations and reduce disappointment. One of the central messages of the Lei Feng campaign was that the ordinary cog-in-the-wheel manual jobs were 'glorious'.

Lei Feng was only the most prominent of the heroes of socialist construction. The portraits of other heroes of the same genre were presented in a widely-read book for teenagers.[15] All of the eleven heroes in the book had, like Lei Feng, been born a few years before

Liberation into impoverished working-class families. Their class stand, like Lei Feng's, was unswerving; their gratitude to Chairman Mao and the party was profound; their commitment to the revolution, total. Four of them were armymen; but almost all the rest were ordinary workers. They were conscientious, hard-working people who took pride in fulfilling their duties. They were self-confident, determined to overcome all physical hardships, not discouraged or ashamed at being manual labourers. (Only one hero, a woman, was described as having had feelings of self-doubt or inferiority.) They all studied Mao's works avidly and constantly reminded themselves to raise their own proletarian consciousness. Those heroes who came after Lei Feng had taken him as their own model. They, like him, were glorious cogs in the wheel.

A campaign was launched in the schools and even the universities to emulate the type of anonymous mundane chores that Lei Feng had engaged in. Ironically but ineluctably, however, this exercise in humble chores-doing soon became subverted by the student contest to be upwardly mobile. In classrooms where students were competing to get into the league and through that into a university, Lei Feng's type of good deeds provided concrete standards by which league members could appraise the political performance of would-be candidates. The writing of diaries and the circulation of them for public criticism, above all to league members, became an important way to show activism; so too did the secret washing and mending of classmates' clothes and sheets and the anonymous cleaning of windows and sweeping of floors. Teenage activists often became hard pressed to think of new and ingenious ways to outdo each other. They vied to think of new types of anonymous good deeds that classmates were likely to catch them doing. The emulate Lei Feng campaign was pressuring the young people to engage ever more intensely, for ulterior motives, in trivialized activist pursuits.

This was especially true of the prestigious boarding schools that drew students from throughout the city. The students there were continuously in each others' presence, constantly in a competitive atmosphere. Interviewees recall how, under the pressures of the Lei Feng campaign, troubling and amusing incidents of opportunistic play-acting began to crop up. For example, 'At about ten o'clock in the evening, when everyone was in the dormitory, one of the kids pretended to be asleep and suddenly, very loudly, called out, "Long live Chairman Mao." That was to prove how deep his class feeling was, that even in his dreams he loved Chairman Mao.'

Students had become extremely self-conscious of every action they took, out of an anxiety to please league members and to avoid being criticized for being 'backward' and nonconformist. Should I hide my laundry to prevent classmates from 'anonymously' washing it for me? What should I write in my 'private' diary? Should I cry aloud now in the 'recall bitterness' meeting? In order to show my activism, must I studiously avoid ladling up a piece of meat from the communal soup pot? How much about myself should I reveal to my league sponsor in our next heart-to-heart talk? The young people felt they were constantly being forced onto a stage to perform. Some felt their inner integrity was being challenged. They were convinced of their own genuine devotion. But at the same time they could not rid themselves of the guilty feeling that in their activist behaviour they were careerists and hypocrites.

Among those of a more rebellious character there was a growing ill-defined desire to rise above the petty posturing, a strong urge to do something unconventional and sincere. When they could muster up the courage, several of my interviewees openly and deliberately broke the league's code of 'revolutionary' behaviour. One of them daringly pinned up a poster in his classroom stating that there was much more to being a revolutionary than the 'petty details' for which Lei Feng was admired. A second interviewee led a group of classmates to a mountaintop on the eve of final examinations to spend a night reciting poetry and marvelling at the sunrise. Such interviewees wanted to repudiate the mundane pettiness of schoolroom activism; they wanted to prove their revolutionary devotion in a sincere, grand, romantic way, and saw no avenues to do so. Their sporadic acts of stubborn nonconformity stirred up commotions in their classrooms, inviting criticism from the league branch. Inevitably they had difficulty getting into the league.

HEROES AND THE THEME OF DEATH

The one quality about the heroes of socialist construction which captured the imagination of such young people was the heroes' willingness to die grandly. Though they had not been provided with a battlefront to prove their ultimate devotion, the stories about these heroes often stressed that in their everyday work they were prepared to lay down their lives for the revolution and the masses; and most of the models of this sort literally did sacrifice their lives. Of the eleven

heroes of socialist construction who were included in the above-
mentioned book for teenagers, nine had died in their twenties in fires
or floods while saving comrades or state property. They had chosen
to risk death; Lei Feng was one of the very few who had died
accidentally. But the very fact that Lei Feng, the most important of
all these heroes, did not perish heroically conveyed the message that
lifetime dedication alone can earn the title of hero, and that the
dedication need not result in any great accomplishment. So long as
one is willing to be a cog in a wheel one could become a hero like Lei
Feng.

Yet this theme of death remained an important element in the
portrayal of heroes, so much so that many of my interviewees had, as
teenagers, given much thought to the subject of death. One would
have imagined that in a time of peaceful economic development the
message of selfless hard work would have been utilized alone in the
effort to maintain revolutionary commitment among the populace.
After all, in a time of peace, how often does a person, even in a
lifetime, encounter catastrophic incidents? But obviously the Chinese
authorities realized such a humdrum vision was not enough. End-
lessly the accounts were of ordinary people flinging themselves into
leaping flames or into raging rivers to protect or save collective
property, becoming heroes by dying.

Here is a typical description of how such heroes sacrificed their
lives. Two good friends were attempting to stop the flames of a
burning truck full of gasoline from spreading to the surrounding
factories:

> Little Lung reached it a little before Little Han. All they could see
> were flames leaping from the truck. The gas at the back of the
> truck was already in flames, with only six or seven barrels still not
> yet on fire. As Communist Party members, concerned with the
> people's benefit and the state's interests, to see barrel after barrel
> of gas burnt off like this; oh how agonizing it was for them! . . .
> The two young workers gave each other a look, and without
> hesitation, really with one heart, Little Lung gave a push with his
> hands, a hop, and up he jumped onto the vehicle. He grabbed hold
> of the scorching rim of an oil barrel and with all his might pushed it
> off the truck. Little Han, too, hanging onto the truck's side, had
> just leaped aboard when suddenly an enormous explosion erupted
> from the vehicle. . .[16]

This, then, is the way to die. One should live and die for the people.

Since a person has to die anyway, why not a meaningful death, for the revolution? Some of my interviewees genuinely took up this view of death. Ao, for example, recollects her attitude towards death as a teenager, after she graduated from junior high school and had gone to the countryside to settle.

To the model heroes, dying was all right. I thought I could do that as well, if necessary then die. Such as dying while saving others, dying while putting out a fire, preventing floods, mending dykes. That is, dying can come under any circumstances. Even pulling a cart can lead to death! Anything can happen, the cart overturning, crashing on top of someone. That is to say: live to work, work while you live, work at all risk. If you die, let it be. And actually, wasn't that the case then? You were to work till you grew old, work risking your life. 'For the revolution we pull carts.' That was the kind of thought that was injected. 'As long as the cart hasn't toppled over, the only thing is to push.' If you are to plunge yourself without limit into the business of serving the people, you work! And if it was necessary for you to die, then give it up, you have to give it up at the very end anyway . . . At that time I was so stupid. There was a fire. A girl like me climbing all the way up to the roof of the building. The fire was burning the tiles already. The roof was already collapsing, with only the planks left behind. I climbed up. But thinking about it now, it was really dangerous. While climbing up I didn't realize that. My heart was red, you know. Ha, to be heroic. That was the mentality at that time. And then there was protecting the dykes from floods. Those scenes were really grand. Those boys jumped down, and arm in arm formed a human wall so that openings could be patched up. And when a typhoon was about to come, in the fields we cut and cut to get the rice. If we didn't, then the whole harvest would be gone. That was another kind of big scene. It was always like being in a battle.

The main purpose of instilling this philosophy of death, in short, was that it was the corollary of the philosophy of life. By downplaying the horror of death and magnifying its social value, life can cease to the individual to be a private possession. When death loses its individualistic component, so can life also. An individual with such a view of death will find it much easier to submit to the collective spirit and the collective will. It will be of some interest to us to see later how the other three interviewees viewed this philosophy of life and death.

HEROES AND INDIVIDUALISM

In addition to the two types of heroes that were prescribed as role
models for adolescents, the youth magazines and books portrayed a
third genre of hero: the great heroes of history, ranging from well-
known Chinese historical figures through great foreign scientists,
generals, theoreticians and contemporary revolutionaries. Of them
all, Mao was the most venerated in the eyes of the young people.
Stories about these heroes often emphasized their individual talents.
resourcefulness and courage. But the decisive difference between the
first two categories (the war heroes and heroes of socialist construction) as against these latter heroes is that the latter, by their innate
individual qualities and the force of their personalities, had pushed
the wheel of history forward. Notably, these were not the heroes
singled out as emulation models by the Chinese authorities. Mao, for
instance, was presented as a fatherly figure to the children and under
the Mao cult he was hailed as the 'great leader', 'the helmsman' and
'the red sun in our hearts', but never was he presented as a model to
emulate.

For one thing, encouraging the pursuit of personal greatness provided room for the pursuit of individualistic interests. The type of
heroism that was officially encouraged was supposed to be bound into
the collective framework, whereas 'individual heroism' (*geren ying-
xiongzhuyi*) was specifically condemned in party teachings. Even
more pertinent, yet left unsaid, was the fact that great heroes, and in
particular revolutionary heroes like Mao, became great by changing
the established order through acts which were basically unconventional or even rebellious in nature. In the period of socialist construction, such creativity and rebelliousness were not appreciated.
'Revolution' now meant conforming to established norms; suppressing all unconventional and individualistic inclinations; surrendering
the whole being to the party and Chairman Mao; and a willingness to
live an ordinary methodically hardworking life. Revolution had become the antithesis of rebelliousness. This underlay the official support for the Lei Feng model, and why Mao was to be venerated but
not emulated.

But some young people, through their private reading, did choose
some of the great historical heroes as their models. Several interviewees had looked precisely to the rebellious young Mao in an effort to
affirm both their individualism and dedication. The kind of model a
young person emulated revealed much about his or her attitudes

towards the established norms of political behaviour. Emulating Lei Feng would be recognized as activist behaviour, but openly emulating certain aspects of Mao Zedong as a rebellious young revolutionary might land you in trouble with the arbiters of correct behaviour in the classroom – the Youth League members.

Several interviewees, to prove that their inner integrity and revolutionary devotion were far superior to the petty activism around them, copied the harsh physical tempering to which the young Mao had subjected himself. They practised exercise routines that required austere, stringent self-discipline. and cultivated a self-image that through this self-tempering they were different, tougher, more genuine than the rest of their classmates, especially the league members. They told themselves that they were toughening their willpower for a 'revolutionary' moment that would come one day; and that when it came they would be able to achieve something truly great, unlike those 'docile tools' such as Lei Feng who limited themselves to being no more than a screw. The Cultural Revolution would soon provide them with their long-awaited opportunity to act out their dreams on a grand violent scale. Violence, and the risk of death, would become to them a liberating experience.

Ao, Bai, Chang and Deng, each in their own way, had wrestled with the questions of conformity, dedication, heroes and death. In the following accounts, one of our interests will be to see what heroes and which aspects of those particular heroes each of them emulated, and why.

THE CONFORMING ACTIVIST AS AN ADOLESCENT

By the time of her graduation from primary school at the age of twelve, as we have seen, Ao was a highly conformist and genuinely committed political activist, alienated from her peers and family. As she grew older Ao remained Ao, with the same temperament and ambitions. Adolescent activism placed greater demands on her leadership role. Her weaknesses remained with her, but she was beginning to develop an ability to 'struggle' with conscious effort to overcome them.

As in primary school, Ao remained academically superior to most of her peers. Her suburban junior high school was considered by most informants as above average, but she herself, being overly ambitious, felt it a third-rate school that was beneath her. In Ao's class, 40 per cent of the children came from peasant homes and another 40 per cent from workers', but the several middle-class families provided a majority of the best students.

In those years before 1964, when academic superiority still overshadowed good class background as a measure of leadership potential, Ao's official political standing went unchallenged. Obedient and politically active, she again was the teachers' favourite. But once more, because of her unpopularity with the classmates, she was not elected as class-head and had to take up a lesser position as classroom committee member in charge of academic studies. She put all of her activist devotion and ego into raising her classmates' academic standards. She spent time coaching the backward students. She promoted the study of Russian, the most difficult and disliked of the school subjects, by introducing flash cards. She even organized her classmates, both boys and girls, to cooperate in visiting sick schoolmates. She was particularly proud of this achievement, since students of the opposite sex in Chinese classrooms rarely talked to each other, let alone showed collective spirit in visiting ill classmates together.

Ao avidly continued to consume revolutionary novels and faithfully followed the news put out by youth magazines: 'These had their attractive side: laying down plans for action, talking about school activities and how one can become a good student, and about going down to the countryside to temper oneself.' It was her search for proper activist action that attracted her to the magazines. She never raised a 'why' question. Her paramount concern was always *'how'* – how to conform to the norms, as instructed, to the best of her ability.

She had no interest in keeping up with the sweep of national political developments. When she did read a newspaper, it was either to fulfil some class assignment or to satisfy the minimal requirements for politics class; after all, she says, 'in politics exams you didn't have to know a lot about current affairs to answer those questions'. What mattered to her were the cues for political action, not the content of the policies.

In junior high school, politics was not placed above other school subjects nor did a high grade in politics count towards activism. In schools that were concerned to keep up a good academic reputation, the schoolheads even encouraged students to concentrate their time and energy on their other subjects at the expense of the politics class. In some schools, the politics class was relegated by students to the same footing as music classes and physical education. Interviewees generally found the subject easy to pass. One merely had to memorize the teacher's notes, read several assigned articles, remember a few dates, and when the examination came, regurgitate them in the appropriate phraseology.

Though lacking interest in political knowledge, Ao had absolute faith in the chairman and the party and unquestioning trust in the socialist system. She felt willing to subordinate her personal interests (though not without some internal struggle) to the collective good. If the occasion arose for her to die for the nation, as we have seen, she romantically felt herself ready to do so without hesitation, just like the heroes she read about.

A genuine revolutionary was supposed to cultivate consciously a proletarian worldview. Ao did try to do so, but she had a difficult time of it, partly due to her ashamed awareness that she was not from a proletarian family. She was disturbed when she could not cry in 'recall bitterness, contemplate sweetness' meetings or when playing a tragic role in acting. Today she recalls the strong social pressures and her repeated frustrations at not being able to cry:

> How could I cry when I just couldn't? I was acting in a propaganda team. Tears just wouldn't come out. They could criticize you for that, even though it was only acting, for not having a class feeling. And I was angry with myself for that. I thought it was due to my father's influence that I didn't have class feeling.

When older, she understood why she could not cry:

> The sufferings of the formerly exploited classes had nothing to do with me. They weren't my mother, nor my father, nor my grandfather. Mao Zedong was right. I did not have that sort of class feeling.
> Q: How about some of your classmates who came from the 'good' classes? Did they cry?
> A: Crying or not crying isn't the point. They were moved. If it hadn't been for the Communist Party, they might still be suffering. We had had no worries, so we didn't so readily care. It's really like this – this thing – class feeling!

Ao might have had difficulty cultivating 'proletarian class feeling' but she had no difficulty drawing a clear line between herself and her parents. As the cause of her lack of class feeling, she tried her best to absolve herself of this political equivalent to 'original sin'. As a child, she was ashamed of her parents; in junior high school she was contemptuous of them. She hardly spoke to them, still less asked them for advice on important decisions. In her 'league application meeting', in front of several dozen people, she drew the class line with her family without any qualms. She publicly declared that she would not allow them to corrode her thoughts, and would help them to reform theirs.

Ao had no personal contact with landlords or capitalists, but she and other middle-class interviewees had had a genuine fear of them. This class hatred of the 'five-category elements' was officially encouraged, and Ao herself tried consciously to cultivate her hatred. The first time that Ao had direct dealings with any of these enemies of the people was when, after graduation from junior high school, she was sent to settle in a peasant village. All of the village's bad-class family heads were lined up in front of the newcomers for careful scrutiny. The exercise was to ensure that in the future they would direct their 'class hatred' towards the appropriate neighbours. For a number of years thereafter, Ao treated these people with both contempt and fear. She found it distasteful even to look at them, convinced that their faces were literally ugly.

To make a public show of their class stand, Ao and many other students avoided close contact with classmates of bad-class heritage. Aware of her own lack of 'proletarian class feelings', Ao was convinced that those from family backgrounds worse than hers were likely to possess an innate antagonism towards the government. She and her fellow league members made it extremely difficult for bad-class classmates to enter the league, at the same time approaching red-class schoolmates to join their ranks. Whereas in primary school the class labels of schoolmates had been of little significance to children, by junior high school these had become a matter of concern to everyone.

At school, the greatest test for Ao in her attempts to adopt a proletarian worldview remained her patronizing attitude towards her peasant-worker classmates, who tended to be academically inferior and had lower aspirations for their futures. Intellectually, she believed the party's teachings that the workers and peasants were the most revolutionary of classes; that it was they who had created and sustained the world; and that the children of such classes shared in their parents' virtues. But emotionally she could not accept any of this. Influenced both by her family and the school's continuous emphasis on academic achievement, her dream was still to become some sort of specialist. She rationalized that her contribution to the workers and peasants would be to 'help them improve their thinking', her own patronizing misinterpretation of the party's line.

For an ambitious believer like Ao, activism alone was not sufficient. In her second year of junior high school, encouraged by the teachers, she applied to join the league. She tells of her reasons:

> It was glorious, prestigious. As a league member or a party member you'd have a *lot* of opportunity to have power. Without power how could you do anything? How could you achieve anything all by yourself? I wanted to be a revolutionary successor, that is, a cadre, and without these political credentials how could you rise? But it wasn't entirely for fame and privileges [*ming-li*]. My interpretation was this: as a member of it I can do work within the organization. Outside the league you float around all on your own, but once inside you have something to rely on. Unity is strength; you could all work together. There are constant meetings, directives, opportunities to discuss things together.

In her consuming desire to join the league, acquisition of status and power were the foremost incentives and, understandably, she mentioned them first. To justify herself, she had been careful to append two further reasons: the sense of solidarity and of efficacy. But she still had left unsaid what Chinese ideology deemed the most important end – 'serving the people'. What should have been the means had become, for her, the ends. I do not wish to imply that she had no interest in 'serving the people'. But forgetting to mention this goal was no mere slip of the tongue. The same question was asked of her on several occasions, and each time prestige and power came first. Ao had developed great dependency on established authority, which effectively offset feelings of individual weakness. By being part of the established order she could be endowed with a part of its power, and for that she was willing to surrender herself to the organization.

Ao's ultimate aim was to become a 'revolutionary successor, that is a cadre'. A Chinese youth's interpretation of this phrase 'revolutionary successor' provides a very good indicator of his or her attitude towards power and the established order. The term 'revolutionary successor' semantically was open to two interpretations. The way it was generally understood by the Chinese broadly meant a new generation trying to carry on the revolutionary ideals of the old revolutionary generation as the latter gradually died off. Accession to power and to official status was not part of the the definition offered by any of my interviewees other than Ao and Bai. In fact, interviewees often expressed surprise when asked for their interpretation of what they considered a simple and straightforward term.

Ao's definition, which spells out specifically 'that is, a cadre', assumes that a 'revolutionary successor' possesses power and status in an established institution. Yet it is Ao's understanding of the term, and not the popular interpretation, which came close to the official meaning as laid down by Mao in 1964. In instructions to party cadres, Mao had specified five requirements for 'revolutionary successors'.[17]

1. They must temper themselves to become genuine Marxist–Leninists.
2. They must be revolutionaries who wholeheartedly serve the overwhelming majority of the people of China and the whole world.
3. They should succeed in learning how to unite and work with the overwhelming majority. Not only must they unite with those who agree with them; they must also be good at uniting with those who disagree with them.
4. They must succeed in learning how to apply the party's democratic centralism, and must master the good workstyle of listening to the opinion of the masses.
5. They must be modest and prudent and guard against arrogance and impetuosity; they must be imbued with the spirit of self-criticism and have the courage to correct mistakes and shortcomings in their work. They must not cover up their errors and claim all the credit for themselves and shift all the blame onto others.

Conditions 1 and 2 are broad precepts that generally could be practised by any ordinarily conscientious individual. Most of the interviewees had misinterpreted the meaning of 'revolutionary successor' by focusing upon these two conditions, which they had seen as compatible with their own perception of genuine activism. It was from the last three conditions, contrarily, that Ao had derived her understanding of the term. Even though still a teenager, she had already assumed the perspective of an up-and-coming cadre. 'Cadres' and 'the masses' are exclusive entities: once a cadre one is no longer part of the masses; one's task thereafter is to work towards 'guiding' and 'uniting with the masses'. This was the mission to which Ao had committed herself.

Mao was keenly aware of and worried by the gap between leaders and led and the resentments of the latter. That is why his third, fourth and fifth conditions were instructions to cadres to assume a democratic workstyle and be willing to be self-critical, trying always to guard against bureaucratism, commandism and arrogance. Yet it was these very pitfalls to which a member of an elite Leninist organization was most susceptible.

Ao was aware of her weaknesses. She tried earnestly and consciously, though not always successfully, to suppress her flaws, disciplining herself. Of all the interviewees, Ao was the only one who seriously began self-discipline as early as in junior high school.

Her efforts at self-discipline intensified when she applied to join the league. Since there were not yet any league members in her class, she had chosen two teachers as her league-entry introducers and dutifully handed 'thought reports' in to them. She preferred this rather than having heart-to-heart talks with them. She says she could not bear hearing them criticize her face to face, for she had been used to hearing only praise. None the less, she had great trust in her teacher introducers and honestly discussed with them her problems and anxieties:

> We talked about my recent performance, problems that I couldn't solve; my worries, my inability to work with the classmates; or how I couldn't successfully push forward my work as the committee member in charge of study, how some people failed in a test and how I felt responsible for it; how I was arrogant and complacent, how I didn't take the advice of the teachers, how I angered the teachers; my inability to fulfil my duty, etc., etc.

Q: How about more political, theoretical things?

A: I didn't talk about that. I was the more pragmatic type. I was worried about what I could achieve and what I failed to do. I thought about these all the time, always measuring – measuring with a ruler.

The self-discipline Ao practised was, as can be seen, mainly concerned with correct modes of behaviour, relating, for example, to her relationships with her superiors and her peer group. She realized that in the eyes of her classmates she was the teachers' 'running dog'. She counted the two teachers who were her league introducers as her only friends. Despite the vows she made to herself to develop a close sense of comradeship with schoolmates, her sense of competitiveness, her yearnings to surpass them, kept her friendless. She has always spoken disparagingly of those among her peers whom she took to be her activist rivals.

She kept a diary, but it was not a Lei Feng style diary. As she says with slight embarrassment, it was not 'proletarianized'; it was full of 'petty-bourgeois' flavour. Her diary became her closest companion. She recorded in it her flow of emotions. Without a friend in class to confide in, and alienated from her family, diary-writing became the only channel by which she could work out her private emotions. Twice, she let her introducers read it, for she believed that by knowing her private self better, they could better guide her. It reflected a certain candidness on her part, but she admits, too, that there was 'a bit of dishonesty'. She had included among her confidential thoughts all the good deeds she had done, calculating that one day her introducers would be reading it.

Her anxiety to conform and her constant fear that she would not win social recognition and the authorities' approval weighed her down with nagging self-doubts. She practised self-cultivation[18] principally to restrain her spontaneous behaviour. But this was not always easy. Subjected to intense moralistic pressures which constantly pitted her against her less noble side, her behaviour became erratic. She could be kindly or supercilious, generous or selfish, frank or calculating, forgiving or jealous, humble or proud, depending on how firmly she applied self-restraint. The moralistic teachings first heightened her awareness of her own individualistic weaknesses, and then had her consciously suppress them. But in these efforts, she was caught in a paradox. The elaborate reward system that was devised for those who succeeded in containing such weaknesses served only to revive the very weaknesses that had been suppressed. Because she was rewarded for acting in a kindly manner, her feelings of superciliousness were aggravated; when she acted in a forgiving manner, it ended up preserving for her the special status that she was so jealous to guard; when she was humble she received praise that fed her pride. Individuals like Ao who so ambitiously aspired to be rewarded were trapped in the system's own contradictions.

It was within the context of her never-ending daily struggle to contain her weaknesses that Ao encountered the first great predicament in her life. She was caught in a dilemma between volunteering to settle in the countryside, which would grant her glory and the self-satisfaction of showing her true devotion to the revolutionary cause; or continuing into higher education, which she had always taken for granted but which would bring her the dishonour of seeming a 'phoney activist'.

By 1963–4, the government was preparing to send young people to settle in the countryside in larger numbers than previously.[19] During the school year, especially in the last term, school authorities mobilized the forthcoming graduates of both the junior and senior high school systems to prepare to volunteer. The slogan was 'one red heart, two types of preparations': be prepared either to settle in the countryside or to receive more education. The slogan betrayed no official preference for either choice. In reality, however, going on to higher education took priority. The rhetoric of school authorities amounted to the following: 'Study hard. Have more education so that in the future you can contribute more to the state. But if you fail to get into the next higher level of education, don't lose heart. Go to wherever the nation most needs you. Go to the countryside. There you can contribute as much, and even more gloriously.' But whatever the glory promised for those who volunteered to go to the countryside, the implication was clear: that this was still the second choice.

The efforts to prepare students to accept this second choice were intense. They were asked to sign pledges of intention at school. To declare whether they would go or not became a major dilemma confronting high school students, especially those who had been set on going to university. For academically good students, the mental pressure was less intense since their chances of getting into the next higher level of education were greater. Those who most soberly had to face the decision were the academically marginal students and the young people of bad-class backgrounds, who knew that they had little chance of advancing to higher education. But the possibility of failure faced everyone; and most of my interviewees, though academically above average, did have 'one red heart and two types of preparations'. Despite their expectation of going on to university, they were willing to go to the countryside if need be, to temper themselves[20] and to contribute to the motherland's development.

Mobilizing classmates to volunteer became one of the league branches' major tasks. Ao, as one of the foremost activists in her school, performed her duty well. She arranged for older students who had already settled in the countryside to come back to their alma mater to deliver speeches. She went out to the countryside to observe personally the contributions that educated youths could make to the construction of a new socialist countryside, and reported back to the school on her findings. She took the lead in making a solemn pledge, in front of the whole school, on her willingness to go. A boy from her school who later went to the countryside with Ao recalls how ordinary students found her determined declarations persuasive. He himself went with enthusiasm, not least because he was inspired by Ao's activist speeches.

But what was Ao's real attitude towards going?

Q: Did you think you might have to go?
A: Actually I was thinking I would go. Why should I be afraid since it was so glorious. That was how I thought.
Q: You really thought you would go?
A: Actually, in my heart I was convinced that I could go on to senior high.
Q: So after all you thought you didn't have to go?
A: If I failed to go. I was prepared to go if I couldn't go to senior high. But then I knew I would definitely pass . . .

But Ao did not pass. She could not believe her ears when the teacher quietly broke the bad news to her. She had made a major tactical error out of overweening conceit. Students were permitted to apply to four schools and no more; Ao applied *only* to the best four senior high schools in the city, schools to which only children of either the reddest of family backgrounds or students who were exceptionally bright dared apply. Ao was rejected by all four. (Most of my other interviewees, several of whom were probably better than Ao academically, had not had the presumption to apply to any of the four elite schools.) Yet even today she refuses to believe that her error of judgement was the cause of her failure. Instead, she prefers to hang onto an illusion that she was rejected for her non-red family background, an excuse which is both face-saving and rids her of self-recriminations that the failure was actually of her own making.[21]

Ao finally did volunteer to settle in the countryside. She went not because there was no alternative. She could have stayed in the city and taken the senior high school entrance examinations again the following year, as many did. She rejected this alternative against her parents' wishes. She likened her situation to the Chinese saying, 'He who rides the tiger cannot dismount.' Having so devotedly pledged her 'two types of preparations' and so actively persuaded others to make their vows, she could not retract now without being sneered at as a phoney activist. She felt that she had to make herself 'pass this difficult gate' to continue to hold onto her self-image as a genuine activist. Once again – this time as a model failure calling on the other failures to volunteer – she announced her decision in front of the whole school:

> I did not speak emotionally. I spoke quietly. After all, it was not a very glorious thing. My heart felt uneasy. Why have I failed? My grades have always been so high. I'm a league member, and how many league members are there? . . . My heart already had a small shadow.

Out of 100 failures from the graduating class, only twelve students signed up to go, and among the dozen she was the only league member. Reconciling herself to her situation, she convinced herself that by going to the countryside she could achieve a special glory, and as the only league member in the group she took upon herself the mission of taking care of the other non-league members. She was determined to accomplish something great, 'on the one hand to work for the countryside, and on the other attain some achievements for myself'. In fact, three others in the group of volunteers could claim more 'glory' than Ao. They had had 'one red heart and only one preparation'; unlike Ao, they had not failed to get into a senior high school.

On the day they left, an impressive farewell was organized for them. The whole school saw the group of sixteen-year-olds off amid the beating of gongs and drums. Ao recalls the group's romantic and idealistic but somewhat mixed emotions.

> On the train we wept and sang at the same time:
> 'On that bright and lovely spring morning,
> The carriages carrying our youthful friends
> To build up the mother country,
> To change the mother country into heaven'.
> We sang all the way, crying. After all, we had never left our homes before, and who knew where it was we were heading for? When the train started my heart jumped a little. My eyes were a bit wet, but I knew my responsibility was very great. Being the only league member I had to take care of the others. They were crying, and I made them sing to brighten up the atmosphere.

THE PURIST ACTIVIST AS AN ADOLESCENT AND YOUNG ADULT

Bai, our second official activist, did not become one, by joining the league, until he was in senior high school. Yet Bai, as we recall, had had activist potential as a child in the orphanage. All those qualities – gratitude to the Communist Party, proletarian class consciousness, solidarity with the peer group, love of collective life, a proclivity to labour – which Ao consciously had to cultivate with very limited success, were integral to Bai's personality by the time he was an adolescent. However, by the party's standards these qualities were inadequate. They were merely 'spontaneous' (*zifade*) and 'unconscious' (*wuyishide*) and could easily degenerate if not properly channelled into 'conscious' political activism. Bai provides a good case study of the transformation of an adolescent with merely activist inclinations into a 'socialist youth with consciousness'.

The junior high school which he entered in 1956 was not a good school, largely because it was new, so new that the students had to spend the first few months of the semester helping to finish the school building's construction. The academic quality of the students was below average, and the school was too new to have established much discipline. Chaos often reigned in the classrooms. Influenced by the rowdiness, Bai soon learned how to fight. By the second year, he had established a reputation as one of his class's best fighters. He never ventured out of the school grounds without pocketfuls of pellets.

To be pugnacious was not uncommon among boys of his age. But Bai, though still proud of his prepubescent exploits, was quick to assure me he was no social deviant. For two hours he gave an animated blow-by-blow account of a junior high school career punctuated by fight after fight, each with a self-explained justification. By the end he had left his exhausted listener with the conclusion that even at that age he had had a compelling sense of righteousness. From his own recollection, he had seldom picked fights. He usually got involved either in protection of the meek or when forced to put up his fists when notorious bullies came to test him out. His opponents were invariably described as obnoxious, antisocial troublemakers. He had to make public self-criticisms repeatedly for his involvement in these brawls, but his self-image was untarnished.

In these years Bai demonstrated a second quality: a compelling sense of responsibility. Having proven his willingness and skill at labour, he was voted the labour committee member of the class. In a nationwide campaign in 1958 to 'work while studying', Bai's class participated in an inter-school competition to produce nitrogen fertilizer by cultivating a kind of bacterium:

> All classes had to do this. But in the other classes the students were lazy and didn't mix the chemicals and manure in the correct proportions or stir them up well. You can imagine that few took the trouble to mix the human manure well. But I was very strict with that. I directed the classmates to do it, and I myself used my hand to mix it. Using a stick wasn't good enough, couldn't mix it well enough. And somehow the classmates listened to me and stirred with their hands too. And I was very demanding, too, going around to make sure they watered it. Tap water had chlorine in it and could kill off the bacteria. I insisted we use well water. I also paired one girl off with one boy to handle the watering to make sure there was no joking around. That's why our bacteria was taken around the whole city to be exhibited. Oh, it was beautiful!

In the final year of junior high school, he revealed a further quality: the ability to impose strict self-control. He had not only fought but had become foul-mouthed. Almost every sentence he uttered was laced with swear words. However, influenced by the propaganda of the 'Security Education Campaign' in 1959 about restoring law and order in society,[22] he became determined to turn over a new leaf. He restrained himself from fighting back even when provoked and publicly made a promise in front of the whole class that 'as of this day no foul language will come from my mouth'. None did. For two weeks he dared not speak, and whenever he had to, he drew out the words one by one.

Yet he had little political 'consciousness'. He had little interest in politics as an academic subject. He found the class 'boring' and 'empty'. But he avidly read revolutionary novels. Too poor to buy any, he often ran over to a book store across the street from his school to read during lunch hours. He respected the chairman and the party and loved the country, but it was still, as he puts it today, 'a very spontaneous love, not through intellectualization. It was only a spontaneous passion of feelings.'

He held the league in esteem as an abstract entity. But like many of his classmates, he had no interest in becoming a member because the only league member in his class was the class's 'greatest ass-kisser'.

Under the influence of his father, Bai had come to take university education as a natural goal. He wanted to become a doctor in traditional Chinese medicine or a great scientist. When it was time to consider what type of senior high school to go to, he applied only to schools which provided continued general education, without giving a second thought to the possibility of a vocational school. Apparently he did well in the examinations, for he got into one of Canton's better schools and was placed in a 'keypoint' classroom: a model class for the whole school, handpicked for the 'cultivation of the state's talents'. At the beginning of the school year the principal imparted to this select class his great expectations for them.

In his class, the children of party officials made up half the students. Academically and politically, the class was unusually 'progressive', with a total of eight league members, seven of whom were cadres' children. From the first day of school there were already enough members to form a league branch, and enough activist students to generate an atmosphere of classroom activism. But Bai paid little attention to the political activities around him. His only concern was to do well in his studies. Soon after the term began, however, when the whole school went to help build a railway station, Bai distinguished himself in his enthusiasm and ability to labour, and quickly drew the attention of his class's league branch. He became a 'target for the expansion of the ranks of the league'. League members were sent to 'come close' to him, to 'understand' him. They invited him to sit in on their activities and incessantly asked him questions on his opinions. They began hinting that he could apply for membership, and later formally extended the invitation.

Initially Bai was indecisive. In the late 1950s it was not yet difficult to enter university, as it was to be in later years when the numbers of students in the senior high graduating classes had expanded. There was still a place in university for almost all senior high graduates, and hence students had little need to enter the league for careerist reasons. From his junior high school experience, Bai retained a negative image of league membership. Nor did the invitation by the league branch to observe 'league life' close-up change his mind. In fact, he was shaken to see the stringent discipline that was demanded of the members: 'It seemed as if you were appraised in every step you walked.' Above all, he was worried that league activities would interfere with his studies. He was unlike Ao, who took anything of the established order as glorious and vied to partake of that glory. He finally consented to join, but for reasons that had nothing to do with heightened political consciousness. 'In that first year of senior high school, I got sick and had to stay in the hospital. I was bored by myself. Wow, the whole league branch came to see me. I was delighted. They were so nice to me that I applied to join.'

It was that brotherhood of collective concern which most attracted him. After he applied, two 'league-entry introducers' were assigned to him, and through them his image of the league began to change. Their concern for him and their efforts to strive for personal virtue drew him closer to both them and the Youth League. Whereas Ao was reluctant to give credit to her peers, he speaks of the two introducers as his spiritual mentors. He established lasting friendships with them:

> They had a great influence on me. They stamped on me a finely engraved political seal. It was because they acted according to what they preached. That revolutionary spirit! We corresponded even in university, and their letters were filled with very pure and correct political sentiments. I kept all the letters. I underlined in red all those moral precepts, and read them almost as if I were reading Mao's selected works. Ah, their thoughts were really wholesome.

It was through the influence of the two introducers that he began seriously to adopt a 'political consciousness'. The transition from spontaneity to deliberate consciousness was almost like a religious conversion for him. It was a rebirth, a new vocational calling:

> After joining the league, my great aim was to heighten my ideological awareness. Through that, I hoped to be better able to follow in the footsteps of the party. Through the league members I began to understand a lot of things, such as how to view life. Why do people live? It became a very concrete question, and caused me to consider my views on clothing, eating and everyday acts of daily life, my views on disease, and what to do when encountering difficulties. Life was fuller and more meaningful – unlike before, when life was without a purpose. Now, no matter what I did, I thought it over carefully or found some reference books to see how I ought to resolve the problems . . . I began using political knowledge to direct my own actions, consciously going after new knowledge, such as in Chairman Mao's works.

His love of collective life found its realization in league activities. Ao, with her strong individualism, had never experienced that same feeling of communion:

If the collective is very good it absorbs you into it. You feel the collective is very warm and that all the people around you are concerned about you. It's very meaningful living in such an atmosphere. And then the whole of you melts into the collective.

He became totally immersed in league activities: putting up wall posters; going from door to door to persuade old ladies to join the 'city communes'; 'working on the ideology' of classmates (i.e. pointing out classmates' incorrect ideas privately and persuading them to change); seeking out non-league members for heart-to-heart talks; helping in the cultivation of new members as he himself was once cultivated. He tried to understand the significance of every campaign and attempted to increase his political knowledge by carefully reading Mao's *Selected Works* from cover to cover, an unusual undertaking for a high school student. In a single week he read through the entire first volume, only to find himself criticized by the league branch for reading too much too fast to be able to unite theory successfully with practice. Organizational discipline penetrated to the minutest detail of a member's daily activities and thinking, but Bai accepted that completely. In fact he enjoyed it. He loved being disciplined, convinced that only with 'organizational nature' could things be accomplished properly. He was similarly happy to impose rigid demands upon others, at times with an insistence that reached authoritarian proportions. Jokingly he says of himself: 'I was sort of – ha, ha – like a fascist: I forced people to act correctly.'

Before he became a member, he had not known and had not really cared to know the class background of classmates. But as a member, he had a comprehensive idea of each classmate's family. He began to take a more 'proletarian class stand'. He followed the official formula, that when evaluating people the emphasis should be on their actual behaviour, not their family background; but he none the less regarded the motives of bad-class and even middle-class youths with suspicion. In interviews he tried to give the impression that he had not avoided being friendly with classmates of non-good-class background: since, as the argument goes, they too could be educated to hold the proper political views. But his attitude, it is clear, was somewhat equivalent to saying: 'He's a nice fellow even though he's black.'

Practising self-cultivation intently, he kept a diary in which he recorded his innermost thoughts – and gladly let the other league members see all his diary entries. The period predated Lei Feng, and diary-writing was not yet prescribed or stereotyped.

> I was very innocent and really wrote down what I thought. And the branch members, because they understood your personality, could always criticize you correctly. Gee, I loved that then. Looking back at it now it was so stupid of me. I told them everything and let them criticize and do anything with me.

More confident of his own virtue than Ao was, less calculatingly egoistic, he was not much troubled by the anguish of gains and losses. He found self-realization in a meaningful collective life and, within that context, was beginning to see himself as a moral force. In keeping with this, his interpretation of the meaning of 'revolutionary successor' both coincided with and differed from Ao's. As league members, both of them possessed the power within the hierarchy of the classroom to control classmates' activities. They were already learning the skills of a cadre and already held vague aspirations for some sort of future leadership positions. Ao equated revolutionary successors with cadres. Bai defined the term slightly differently – as a model figure whom others could emulate. His interpretation contained the element of leadership, but did not necessitate an official cadre position. He admits that in his strivings to serve the state, the idea of becoming a cadre came naturally. This was, he declares, after all the official interpretation of Mao's five conditions for revolutionary successors. He is quick to moderate this, however:

> I mean it included the idea of being a cadre. But it didn't mean desperately fighting to become a cadre. No such thing, unlike the way people in the West campaign and fight for such things, pushing aside people above and below. No, no such thing. If so, then it would fall short of the conditions.

With Ao, becoming a cadre was the ultimate goal. With Bai, such an individualistic ambition was relegated to a secondary position. When asked what personal advantages accrue to cadre positions, Bai dismissed the question as irrelevant:

> Aya, at that time we didn't think what advantages there were for oneself, but what advantages there were for everybody. To attain a

position of responsibility was merely for making bigger contributions to society. Thinking of oneself all the time! Like in Western
ideology, always thinking of one's own interests, of fame and
benefits? No, the method of thinking was different in China . . .
Whenever doing anything, the first thought which sprang to mind
was to serve the whole school, the whole country, the whole
classroom.

Righteous and devoted, Lei Feng had not had to exert self-
restraint, whereas it was central to Ao's daily exercises of introspection. Bai, in this respect, was much like Lei Feng. He had class
feelings and gratitude to the party, which Ao hadn't. Though not
even officially classed as of the 'proletariat', he was self-confident
enough of his proletarian identity to be spared Ao's insecurity and
uncertainty. Bai's feelings of gratitude to the party actually deepened
as he grew older, when he received financial aid from the state and
was allowed to sleep in one of the school's classrooms, after his
teacher discovered his family's financial plight and overcrowded
living conditions.

Bai, as noted, shared with Lei Feng an uncommonly strong sense
of righteousness. It was, ironically, the trait which Bai most had to
overcome, for it overspilled into self-righteousness. Self-righteousness brings 'subjectivity' (*zhuguan*).[23] In Chinese ideological belief, it
breeds stubbornness, an inability to evaluate situations correctly, an
inability to understand and listen to other people, and therefore an
inability to cooperate with others. Bai was the 'ultra-leftist' in his
league branch, whose self-righteousness led him to impose narrowly
rigid demands on others. He was the one who most often objected to
the admission of applicants to the league, even when the majority of
the league members had agreed to overlook small inadequacies. He
saw himself as the incorruptible arbiter of correct and incorrect
behaviour. When everyone, including the league cadres, plunged
into their books to prepare for the university entrance examinations,
he was the one who kept righteously to his political work. He held a
one-man investigation of a classmate who had encouraged others to
go to Hong Kong (this was in 1962 during the economic depression,
when thousands of people flocked across the border every day) and
had the boy locked up for a week at a police station. Many in his class
found that going too far. Later, the classmate sought revenge. A
fierce fight ended with the classmate seriously injured. This was grave

misconduct on Bai's part. As a league member he was always supposed to persuade, never turn to force. He was subjected to disciplinary criticism in which he verbally recognized his fault, but deep down he barely felt sorry:

Fighting was wrong. But I was convinced I was correct in gathering materials [investigating the classmate in question]. He was the guy who had spread rumours about going to Hong Kong; he dared use a sling shot to bore a hole in Chairman Mao's photo; after returning from the police station he went around saying we northerners were eating Guangdong rice [Bai was not originally from Guangdong], yelling 'down with the northerners'. I had to run after him with a pick . . . The league branch asked the party branch for advice. And who could have known? The headmaster said I had done a good job beating up that guy! Ha, ha, he said this guy deserved being beaten. So I didn't get into trouble . . . I had to write several long self-criticisms. No, I didn't really admit I was wrong. That was why I fought again in university, ha, ha.

Bai considered himself the crusader of a true faith. Just as Ao had difficulty restraining her arrogance, Bai had difficulty controlling his compulsive self-righteousness. Both of them could make public promises and write appropriately worded self-criticisms in a format conforming impeccably to the required standard, but they never altered their behaviour. Yet we should not conclude that their public self-criticisms were insincere. They did honestly confess. Their intellect told them they were wrong, even though they let their weaknesses overcome them.

By the time students were well into high school they had, like Ao and Bai, mastered the technique of public criticism and self-criticism, a result of years of training. In primary school they had begun writing essays and weekly diaries that conformed to a rigid formula of moral posturing. (Similarly, in Hong Kong and Taiwan students have to pen essays heavy with moralizing.) By secondary school, they knew what phrases to use, how to support their argument using the appropriate quote or slogan, and how to make criticisms and self-criticisms neither too extreme nor cutting, but strong enough to be convincing. They were adept to the extent that, as we earlier quoted another interviewee, they 'could spurt those things out naturally'. This Chinese style of learning, using constant repetition of highly stereotyped moralistic phraseology to inculcate political and moral values, was in fact quite successful. The incessant hammering of earnest rhetoric – as Bai puts it, like 'invisible X-rays pounding on you' – achieved more than overt conformity. One's daily vocabulary, one's very mode of self-expression, was incorporating the premises of a specific set of values.

Bai was not a worshipper of men – any man. He respected Chairman Mao, his ideas and achievements, and tried seriously to follow his teachings, but he never made Mao the object of religious devotion. In senior high school, when reading Mao's works, he scribbled his own comments in the margins, much as he did when reading lesser mortals.[24] In university, where he majored in political economy, he tried similarly to maintain a more independent frame of mind when studying Marx and Lenin. The professors were careful to present the writings as axiomatically perfect, and Bai had to teach himself never to mention any discrepancies or problems in the Marxist classics. Political truths were to be learned by rote study. Students were instructed that Marx's *Das Kapital* was to be read from cover to cover seven or eight times, so that the concepts could be near-memorized; and some studious souls claimed to have pored through every page up to fifteen times. Bai considered himself independent-minded because he stopped after three readings and told the professor that further reading would not enhance his understanding. Mao Zedong, in his many talks and conversations during the 1960s on the problems of the Chinese educational system, lamented that university social-science students no longer could write intelligently because they did not 'unite theory with practice'.[25] But Mao never chose to observe that the deliberate conversion of Marx's, Lenin's and Mao's own writings into unquestioned dogma, as in the growing Mao cult, was equally stifling intellectual development.

Ironically, Bai's comparative reluctance unquestioningly to accept dogma resulted partly from the fact that he had strongly tried to pattern himself upon the young Mao. In a widely-read book on Mao's youth, great play was given to the young Mao's critical and independent thinking, and to Mao's early habit of scribbling his own notes and comments in the margins of whatever he read:[26]

In a book of 10,000 words he [Mao] had written more than 12,000 words of critical comments. In addition, throughout the whole book every character and sentence was marked in brush with such signs as circles, dots, single lines, double lines, triangles, crosses, etc. This, in the history of studying, is deserving of wonderment.

Several times Bai tried to impress me with the vast quantity of comments he had written in his own books through the years. As for his rejection of Maoism as pure dogma, he quoted Mao himself:

Mao Zedong himself had said no matter who you were, you were bound to have faults and make mistakes. This statement should be used as a directive to study his books. This was how I looked at it. Since everyone has mistakes and faults, your books might not be completely correct. Okay, your books are great, they directed the revolution to success. They are 99 per cent faultless, but there is still that 1 per cent.

Yet, though he might have had mild queries about Mao's teachings, he never questioned the teachings of the party, because to him 'The party is a huge organization. All its mistakes it could rid itself of. So its direction is always correct.' By party he was not referring to individual party figures in posts of authority. Party members as individuals he did not hesitate to criticize, as we will shortly see when discussing his days at the university. In his conception, the party was an abstract entity, the epitome of collective truth above mortal failings.

Despite this conviction, Bai, unlike Lei Feng, was not willing to be a 'screw'. He had even been critical of Lei Feng's lack of ambition:

Though I thought that the spirit of wanting to become a screw was valuable, in looking towards the future one should analyse one's own ability and the objective needs of the country, to try to become more than a screw if possible. Only when it was impossible should one be willing to stay a screw. Lei Feng limited himself to the role of a mere screw, and didn't aspire to something more than that.

He had held to the conviction, as had Ao and the rest of the interviewees, that their contribution to the state could be greater by becoming an expert, not by becoming, say, a mere peasant in the countryside. To strive to go to university was ideologically justifiable – as well as fulfilling personal desires.

There was a time, however, in senior high school when Bai appeared willing to become a screw. Swept along by the extreme activist atmosphere of his league branch, in which he himself had staked out a righteous role as the branch's purist 'ultra-leftist', he found himself clamouring loudly – and sincerely – that students should volunteer to settle in the countryside without taking the university entrance examination. Pledging 'one red heart and two types of preparations' had not been revolutionary enough for him.

Bai was prepared to go of his own volition, this being the crucial validating point for him. But his application was not granted. The school principal, in Bai's senior year, came expressly to the class to explain that theirs was a key-point class, that the nation was in need of talents, and that they as students could serve China best in the future by entering university. Pacified, Bai relented in the face of an official party pronouncement that happily coincided with his personal aspirations. He plunged into cramming for the entrance examinations like everybody else.

Bai perhaps half believed that he was devoted and prepared to sacrifice himself, but all along he must have known that the official press was urging activist young people to take the exams and let the state decide for them how they could best serve the country. He had, perhaps, been accumulating 'political capital' for himself, knowing that he would not be going to a village. Yet two years later, when he was in his second year of university, he applied to quit school once more to go to settle in the countryside, forfeiting an enviable career. He did so vociferously, and with at least some chance that his request would be granted. In the eyes of his classmates, he was no longer simply extreme but verging on the abnormal.

This second application was made in 1963, when university students had had to go down to the countryside to participate in carrying out the Little Four Cleanups, a campaign to stem corruption in the peasant villages.[27] In the course of compiling a village's history, Bai became involved with the villagers and developed good relationships with them. He saw himself 'tying his roots' there, and explains why:

> My dream was to change it so that it could in future become a model brigade, a very famous brigade. Because this place was quite good in climate and geography, I had a plan for technological innovation and a programme for future mechanization. I felt this place had great potential . . . I knew where to put my hand in to change it.

It was an ambitious plan. He had in mind to build up a model brigade as famous as Tachai. To give up finishing university would be a sacrifice. None the less, his dream could not be considered an unconditional subordination of personal interest to collective interest, either. If he succeeded, he would become a famous activist.

Liu-Shaoqi had called this type of ambition one of 'personal aim harmonizing with party interest'; personal interests are permissible so long as they are not 'independent personal aims'.[28]

So long as Ao and Bai were given the chance to express their devotion, to feel their actions efficacious and prove their own superiority, both of them were willing energetically to play the role of dedicating themselves to the collective. Ao, always measuring herself, became aware of an inconsistency in her self-image. At times she believed that she had really been selfless; at times she was aware of her self-seeking motives. Bai, a less introspective person, perceived himself to be entirely selfless.

Ao and Bai set themselves off from the rest of the inteviewees. They belonged to a different breed. They were the recognized activists. As a consequence, their sense of political efficacy was considerably stronger. They had high expectations to play the leadership role and, in that position, were confident they could change things, could organize 'the masses', get things done. Furthermore, more than other interviewees, they identified themselves as part of the Establishment, a perspective they had gained as league members. The league was the training ground for future cadres. Bai saw his dedication not in terms of wielding a hoe but rather as a dynamic rural leader poised to move up the hierarchic ladder to glory.

In the league they had learned the techniques of governing. They were aware that they should assume a correct disposition when approaching others; they knew how to point out mistakes without alienating others, when to be soft, when to be firm, how to coax others to talk, what quotations to use to bolster their own arguments. Despite this knowledge, Ao never did overcome her condescending attitude; and Bai could not rid himself of his rash and sometimes dictatorial work-style. This was because, finally, their perspectives and self-perceptions as 'leaders' insensitized them to the grievances and resentments of peers who enjoyed no power.

Ao and Bai entered the league among the earliest of the chosen few. They did not have to make concerted endeavours to get into the league. More cynical classmates would say that they were 'dragged' in. Those who came after them had to compete desperately to join, with the anxiety, self-doubts and resentments which that contest entailed. Ao and Bai still talk of their league branches with idealized nostalgia: how much their branches had achieved, how principled their league branches were in their enrolment policies, how important the activities were that they initiated, how in meetings they dissected the cases of non-league members, how they had inspired others' political thinking, how they had scrupulously investigated family dossiers, etc. But they talk little of the hostility some class-mates had felt towards the branch. They had no empathy for the subdued classmates of bad-class background who had been pushed into a grossly inferior status. They were insensitive to the fact that as league members, no matter how kindly, objectively or correctly they criticized the non-league members, no matter how principled they were in their selections of new recruits, no matter how much they thought they were at one with the 'masses', the latter were constantly on edge in their presence; and that no matter how well-intentioned they were in their moralizing, there were some who found them patronizing. This other side of the story we shall shortly see when we come to discuss Chang and Deng.

As official activists, Ao and Bai differed significantly from each other in one respect: in their attitude towards authority figures. Ao *always* submitted to her immediate superiors. Bai did not. Once he sensed hypocrisy, he was ready to despise his superiors and rebel against them on behalf of his sense of purity. When he entered university, the righteousness which in high school had been mani-fested in a guise of 'leftist' extremism surfaced as a series of rebellious actions.

In 1962, Bai had gotten into the political economy department of one of China's best universities. To be admitted to a good national university was highly prestigious, but to be allowed to major in Marxist economics was doubly so. The class background and political records of the students were excellent. Of some thirty students in the class, four were party members and more than half had been league branch secretaries. Bai describes how, having gained entry to an elite institution, with excellent careers ahead of them, most of the students thought they had become mandarins. They assumed stern faces and tried to look important.

Most of the students were striving to achieve two goals at univer-sity: to get into the party and to lay the groundwork for acquiring a good job assignment after graduation. To attain these, two things had to be done: academic cramming and a show of political activism. As a result of frenetic efforts to succeed simultaneously in these twin efforts, the students' health deteriorated dramatically.[29]

The political competition was not only intense; it was calculating. Every word and sentence the students uttered, Bai reminisces, was a

Marxist–Leninist catchphrase. In league branch meetings, members tried to show off their own good points and stepped on one another. The period coincided with the height of the emulate Lei Feng campaign. Bai recalls, with contempt in his voice, the hypocrisy that enveloped the class:

> During this emulate Lei Feng period, a fad built up in class to write diaries. But these were diaries for others to read. They were stuffed with all sorts of abstract empty sentences – that university students should be well-versed in Marxism–Leninism, etc. Several empty slogans as each day's entry . . . No, I wouldn't exchange mine with anybody. Some purposefully used theirs to advertise themselves, gave it to the league branch and party branch to read. When I read these, they made me want to throw up. So hypocritical.

What upset him most was the low level of solidarity and comradely concern, the things which had most attracted him in his former high school league branch. He not only stopped revealing himself to his classmates. He attempted to show he was above such self-seeking by engaging in a series of nonconformist actions. While everyone in the class tried to impress the party branch in order to get into the party, Bai assumed an ostentatiously couldn't-care-less attitude – the only one in the class who declined to apply.

In meetings he did not hesitate to speak his mind. His criticism of classmates went beyond what was deemed acceptable etiquette. He incessantly brought up the virtues of his former league branch despite the other students' ridicule. When a classmate contracted a serious case of tuberculosis and no one else dared come close to him, Bai purposely shared a room with him, ate with him and accompanied him everywhere as a reproach to the other classmates – and in particular the party members. He aimed to make it clear that they had shown a lack of concern for a comrade in distress, though in meetings they clamoured about concern for others. When the campus was caught up in the craze to emulate Lei Feng's 'tolerance of hardship and simplicity', with everyone competing to put on the oldest and most tattered rags they could find, Bai instead walked around in smart new clothes he had acquired in exchange for his old ones – an exchange with a well-off friend who had never had to wear old clothes and had become anxious to ward off criticism. By making himself look conspicuous in a sea of rags, he mocked the faddism.

He must have become a considerable nuisance to his classmates, always cornering others into embarrassing situations, always launching unreserved criticisms. He created enemies with his righteousness; and later, when the Cultural Revolution broke out, he would become a target of the party branch in his class.

Disappointed though he might be to see the phoney activism around him at university, his fervour was not dampened. This was the same year that he had applied to remain in the countryside. A year later, as a consequence of his continued righteousness, he tumbled into serious trouble, sufficiently serious to jeopardize his whole career. He was obliged then to make an important choice, putting his beliefs to the test.

It was during the nationwide Big Four Cleanups Campaign, when a great many university students had to go down to the countryside to help 'carry out class struggle' and help clean up the grassroots corruption rampant throughout the rural districts in the wake of the economic depression.[30] Mao had in mind that such an experience of 'uniting theory with practice' for several months would provide the students with a 'proletarian eduation'.[31] At the end of 1964, Bai, together with several other students and some twenty cadres of commune and county level, forming one Four Cleanups workteam, went to carry out the campaign in a north China village (production brigade). In a workteam comprised of such mixed personnel, the status of the university students was subordinate to that of the cadres. It was in the self-interest of the students to defer to the wishes of the cadres. The workteam's report to the university on the performance of the students might have grave repercussions on their future job allocations and careers.

Students, new to the work, tended to be more idealistic than cadres. Bai, in particular, was disturbed by the cadres' laxity and their susceptibility to flattery and small presents. He tried to be more active than the others, labouring with the peasants in the fields as often as he could, and in his spare time organizing local youths into uplifting activities. He was the 'rate buster'. But he did not raise his colleagues' hackles until Bai disagreed with the measures taken by the leaders of the workteam to extract information from grassroots cadres suspected of corruption. The workteam was trying to accomplish this mission by threatening the grassroots cadres during 'struggle meetings', extorting blatantly exaggerated confessions from them. By normal campaign guidelines, this was forbidden; Bai had learned at school that persuasion and education were always supposed to be the tools employed in soliciting confessions. But there was a built-in momentum throughout the nation towards 'ultra-leftism', each work-team trying to outdo the others in rooting out as many corrupt cadres and uncovering as many cases of gross corruption as possible, so as to show off 'great achievements'.[32]

The ensuing disagreement between Bai and the workteam finally exploded over the selection of new grassroots cadres to replace the former corrupt ones. Some workteam members had coerced the peasants into accepting several new village cadres who had no mass support and no noticeable competence in agriculture. Bai, having solicited the opinions of the peasants, felt that the unpopular choices would have spelled disaster for collective production. Acting as a crusader on behalf of the masses, he encouraged the peasants to repudiate the decision – which they did. Serious differences of this nature among workteam members should have been reported to superior party levels, but the workteam cadres, eager to hush up the matter, tried to force Bai instead to make a contrite self-criticism in front of the peasants. He was faced with a difficult dilemma. If he refused to do so, the consequences were grave. The whole workteam might get into trouble for breaking workteam discipline, perhaps himself included. He did not want to push the workteam to the brink. But to renounce what he had done would mean betraying his own integrity, losing face in front of the masses. That night he could not sleep:

Q: You were a bit worried?

A: No, the whole night I was reading Mao's *Selected Works*. Really reading Mao's *Selected Works*, hoping to find a solution from Mao Zedong's thinking. Ah, I was really so faithful then. As I was leafing through, from volume I to volume IV, I looked for an answer. But I couldn't find any.

Q: Was this your usual method of coming to decisions?

A: Oh. often, when learning from Lei Feng that was the method. Oh, yes, I often did that.

Q: You mean to pull out a sentence which looked useful . . .

A: No, only to get the idea, to see how Mao Zedong at that time solved a problem and then apply it to my own situation: especially on a problem of line struggle, such as in the 6th Plenum of the 6th Party Congress or 7th Plenum of the 2nd Party

Congress. In this struggle I was convinced that I represented the correct line. I was subconsciously convinced that what that group of people was doing was revisionism. I read till very late . . .

The next morning he found a way out of his problem, though if his luck turned against him it would cost him his career:

After breakfast they told me to go make my self-examination. The more I thought of that session, the more uncomfortable I felt. So I gathered up a few of my meagre belongings, a few books, took up my school bag, went up the hill, and facing east, I ran. I climbed up to the main ridge of the mountain, to the very top. There I contemplated for a long time. 'What should I do now?' I had several ideas. First, I'm tired of university life. I'll drift till I find some new place to tie down my roots. At that time I wasn't thinking of my family, etc. Second, I thought, those party members and league members were all not my type. Let the workteam taste it this time. I'd tasted enough. This time it's your turn because you've broken the rules . . . Third, this way I'm proving to the masses that I refuse to submit. If I disappear, this proves I will not submit, that I hold onto what I'd been advocating all through. So regarding the masses, I won't lose much. Ah, but I felt bad leaving this place because I had worked there for so long, put in so much effort and sweat. It was difficult; but I just left.

It was a principled but emotional decision. For three weeks, concealing his identity, he wandered aimlessly from county to county, city to city. There was a romantic impulse to it. He had always envied how Chairman Mao in 1927 had travelled through five counties in Hunan Province, making a first-hand investigation which resulted in the essay 'Report on An Investigation of the Peasant Movement in Hunan'.[33] Bai had lamented that in his own generation they did not have an opportunity to do similar first-hand investigations for the revolution. To fulfil this wish was not his original intention, but now that he was on the road he carefully noted down what he saw, as Mao had done. Despite his love at being part of a collective, it was the first time that he experienced the lightness of being temporarily cut off from all social, personal and political ties.

But in China there is tight control over a person's residence, and wandering is illegal. For more than a week, he spent time in two prison-like detention centres. For the first time, he had contact with and experienced the life of the lowest stratum of Chinese society. He saw beggars and vagrants, elements which he thought had long disappeared from the soil of socialist China, locked up, kicked, punched and beaten up by prison guards.[34] He saw hordes of peasant refugees, old and young, men and women, fleeing from a drought in the next province, begging along the way, finally rounded up, given a meal and then packed into trucks and driven back to their places of origin. New ideas began to creep into Bai's mind:

> I felt socialism needed serious re-thinking. I also had other weird ideas: why didn't the newspaper report this? Why was it never reported that such and such a place had a natural disaster? Had refugees, etc.? Why only report great achievements, excellent situations? I thought this kind of thing should be reported, so that all the people would shoulder a heavy responsibility. Let the intellectuals know that the country still was filled with disasters and calamities, and let everyone strive for progress. I was very perplexed. But it could be said that I had, as yet, only a bit of doubt. I was still what Chairman Mao said: a piece of white paper on which could be written the newest and the most beautiful pictures.

Released, wandering again, he contracted a disease and was found on a deserted hill by two shepherds, weak with fever and diarrhoea. His identity was revealed and he was shipped back to the university. In his absence, the conflict with the workteam had ended in his favour. Several workteam cadres had been penalized and the peasants allowed to reelect their leadership in the manner Bai had been advocating. By good luck, Bai's 'purist' notion of activism had been vindicated.

THE REBELLIOUS ACTIVIST AS AN ADOLESCENT

Ao and Bai had the opportunity to play the role of official activists. We have seen how, despite their personal failings, they had internalized the political values and abided by the activist norms. Particularly important was their willingness to submit themselves to an organization and its discipline. Few of the other interviewees ever became official activists. They failed to get into the Youth League either because, when the class line intensified, their non-red-class background torpedoed their chances or because they could not bring themselves to perform 'docilely' as required by their league branch. Ao and Bai had joined the league just when the classline was beginning to tighten; and, as we have seen, they were spared a cut-throat competition to join the league. Chang was one of those who failed in this competition – more because of his personality, perhaps, than his parentage.

Worried that the record of his poor conduct in primary school might affect his application to high school, Chang had chosen a second-rate neighbourhood junior high, the type to which only children of ordinary academic grades and class background would apply. His new classroom happened to have a particularly high percentage of children from capitalist class origin: about twenty in all, out of about fifty students.

During the first two years of junior high school, he continued to let his rebellious tendencies rule his behaviour. He quarrelled with teachers, fought and gambled in the streets. In class, he paid little attention to the lessons. But he managed to maintain a good academic record, particularly in essay-writing and politics, and distinguished himself in chess and calligraphy.

In the third year of junior high he experienced a period of emotional turmoil. Chang was entering an unusually disturbing phase of early adolescence, which coincided with the inner confusion that Kenneth Keniston found some of the young, middle-class, anti-Vietnam War radical American student leaders had passed through at the same age.[35] Of course, the Chinese and American social settings and socialization processes are very different. But there was a parallel in the personality development of these young radical Americans and the rebellious Chang. Keniston's description of this turmoil-filled adolescence well describes Chang's psychological state:

> the preadolescent pattern of outgoing activity changed, often in a few months, to a new style of seclusiveness, a feeling of social awkwardness and moral inferiority coupled with intense intellectual concerns and, at times, with extreme religiosity . . . Others mentioned their anxieties about masturbation, about their sexual fantasies, and about their feelings towards girls . . . In early adolescence, too, feelings of loneliness, solitude, and isolation came markedly to the fore. Several young men and women began adolescent diaries, which they kept for many years, prefacing them with such thoughts as 'since I have no one to talk to, I will have to talk to myself'. Turning toward themselves rather than toward

their peers, these young radicals began a habit of self-analysis that continued in later years.[36]

Chang, similarly, was increasingly turning in on himself. He rarely spoke, always contemplating. Time and again he describes his thinking as 'complex'. He regarded his intense feelings as beyond the understanding of his peers. He was aware that his peers found him strange. In a society where there is enormous pressure to be part of the group, he felt himself isolated. Brought up under strict puritanical values, his sexual fantasies disturbed him: 'I felt very painful deep down. I thought I was very contemptible. I felt myself confused and becoming clumsy.' He was so filled with passions that the slightest incident could throw him into an emotional state. He had to express himself. He began learning poetry as an outlet to release his feelings. He felt idealistic and consumed biographies on heroes in large numbers. He felt yearnings which he could not articulate.

Several external factors plunged him into even deeper emotional conflict. The strengthening of the class line was being felt. Several classmates of working-class background who had been as naughty and as apathetic towards activism as himself were suddenly invited to become league members. A few 'red' parents were invited to school to 'pour out class sufferings'. In a classroom containing such a large number of bad-class students, there was a particular sensitivity to these changes in official policy. He noted that among his classmates, some who used to be lively became quiet, some who were inactive suddenly became frenetically activist, some began to look as if they had a lot of worries.

To be sure, the bad-class students had always been in a somewhat precarious position. My only interviewee of capitalist background had learned to be cautious from an early age. As a social group, they were quiescent, politically inactive, studious and burdened with a sense of social inferiority. They could not readily try to demonstrate activism without arousing suspicions. With the advantages of a literate family heritage and thus a strong academic achievement orientation, they had striven hardest to use academic success to secure careers. When they saw the effect the class line might have on their future, they became alarmed and anxious. They increasingly identified themselves as a group and complained among themselves privately.

Chang did not come from a bad-class background. However, that same year something happened to his family which tarnished his dossier. As the size of his family had expanded, his parents' financial situation had deteriorated. When his mother contracted a liver disease, she found the weight of their economic problems too great and left for Hong Kong with a few of the children. As a result, Chang, though of passable class background originally, became 'smeared with a layer of grey'. He began to share some of the anxiety felt by his bad-class schoolmates: 'We all felt that we were of a different type from most children, people of a different class status. I was beginning to form this kind of feeling. We had a different kind of future, a different kind of fate.'

As the emulate Lei Feng campaign gathered momentum, Chang noticed that the middle- and bad-class classmates became more activist, even those who had little chance of getting into the league. Chang considered many of his classmates to be phoney activists. He might have exaggerated the extent of phoney activism as a projection of his own personal anxiety; but this issue of phoney activism haunted him. The pressing problem facing him was whether he, too, should throw himself into the activist contest so as to safeguard his future. That year, as he graduated junior high school and entered senior high, the effect of the class line was self-evident. Most of the bad-class classmates had failed to get into any senior high school. The decision to begin to fight seriously to get into the league was imminent if he still wanted to enter university.

Why this hesitation, as if there was something wrong in becoming politically active? Why this greater fear of phoney activism than his classmates? The root of Chang's dilemma lay in his strong desire for spontaneous self-expression, his inability to surrender himself at all to authority and organizational discipline. He was an activist, but only on his own terms.

Chang had retained a passionate interest in and concern for politics, national, international and theoretical. He read the Marxist classics, as much as his intellectual faculties would allow him to absorb. He daily spent time in the school office perusing a limited-circulation newspaper which carried unabridged articles from foreign news agencies, because 'I was interested in the new inventions of the West, but interest is not the word for it. I always placed China at the very top. I liked reading how other countries evaluated China, to satisfy my national self-respect.' Though normally a non-activist in formal political discussions, he so '*bitterly hated*' the Russians that once he burst out in class with a vehement condemnation of revisionism that astounded everyone. To him only such 'far-sighted' political concern was real activism. His understanding of 'revolutionary successor' was to steel oneself, to serve the nation and to read Marx and Lenin, laid down in the first two of the five conditions. It never occurred to him that one had to be a cadre or necessarily play a leadership role to be considered a revolutionary successor.

His patriotism and his internalization of the political values stood the test of real life. When his mother left for Hong Kong he could have joined her. His parents, especially his father, tried to convince him that a better future was possible for him there. But he refused to go on the grounds that 'I didn't like capitalism. I also thought leaving the mother-country would be an agonizing thing.'

He practised self-cultivation, but in a manner different from Ao and Bai. Ao and Bai dutifully wrote diaries and introspected. The standards against which they diligently measured their own conduct were slogans, Mao sayings, Central Committee directives and officially-prescribed modes of behaviour: whether they had accomplished a good deed that day, and if not, why not? Why had they not swept the floor but instead left it to the monitor? Why did they lose their temper? Why could they not act as selflessly as Lei Feng? They placed stringent demands on themselves to be 'docile tools' of the party and the chairman. Chang also subjected himself to daily self-examinations, though only making diary entries when there was an inner urge to do so. But the arbiter of what he considered as correct behaviour was not a current slogan or league instruction, but rather – or at least that was the way he subjectively perceived it – his own conscience. It was to himself that his own actions had to answer. He did not feel he had to accommodate to standards external to himself. But having developed a habit of self-cultivation, even Chang finally attained what the Chinese called 'self-consciousness'. He brought his defiant outbursts of rebelliousness under control.

Chang devoted himself assiduously to physical tempering and asceticism. In China, strenuous physical exercise has long been considered a politically moral commitment. As early as the beginning of the century (in Liang Qichao's time), when the Chinese took the term 'Sick man of East Asia' literally, attaining physical fitness had been included in the programme of liberal reformation. Today, the precept that children should simultaneously acquire a 'moral, physical and intellectual education' is a cliche as often quoted in Taiwan and Hong Kong's more traditional schools as in China. But only in China was physical education still taken seriously. As we have observed, the government strongly promoted tempering through strenuous exercise as a means to develop the fortitude of character helpful to the construction of socialism. Though city-bred, during the seasonal harvest-help my interviewees forced themselves to withstand a degree of physical exertion that young people brought up in a 'bourgeois' system of education would normally find beyond themselves.

Linked with this view of physical exercise and physical tempering was a notion of asceticism embodied in the slogan 'tolerate hardship and live simply'. Chinese students generally led spartan lives. Frugality was upheld as a necessary revolutionary virtue. Going barefoot was common and had even become fashionable. Leather shoes were a source of shame rather than of pride. Students dared not wear new or colourful clothes for fear of being criticized as 'petty-bourgeois'. Spending pocket money on sweets and snacks was disdained.

In general, then, Chinese students sought to be physically tough, puritanical and frugal. Some merely tried to stay with the tide, some did so conscientiously and enthusiastically. But Chang, compared with the average student, was fanatical. Again, as in acquiring political knowledge, his unflinching pursuit of physical tempering was not in conformity to the peer-group norms; indeed, anything in excess of the required standard only made one stand out as abnormal.

Chang was inspired in his efforts by stories about the young Mao. Mao as a young man was a devotee of physical exercise and toughening. Mao had taken cold baths and gone swimming in winter, had purposefully drenched himself in winter storms, slept unsheltered in the wilderness and embarked on exhaustingly long hikes.[37] In one of his earliest essays, Mao wrote of the purposes of such physical tempering: (1) to attain a health which he considered in 1917 as absolutely necessary for the nation's survival; (2) to restrain one's spontaneous emotions, which he saw as weaknesses; and (3) to steel one's willpower in order to cultivate a fearless character.[38] This captured Chang's imagination: a steeling of the physique was an essential foundation for a steeling of the spirit.

> I could be very undisciplined, unkempt, but I could also be terribly ascetic. I worked very hard to be progressive. Those other people were very progressive in joining the league, doing good turns and whatnot. But there was a qualitative difference. I read of Mao Zedong's youth and I was very moved, so I swam and took cold baths in winter, which many people could not do. Jogging – they couldn't stand it; I could. You push yourself and push yourself.

Sometimes it became so very painful. But if you could run just that one extra step you have already increased your willpower by one millimetre. If you gave up, then you couldn't go any further next time. This determination was very difficult. My desire to be progressive was so strong, so idealistic. Different from theirs. I was like a revolutionary tempering himself when young.

He was emulating Mao as a young man preparing himself for the revolution. But what kind of revolution was there for Chang to stage? In Mao's days, the revolution was necessarily a violent revolution, one of rebelling against the established order, for the introduction of drastic changes in the social and political spheres. In Chang's day 'revolution' continued to be employed daily in the vocabulary, but the import of the word had changed. It was phrased as 'continuing the revolution under the dictatorship of the proletariat' in the stage of 'constructing socialism'. Rebelling against the established order, as was noted earlier, was to play no part in this stage of the 'revolution'. 'Revolution' in essence meant conforming to established norms; suppressing all unconventional and individualistic inclinations; surrendering the whole being to the party and Chairman Mao; and a willingness to live an ordinary hardworking life to build up socialism as Lei Feng had. Yet Chang rejected Lei Feng as a heroic model. Lei Feng was a 'docile tool', and those who emulated Lei Feng were banal. His heroes were Mao and great historical figures. He loved Mao's poems and calligraphy. He quoted Mao in his writings, but usually Mao's poems, not his current directives and quotations. It was Mao's romantic style and his rebelliousness which attracted him, not Mao's teachings on 'serving the people'. Mao was a scholar, a poet and a military talent, a great revolutionary. He too would strive for these accomplishments. He had deep admiration for Galileo's efforts to hold to his convictions under persecution. He adored Napoleon for his military talent, and hoped that he, too, if given the opportunity, would prove to have such talents.

Chang was seeking what the state condemned as 'individual heroism'. There was always an urge to prove to himself and to others his revolutionary qualities in exactly the way he himself defined them. He did not aspire to have an established organization shower him with power, status and prestige (to which Ao and Bai, especially the former, aspired), so long as he could prove his own worth in his own way.

Chang had a crying need for self-expression, which his rebellious American counterparts also experienced after that upsurge of adolescent turmoil. Keniston noted that two or three years after that earlier difficult phase, the young people he studied entered a period of rebellion against their parents, whom they saw as restricting them excessively, not allowing them sufficiently to be themselves, trying to control their lives, trying to plan their futures.[39] In Chang's case, the imposing authority was not his parents, since they had had little control over him even when he was a child. But there was 'something' which was restraining him from letting him be himself. This 'something' was the Youth League concretized in the classmates who belonged, who seemed to be trying to control every detail of his daily thoughts and actions: 'It was like a wall, a wall encroaching upon me. I felt suffocated.' And though he had great respect for the party, there was a vague resistance against obeisance to it:

> In writing essays, the sentiments always had to be positive, right? My essays always praised the greatness of the mother country, the greatness of the people, the party . . . no, not much about the party. Somehow I just couldn't praise the party in the same spontaneous way. I felt when something was too demanding, I just couldn't do it. I felt it extremely difficult. I felt it somehow very hypocritical. But as for the mother country and the people, they were different; I felt they were very very different.

It would be a gross mistake to say he was discontented with the system. In fact his faith in the polity was unswerving. He was even convinced that his devotion was more noble, profound and special than that of his Lei Feng-emulating peers. It was the organizational conformity that bothered him.

But 'leaning close to the league' and emulating Lei Feng were necessary if he were to stand a chance of joining the league, which by then was perceived to be an important qualification for getting into university. He had always wanted to go to university to study literature and politics. This way, he thought, he could contribute more to the country, more than if he were to go down to the countryside. But was he to give up being master of himself and conform like everyone else? Was he to allow himself to engage in those petty 'revolutionary' deeds which he detested as phoney? It was not so much the act itself which disturbed him; after all, what was wrong with doing a good deed? It was the motivation behind the act which was troubling to him. He likened his classmates competing to emulate Lei Feng to a 'fight over food'. But finally he gave in and performed at the minimum level required, fully aware of the impurity of his motivation:

> Yes, I went to my league sponsor regularly. The thing is, if you didn't you would be looked upon as not progressing. Raising petty questions with him was nothing special; one had to do a lot of it in studying Mao, such as 'today I had this thought problem, but after reading Chairman Mao's works, oh, I realized this and that . . .' This was so standardized. Everyone did it, so I had to do it also. I also wrote such things in notes; sometimes I did it even in conversations. I raised these questions, feeling very miserable because the questions I wanted to ask were actually not these questions. I thought about big questions, about revisionism, the nation, life, not petty nonsense. As long as one was sincere I thought that was enough. The things they asked were: Did you do a good deed? Did you wash clothes for your roommates? It was so painful. Apart from saying things I didn't believe in, I also had to behave like a kid in front of those league members.

Chang was not alone in feeling this. About half of my interviewees sensed the same pressures forcing them to conform and an internal resistance against these pressures – but among them all, Chang was the most bothered. He felt a phoney activist. Torn by a sense of guilt, he eased off in his efforts to be activist. Ao at times had been disturbed by a sense of shame; Bai, in his insensitive righteousness, had never been.

Whatever a student's feelings, in criticism and self-criticism meetings, almost automatically through experience, students would each criticize themselves to the extent that befitted their personal disposition and class background. Through practice, such sessions had become so formalized, from the perspective of the ordinary student that, after a while, a group dynamics had worked out an informal formula among the students. Students of good-class origin would talk about how grateful they were to the party, how they would try their best to study to repay that gratitude. Those of bad-class background would concentrate mainly on their faults and mouth the standard phrases about how their thoughts had been influenced by the 'backwardness' of their families, and how they were determined to draw a line between themselves and their class origins. Those of middling class background did not have to make as harsh a self-criticism, and would say something appropriately in-between about their faults and their own families. Based on this informally-arrived-at formula, those who found such sessions hypocritical gradually could get used to performing their own part formalistically, as if it were a meaningless rote ritual.

In counterpoint, a demonstration of activist commitment had to go well beyond the minimum requirements. It had to be expressed in one's tone of voice, in one's facial expression, in the kind of detail one was willing to reveal about oneself and the extent one 'drew the line' with one's parents. As one interviewee cynically put it: 'they deprecated themselves till they were like breeding dogs'; and neither he nor Chang would do it. At the same time, such sessions could become so ritualized that even if someone like Chang were ready to make a sincere public self-examination that went beyond standardized trivialities, he would face a different kind of problem.

Sometimes in such sessions I would bring out some of the self-criticisms I made privately in the evening. Of course, I couldn't talk about all of them. Just a bit. Just a portion of it would be enough. Telling all would expose myself, expose that what I thought about was different from theirs. Because at that time the demand was that everyone should be the same, imprinted by the same mould. So sometimes I would just begin to talk about myself, of course within limits, but even then it made them feel as if I was sort of strange, that I thought too deeply. I always felt caught in a very contradictory situation.

Chang had yet another quality which diverged from the standard activist-oriented youth. Strictly speaking, he lacked 'class feeling'. We have seen that as a child he had no romantic notions about the innate revolutionary spirit of the 'proletariat', even though he himself grew up in that kind of social environment. He had never cared to possess the class feelings which Ao so desperately tried to cultivate. He had arrived at his own interpretation of 'class feeling', as when he heard working-class schoolmates talking about their gratitude towards the party:

I got the feeling that there was something wrong with it. From what I could see, they were just manifesting the selfishness of man. It was the feeling that something or someone had been good to me, so I'm now good to him. Yes, that was how I saw it, that it was a kind of selfishness. On the contrary, though it could be said the Communist Party had not been beneficial to me in any particular way, in my heart I knew I understood it even more, better than most people. Mine was not their kind of narrow-minded emotive infatuation. Mine was at the rational level. I even thought that when the critical moment came, well then, see who could – yes, I was thinking – see who could be more loyal to the party. Mine did not involve repaying what you had done for me.

One other interviewee of middle-class status had arrived at the same conclusion: that class feeling was actually a less than noble and less than selfless passion. But most middle-class children had never questioned the validity of class feelings. In everyday life, they never recognized their red-background classmates as more revolutionary than themselves, but where the teachings about class feelings did not impinge upon themselves adversely, they were adherents. Interviewees recall, for example, that usually they were suspicious of their classmates of bad-class background.

The corollary of 'class feeling' is 'class hatred' for the class enemies. And this Chang also lacked. Not that he particularly befriended classmates of bad-class background, since he was very much a loner. But he possessed humanitarian feelings which were not in accord with class hatred. Humanitarianism was condemned in the ideology taught in classrooms. The argument was that all feelings have class content, that there is no feeling which transcends class. The idea of man having humanitarian feelings and the notion of 'human nature' were taken as dangerous 'bourgeois' opiates. There could only be class feeling and class hatred.

One day when his class went to labour in the countryside, Chang was surprised to see his former headmistress, who a few years earlier had been branded a rightist and dispatched to the countryside to labour.[40] She was washing clothes by the river. Her hair had whitened and she looked dispirited and worn out. The sight brought out in Chang a strong sense of sympathy:

At that instant I tried desperately to make sure that my face didn't register a look of contempt, that look of regarding others as strange creatures, as if I were noticing her. Actually I was watching her out of the corner of my eye, because I didn't want to look as if I were staring. Because I thought that it would be objectively equivalent to despising her, as if because she was a rightist I had to notice

her. I wanted to treat her as an ordinary person. I was hit with a
bitterly depressed feeling. It was all just very sad. I didn't quite
understand, but I felt the whole situation was very pitiful.

To have sympathy for class enemies means either siding with the class
enemies or 'not having a class stand'. It is considered a serious
problem, warranting severe criticism. Among my other interviewees
of middle-class background (except for one whose own parents had
been branded rightists), there were no similar memories of compassion.

Chang tried to follow the political rituals as best as he could in
order to get into the league, but his performance was never up to the
mark. He simply could not put on a show of spontaneous enthusiastic
subservience to the league branch, or speak up in meetings with the
required gung-ho cadence, or demonstrate a passion for organized
endeavours in the manner of Ao and Bai. In the second year of senior
high school his teacher, hoping to increase Chang's chances of getting
into university, enquired of the branch on his behalf but without
success.

Yet Chang did gain two posts which were political in nature. He
became the newspaper-reading officer, whose responsibility was to
read and explain the important news items to the class every morning. And when the Study Mao's Works Campaign began, he became
the Study Mao's Works Counsellor. One would have imagined that
league members, considered the political vanguard, should have
been responsible for disseminating and interpreting political knowledge to the rest of the students. But instead, it was Chang, someone
who could not even get into the league. He sums up his position:

> Very strange, though in class I had no political status, I had capital;
> by capital I mean being responsible for the side of political activi-
> ties that required 'expertise'. So in class I didn't belong to the
> group which was despised. It was like in the broader society, where
> there are people whose talents are needed but who have no
> political power or status.

THE PRAGMATIC ACTIVIST AS AN ADOLESCENT

Deng's limited grasp of the state's moral and political values only
very gradually began to mature in junior high school. His school was
a third-rate neighbourhood school, a converted temple. The student

body, composed largely of 'small citizens', i.e. children of the formerly less-educated sector of the urban population, exhibited scant enthusiasm for academic studies. The main tasks of the school authorities lay more in keeping order than instilling knowledge and political consciousness.

Though lacking in both academic and political stimulation, Deng had ended his 'warring life' and managed to maintain an academic record sufficient to satisfy his parents. Yet in class he felt a nobody and remained quite unsociable. The sour-grapes attitude which he had developed in primary school stayed with him.

His first two years of junior high school coincided with the years of economic depression. During that period all of my interviewees temporarily had experienced hunger pangs, but none seems to have been as much preoccupied with the sensation as Deng. It has blurred his memory of all other aspects of his life. It was a difficult period for him. With his father transferred elsewhere, his mother a state cadre too busy for household matters, and a brother sick at home, young Deng had to be responsible for all the household chores, at a time when hours of queueing for every single item was the order of the day.

> The greatest impression I have of junior high school was of hunger and groceries for the house. My sharpest memory is of some of my cabbages being robbed by some guys. I can remember clearly also queueing up for fried goodies before the New Year. My older brother was sick; $10 a catty of pork; and $1.20 a catty of sweet potatoes specially kept for my brother to eat.

It was useless to have him search his brain on other topics. His memories of class elections and his attitude towards the league were fuzzy, lost in time. His mind had never focused on such matters.

Still, piecing the anecdotes together, we can draw out certain personal characteristics which were taking shape in those years. He was already inclined to think independently and had not much deference for authority. In these respects he resembled Chang. Ao and Bai, particularly Ao, had great respect for teachers, and believed in any official message. Not Deng. For instance, when the teacher tried to allay students' discontent during the food shortage, Deng thought the teacher hypocritical for the apologetics and chalked up the episode as a negative lesson. In class he joined with the majority to tease the 'phoney activists'. He had no fear or abiding respect even for the police. Once he was detained in a police station overnight for fighting with a neighbour, and Deng protested by kicking at the door of the room he was locked in.

But he was ambitious, and though he did not, like Ao, fight for officially-conferred honours – for there was also that streak of rebelliousness in him – neither was he indifferent to them, as Chang was.

When the time came to apply to senior high school Deng was sufficiently confident of his grades to apply to a well-above-average school, a boarding school in the suburbs. To play it safe, his father had preferred that he go to a technical high school. His fear was that Deng might later fail to get into a university, which would leave him without career prospects. But his mother, who had had a higher education herself, was ready to take the risk. Deng himself, influenced by his 'expert' family background, saw a senior-high education simply as 'normal', and going to settle in the countryside as 'glorious' but 'abnormal'. He was so confident of success that he had not been perturbed by the possibility of being sent to the countryside.

He succeeded in getting into the school of his choice. Flushed with confidence, Deng was determined to study hard. More than that, in dramatic contrast to his behaviour in junior high school he, too, began a regimen of self-cultivation. He started a diary in the notebook his mother had bought him as a present for his success. He was the first one in his senior high school class to keep a diary, before diary-writing had become a fad. But his self-cultivation was persistently characterized by a comparative lack of idealism of the type so strong in my other interviewees (with the exception of the one of capitalist background, and interestingly enough, also the one of revolutionary-cadre family background). Though Deng's self-cultivation was concerned with personal tempering, it was not predominantly or ultimately oriented towards the collective good. Nor did he have any passionate feelings towards the party, Mao or the idea of serving them:

Ha, ha, of course one should love them. It was like any person born into this world, mother is mother, father is father. Of course you should love them, even if they are nothing special. A person is born into the world, and the leader of the country is Mao Zedong, so of course you love him . . . As for the big problem of loyalty to the party, it comes with birth; the moment you were born you should be loyal to the party. Why should you think about it, right? Like you were born with hair, and you never ask yourself why do I have hair . . . I'm telling you now that I didn't think much about loyalty to the party, though at the same time I was naturally faithful.

He fell far short of the standards required of 'a socialist youth with consciousness'. When Deng emulated Lei Feng:

> Oh, personally I agreed we should be leading a life like Lei Feng. A man should not be afraid of swallowing minor losses in little things.

Q: But apart from this quality there were other qualities in Lei Feng such as his loyalty to the party and worship of Chairman Mao.

A: Oh, this kind of thing had little influence on me. This loyalty to the party was something emotional, right? The most important thing was that I observed Lei Feng's behavioural manifestations.

When Deng emulated someone, be it not just Lei Feng, but also a teacher or a classmate or Mao, he was pragmatic. He had immediate small goals. He observed carefully and selected deliberately what he considered the valuable characteristics of each and went about emulating these in a business-like manner. He would emulate a particular teacher in the way he walked, a classmate in his suave way of dealing with people, another schoolmate in the way he talked. Similarly, in the Cultural Revolution, it was when he discovered his lack of grounding in politics, essential for writing good big-character posters, that he began immediately digging into books on Maoist ideology. In most of the things he did, he was not much motivated by ideals. His predominant concern was that his actions should bear some pragmatic, utilitarian, tangible results.

So when he emulated Lei Feng it was expressed in doing a bit extra, not in trying to cultivate a passion. When the class went to labour in the fields, he would bother to gather up the tools. When no one else swept the floor, he would take up the broom. When talking to people he tried to be patient. This is what he called 'not afraid of swallowing minor losses in little things'. But by no means was he equating these public-spirited performances with a 'revolutionary' spirit:

Q: You considered yourself very red?

A: Of course I was red! [said with much pride in his voice] Not too many impure thoughts. I also had the traditional thought and quality of the Chinese intellectual, feeling personally responsible for the nation and for the world. Besides, I realized I was living in an era of peace, so I must do some small things.

Q: Not big things?
A: Things like what Lei Feng did, what else? [said with a cynical tone of voice]
Q: How about in the future?
A: To design a machine for the country. This is a small deed.

Certainly it is a strange way of putting it, but he had hit on one important aspect of what we have been discussing: that in their era of peaceful revolution – actually evolution, despite the use of revolutionary rhetoric – their contribution was to be of a type different from the older generation. Having been brought up on the glory attached to achieving the victory of violent revolution, they saw little left for them to accomplish. While in school, the only recognized 'revolutionary acts' they could engage in were of the Lei Feng style of insignificant deeds; at the most, when they grew up they could contribute to developing the economy of a still very poor country. Yet in the 1960s, it had become increasingly difficult even to accomplish the 'small things' Deng visualized for his future. There was the imminent threat of being sent to settle in the countryside for life. There was the intensification of the class line, which was increasingly to their disadvantage in the struggle to enter university, the gateway to achieving these 'small things'. There was a shift in what a 'revolutionary' performance entailed – towards a petty show of activism, the mouthing of ritualistic allegiance and increased conformity.

Like Chang, Deng's response was to embark on a frantic programme of physical tempering, similarly inspired by the young Mao. He devised a well-planned schedule for each day's exercises. He rose before everyone else to go jogging and perform gymnastic exercises, and at night rushed back to the dormitory to perform more before the lights went out. He pursued his physical tempering with such systematic and strenuous training that finally, though previously a nondescript athlete, he could boast a championship form in both speed and strength. But what for? Mao, and Chang emulating Mao, tempered themselves in cultivation of a willpower in preparation for the future revolution. Bai did it for health reasons, which he rationalized were tied to the revolution: that to construct socialism – and he meant it literally – one needed a strong physique. Deng had several of his own reasons.

First, physical exercise was one means by which he could regain some of the self-esteem he had lost in being hopelessly poor in ball games. A believer in the survival of the fittest, he worshipped physical prowess, which he saw as power, superior and beautiful. To excel in jogging and gymnastics became channels of self-expression and proof of his worth to himself and to his peers. But more than that, by sticking to his own set of exercises and his own schedule and refusing to participate in the class's daily calisthenic sessions, during which his classmates ran round the playground like a 'herd of ducklings', Deng was really, in his own subtle half-conscious way, competing with the others. He was trying to be different, trying to show them he was not one of the common crowd, that he was 'pure and lofty'. Finally, without originally intending to, he turned it into an opportunity to defy organizational discipline. The league branch began to criticize him for breaking the rules with his individual exercise schedule and for disturbing the others by rising earlier and turning in later. He ignored the criticism and continued doggedly with his planned schedule. As the rebukes from the branch mounted, he did compromise temporarily; but already his reluctance to conform and be disciplined was obvious. In their physical tempering, both Chang and Deng possessed strong willpower, and both were fighting through the physical training to find ways to express themselves.

Deng's physical tempering was also an effort to draw attention to himself as a somebody. He felt his capabilities had been unfairly slighted. His grades were not bad. His performance in manual labour, according to him, was excellent; yet he never so much as got a nomination for being a labour activist, a recurrent complaint in the course of the interviewing. He attributed the 'unfair treatment' to the fact that he did not have a 'sweet tongue' like the others and did not play the trick of labouring more actively in the presence of teachers and league cadres than when their backs were turned.

Though both Chang and Deng felt unfairly treated, for Chang it was mainly for not being recognized for his revolutionary fervour, and Deng for his capabilities. Chang's dissatisfaction was joined to his internal turmoil, whereas Deng's had to be externalized. He brooded over the rejection of his application for league membership in senior high 1, and finally came up with the rationalization that one could as readily or more readily make revolution without joining the league, implying that not all league members were revolutionary. He wrote a small-character poster arguing this and stuck it up on the classroom bulletin board. The move was daring, because it was a direct attack on the legitimacy of the league as the vanguard of youths. The poster stirred up a storm. The class became split over the issue: the league members together with the conformists, mainly girls, on the one side; and the non-activists supporting him on the other. For several days, a spate of small-character posters from both sides plunged the classroom into a mini-crisis.

Such open arguments over basic issues rarely occurred in Chinese classrooms, but the episode was not unique. Another interviewee from Deng's own school had stirred up a storm quite similar to this one during a campaign known as 'revolutionalization'. This was a campaign calling for even tighter discipline, so much so that a special hour was set aside for midday siestas during which monitors toured the school grounds to enforce the new regulations. This interviewee purposely had read revolutionary novels during that hour instead. He was criticized and an argument on small-character posters ensued between himself on the one side and the rest of the class on the other.

A common characteristic ran through these incidents. They were all expressions of independent nonconformity. They were regarded as potentially threatening to the established order among students. As the arguments grew more heated, the intrinsic right or wrong of the unconventional acts no longer constituted the major issue. The main objection of classmates was to the spontaneous nature of such actions, that they were beyond the control of the authorities and beyond the confines of normal expression and that they challenged discipline and the efforts actively to conform.

In both cases the school leadership allowed the storm to subside without intervening, perhaps because the unorthodox viewpoint possessed an internal logic not entirely alien to aspects of the official ideology. A special class meeting was to be held to criticize Deng, for example, but the teacher privately advised him beforehand in a roundabout way to drop the matter. Deng saw it was best to back off, and in the meeting the teacher succeeded in touching upon the issue only lightly before branching off to discuss something else. The incident was brought to an inconclusive end.

Deng's yearnings for recognition of his abilities did not necessarily involve yearnings for power. All evidence, including his Cultural Revolution performance after he achieved a political mass base, suggests Deng did not have great aspirations for power. For example, unlike Ao he saw no connection between the term 'revolutionary successor' and power or cadre status. His understanding of the phrase was simply, 'Well, we are the new generation and of course we are the revolutionary successors.' He would not willingly bend to achieve league membership, feeling it would necessitate a selling out of his integrity. He disdained those who 'lowered' themselves by washing others' clothes or who always left clues obvious enough for the league members to notice their good deeds, or who wailed aloud in self-criticism meetings, or those who 'drew a clear class line' with their families. But then his own situation never demanded such action of him, compared, say, even to Chang. Though Deng's family was not of the five-red classes, his parents were middle-ranking state technical cadres. And academically he was above average in an above-average school.

Deng did apply to join the league once more in the final year of senior high school, since one could keep on handing in applications to join the league after being rejected. Such an act of renewed application was itself taken as a sign of activism. During the interim period between application to the league and the league branch's decision, the applicant was supposed to prove to the league members his revolutionary fervour by his behaviour. Deng knew that he had a serious chance for entry, since he had applied with the encouragement of the teacher, who had a liking for Deng and hoped to see his chances of university admission heightened. Since the teacher was himself a league member and therefore sat in on his class's league branch meetings, Deng finally received the league's preliminary approval one month before he was supposed to graduate from high school. (As the Cultural Revolution gathered steam that May, however, both his graduation and his admission to the Youth League were suspended indefinitely. Deng never did get to play the part of a league member.)

That spring, while his application to enter the league had been pending, Deng had to decide on his future. Weighing all the pros and cons, he applied to an agricultural college:

> My thoughts were more or less progressive. It was my opinion that one should put one's knowledge into practice in serving the society . . . and at that time I criticized those people who had a very sweet tongue [pledging to go to the countryside] but who really were thinking of going to university. Nor did I see the necessity of taking the opposite route, of refusing even to apply to university and insisting instead on going to the countryside. I didn't belong to this type. I took the middle course.

This choice had its practical and ideological advantages. Among urban students, the agricultural colleges were the least desirable of all the higher educational institutions. Deng's decision not to attempt the more difficult strategy of trying to get into a regular university reduced his risk of being sent to the countryside to settle for life as a peasant, a future Deng had no illusions about. Applying to an agricultural college at the same time satisfied the ideal of serving the people. Deng often seems to have tried to tread this kind of middle road, a careful balance between pragmatism and ideals.

CLASS GROUPINGS AND THE TENSIONS OF CONFORMITY

We have observed, in large measure by way of our four case studies, that classroom tensions in the two or three years prior to the outbreak of the Cultural Revolution had intensified along two dimensions. One, the class line, had split students into four recognizable groupings: the cadres' children, the worker-peasant children, the middle-class children, and the bad-class children; and two, the competition for political credentials had divided students into a camp of official activists versus classmates who had been denied official status.

Deng's classroom can provide an example of the emerging schism between class groupings. His schoolroom contained a large number of cadres' children. The school had tried to build a good reputation by getting a high percentage of its graduates into university, so it had made it a point of recruiting the type of students whom university admissions offices normally looked kindly upon: namely, (1) high and middle-level military and party cadres' children; and (2) bright students from the households of the intelligentsia who could not make it into the few top schools in the city. Apart from these, there was a scattering of workers' and peasants' children, a handful of middle-class children from non-intelligentsia homes, and a few bad-class children.

In the first year of senior high school, activities in Deng's classroom had been dominated by those students who had joined the Youth League in junior high school. They had entered in the early 1960s, when class background had not been a very important criterion; children of the middle-class intelligentsia were well represented in their numbers. Ao, had she gone on to a senior high school, would have been among such 'veteran league members', as they were called. The new league members, recruited during Deng's three years at the senior high (1963–6), were largely red-class children. By the last term of senior high school, of all the middle- and bad-class students put together, only about a third were league members, while all but one of the cadres' children were in the league. The latters' standing in the league, based upon their 'natural redness' (*zilai hong*), had soon overshadowed the veteran league members'. The veterans had, until the 1964–5 schoolyear, been holding the league officers' posts, and naturally felt threatened. However, this tension between the veteran and new league members remained below the surface. It was to become evident only during the Cultural Revolution.

The cadre children normally stayed apart from the other students, as a separate group. They seemed to inhabit a politically special world. They were name-droppers, who picked up inside stories through their parents, which they would parcel out authoritatively among their lesser peers. Among themselves, they recognized a status ranking that in large measure was commensurate with their fathers' official positions. The children of high-level army and party-organ cadres stood socially atop the high-level administrative and middle-level cadres' children; children of cadres from outside the province above local cadres; middle-level party administrative cadres' children above those of ordinary level; the latter above the workers' children; and the workers' children above those whose parents bore a good-class peasant label. Though lumped together under the common rubric of 'red class', between the cadres' children and the worker-peasant children lay a vast gap in status, economic situation, social milieu and life-style.

In Deng's school, most of the cadres' children did not board, as the others did, but lived at home in a nearby party cadre compound. They bicycled to school every day; and bicycles, for high school students in China, were a luxury. Some were even chauffeured to the school gate. When Deng visited their homes, he was amazed at the material comforts they enjoyed, despite the fact that Deng's own economic situation was far above average.

Generally speaking, cadres' children were less eager to demonstrate activism than were their middle-class schoolmates. My interviewee of cadre family background was a case in point: 'If I wanted to get into the league I knew there would be no problem.' Sometimes, even if a cadre's child showed no interest in joining the league, the league branch specially 'cultivated' him in the same way Bai had been cultivated. The children of cadres did not have to be anxious about their future. They knew that with 'natural redness' to fall back on, even league membership would not be important to them in getting admitted to a university. They were confident, moreover, that with influential parents they would be able to secure a good career even if they did not attend university. Partly for this reason, cadres' children generally were less proficient academically than were the students of the intelligentsia middle-class. They had less incentive to strive to be the best.

But they genuinely believed that being red by birth meant they were more revolutionary by nature and hence had a natural right to become the 'successors' to the revolutionary cause and to positions of power. Since they believed their redness was innate, they did not feel that it needed to be externalized in behaviour; and since no one openly challenged this kind of belief, there was less social pressure put on them to show their activism. Thus, they rarely had to fake activism. In fact, they were as contemptuous of phoney activism as were the middle-class nonconformists. For most students, activism entailed submissiveness, obedience, discipline; but the high class status of the cadres' children, their feelings of familial superiority, and the respect they were accustomed to receiving from their parents' subordinates had habituated them to a pattern of behaviour beyond the constraining discipline of the league or school authorities. At least a minority seems to have been spoiled and arrogant.

To distinguish themselves from the rest of the students in Deng's school, the military cadres' children developed their own status symbol – the wearing of old army clothes handed down from their fathers. The adventure stories about war heroes had lent heroic connotations to the wearing of such uniforms. With his adoration of physical prowess, Deng was quite envious of the armymen's children. But he and the other students never dared to wear such garb lest they be accused of falsely usurping status. Later, during the Cultural Revolution, when this monopoly of the PLA cadres' children broke down, the military style became a fashion of the 'masses.'

Not only did some of the cadres' children not care much about joining the league; they even looked down on the league as too much of an impure 'mass' organization. In a classroom where, by the end of senior high school, a third or in rare cases even half of the students (as in Deng's class) were league members, the organization lost some of its 'glorious' elitist lustre. This psychology, Deng contends, accounted for why, at the beginning of the Cultural Revolution, the cadres' children organized the first Red Guards as an exclusive preserve for themselves.[41]

At school, the cadres' children and the bad-class students occupied the two extremities in a minutely divided social spectrum. The bad-class children, to compensate for their lack of 'political capital', often studied ferociously. They felt that their only hope was an academic record so outstanding that the authorities would overlook their class origin. But ironically, the more they worked at their studies and the more they distinguished themselves academically, the more did their successes reflect badly upon the academic inferiority of the cadres' children. This invited the antipathy of the cadres' children, who could point to the bad-class high-achievers' indifference to activism as proof that they were in fact 'backward elements'.

Among this stigmatized bad-class group, there were a few who did not drop out of political competition, out of genuine dedication or ulterior motives or a mixture of both. But in order to be accepted as politically reliable, sufficiently to join the league, the test imposed upon them to prove their devotion became doubly stringent and demeaning. The final and most difficult 'gate to pass' was to draw a 'clear class line' with their families, and it had to be a *serious* 'drawing of the line', by exposing the reactionary nature of their parents. The mere mouthing of standardized slogans would not do. It was demanded in order to force them into an irreparable psychological break with their family, prescribed as a prerequisite for cementing the youth's loyalty to the polity.

But most bad-class students were not willing to betray their parents. Even those who were positively oriented towards the system and who genuinely regarded their parents as reactionary could not bring themselves to clear that hurdle. The slogans were 'educate well those children who are educable' and 'unite with all those who can be united'. But generally, the severe psychological pressure put on bad-class children was counterproductive. The greater the pressure on them to distance themselves from their families, the more they tended to identify with their families. The interviewee of capitalist origin noted:

Although many bad-class students didn't have much good feeling towards the Communist Party, it was not to the extent of going against it. But the result of the strengthening class line was to push us to the opposite side. Those who actually did not oppose the national system now felt disgruntled with it. Actually there had previously been a chance of winning us over.

They developed their own subculture, with their own moral standards: 'If we became red we were degrading ourselves.' They had an inner integrity to maintain. As a result, they reacted to political demands with minimal and passive compliance.[42]

The middle-class students, especially the children of professionals, had always been, after the cadres' children, the system's favoured group. During the 1950s they had been granted access to both channels of upward mobility – through the party machinery and the educational ladder. Since they did well academically, children from this group had tended to dominate the posts of student officers in the primary schools. As we have observed, due to the influence of their family upbringing they constituted the most achievement-oriented of all the student groups. They generally accepted the system and were committed to the ideology.

These students prided themselves upon their academic superiority even in ideological terms – as being valuable in building up the country. They believed they were genuinely red and expert: 'red in heart, if not red by blood'. However, with the tightening of the class line, middle-class students began to see their favourable position challenged by the students of good-class origin. Increasingly, they needed to make up for their innate deficiency in 'natural redness' by becoming 'red' through political performance. But as the competitive mood mounted in the mid-1960s, some of the good-class students derided them for not having 'true' class feelings and for acting in a politically enthusiastic manner only in order to get ahead. Precisely for this reason, they were among the most anxious of all the students to prove, to themselves as well as to others, the *genuine* quality of their activism.

The group identity of the middle-class students was less strong than that of the bad-class students. Only when they were challenged *as* a group did they begin to see themselves as such. They did not repudiate the party's premises, however. As we have seen, most of them had been willing to treat their bad-class schoolmates as pariahs, partly under social pressure but partly, also, because they actually believed that members of the outcaste group might harbour 'class hatred'. At the same time, however, they were unwilling to accept that the good-class students were more 'revolutionary' than themselves. They despised those who claimed status merely by ascriptive criteria, without having to show talent or exhibit dedication. The cadre children's sheltered, soft life-style seemed to contradict the image of proletarian simplicity and sacrifice; they saw little of a 'revolutionary nature' in these classmates.

Feeling that the cadres' children did not warrant any great respect, and recognizing how far most of the workers' and peasants' children lagged behind in academic qualifications, many of the middle-class professionals' children believed that they were the most qualified to rise into the positions of responsibility and trust in the next generation. This ambition was not explicitly articulated before the outbreak of the Cultural Revolution, but privately some of them were anxious for China to reject the class line which, since 1963, had progressively been encroaching upon their chances for elevation.

The more ambitious of the workers' and peasants' children knew they could not hope to compete with the brightest of the middle-class professionals' children in the academic arena. But they could expect to achieve an equivalent social status at school by claims to a superior 'natural redness'. Naturally, they welcomed 'redness' superseding 'expertise' in recruitment policies for higher education and the Communist Youth League. Yet, when they were matched up against the cadres' children, they always came off one notch lower: their parents were merely recipients of the revolution, not its originators. By the class-line premises that they themselves supported, they were placed in the position of seeming less 'revolutionary' in nature than the children of the cadres. Not suprisingly, many of these workers' and peasants' children harboured resentment both against the middle-class professionals' children for their academic superiority and against the cadres' children for their successful presumption of political superiority. But they were less ambitious than the middle-class professionals' children in challenging the cadres' children. The only students over whom they could safely claim superiority were their bad-class schoolmates. We shall later observe how, in a frightening display of authoritarian intolerance, they played upon these presumptions of superiority in the early months of the Cultural Revolution.

The second major type of tension that increasingly wracked Chinese urban classrooms arose from the competitive pressures to be conformist. The pedagogic teachings of the 1950s had, as earlier observed, in a self-contradictory fashion wanted young people to be self-activating and creative on the one side, and self-abnegating, disciplined, submissive to the collective will on the other. From our examination of the high schools of the 1960s, it is obvious that, much as in the writings opposing Deweyism, the demands for discipline and conformity had triumphed in the urban education system. Few formal channels existed by which young people could express individuality or show creativity. Most of my interviewees felt stifled by the unremitting demands for behavioural conformity. The majority, not as rebellious as Chang, obediently toed the line, but also, not as conformist as Ao, they experienced a frustrated urge to assert their individuality.

Worse yet, many felt hypocritical in toeing the line. On the one side, as the campaign mounted to emulate the self-abnegating Lei Feng model, an increasingly moral stance was demanded of students; but that same campaign was pushing students towards amoral role-acting. They wanted to show their dedication of their own free will; some even wanted to devote themselves to the activist venture as an uplifting, self-actualizing experience. But their activities at school were instead geared towards gaining a better opportunity to climb the educational ladder by pleasing those who held authority over them. Most of my interviewees, as noted earlier, were perturbed by what Chang called 'this painful experience'.

Those who could perform a self-righteously activist role with the greatest confidence and the fewest self-doubts were those like Bai, who looked to the credo of the party to set the guidelines of right and wrong, or Ao, who looked to her superiors. They never questioned whether the external guidelines were correct or not; they did not submit the guidelines to an inner moral judgement. For that reason, hypocrisy did not pose much of a problem for them; so long as they acted in accordance with the dictates of legitimate authority, they could perceive their actions as moral. Contrarily, the half-dozen interviewees who, in their surface behaviour, seemed hesitant to act in a devoted activist manner, who seemed awkward in the effort, tended, like Chang, to be more inner directed, less oriented towards the standards established by external authority, more given to private evaluation of personal right and wrong. For them, the activist play-acting posed persistent dilemmas.

These several nonconformists often talk in retrospect of having been suppressed by some invisible force they could not pinpoint. Unlike the alienated bad-class students, they fully believed in the political system and so could not put their predicament into perspective. Though disgruntled with the effect of the class line upon their standing and their chances for upward mobility, they dared not consciously oppose the basic premises of the class line, since these premises had been endorsed by Mao and the party. Stifled by the demands of conformist activism, they blamed not the system of political education in which they were entrapped but, rather, directed their discontent towards the membership of their own particular classroom's league branch. Themselves ridden by doubts regarding activist conformity, they ascribed to many of the league members the same hypocrisy they feared in themselves. They gave their own unfavourable twist to 'redness'. They commonly used the term pejoratively to mean mere overt conformity without genuine revolutionary consciousness. When they described someone as a 'big red person' (*da hong ren*), as 'very red' (*hao hong*), 'being at the height of redness' (*hong ji yi shi*), or used the Cantonese saying, 'so red it's magenta', they always implied a scramble for fame, with an element of long-term opportunism. To them, neither official activism nor natural redness was 'revolutionary'.

In the Cultural Revolution, these unrecognized activists would be clashing with official activists, each side asserting its own superior purity. Even more significantly, the different class groupings among the students would be dividing and redividing into hostile political factions. In other words, in the Cultural Revolution the students would be playing upon the various types of frustrations and animosities that had imbued their classrooms during the preceding years. Depending upon their differing statuses, different students would be bringing different sets of attitudes to bear in the conflict, and would be playing different and sometimes opposing roles.

Notwithstanding these major differences, in the upheaval of the Cultural Revolution all of them would also exhibit similar behavioural traits – deriving from the beliefs they had been taught in common, the activist school milieu they had all inhabited, and the similar pressures and tensions to which they had all, to some measure, been subjected. Their frustrations over petty activism would be released in a common frenetic effort to prove the genuineness of their dedication, through a clamorous worship of authority in the shape of the demigod Chairman Mao. Their anxieties would be acted out through a frantic show of righteous intolerance, which would include the organized beating of bad-class 'ghosts and demons' by good- and middle-class students alike. Their competitive efforts to be upwardly mobile would be transformed into a ferocious contest to win political recognition through the force of arms, each Red Guard grouping trying violently to suppress the other. In short, in the heat of the Cultural Revolution (and in particular, during the first half year of that upheaval), the authoritarian proclivities of all of the activist groupings among China's urban student body would be surfacing – dramatically.

4 The Cultural Revolution: a Test of Political Activism

In the period just before the call of January 1967 to 'seize power', the weather was quite cold. But when I walked in the streets the wind seemed like a spring draught wafting toward me. I'd never felt so free. Ah, it was truly exhilarating. I felt myself so lucky to have been born at this time of history in China, born under the flag of Chairman Mao – on the one hand to have been liberated by Mao Zedong, and on the other to have experienced such a sublime sense of freedom.

> Respondent Chang, Deputy Commander
> of Canton's secondary school Rebel
> Red Guards

At the end of the Cultural Revolution in 1968 we were distraught. We simply couldn't figure out why, having plunged into Mao Zedong's Cultural Revolution with completely dedicated hearts, and having followed Mao Zedong's footsteps, in the end we could have fallen into prison.

> Respondent Deng, Commander-in-chief
> of the secondary school Rebel Red
> Guards

When Mao Zedong gave young people the green light to assail the established order in 1966, the tensions, antagonisms, anger, self-disdain and bottled-up frustrations of the preceding years exploded into violence. The conscious basis for the young people's behaviour was to 'defend Chairman Mao's revolutionary line'; but this became, as shall be seen, a rationale for the expression of their personal interests and emotional yearnings.

The two years of student upheaval can be broadly periodized into two distinct phases. From May to autumn 1966, student activities were characterized by an aggressively competitive activism performed under institutional and peer-group pressures: a brutally magnified version of the kind of activism that had plagued Chinese classrooms for the past several years. The second phase, from the late autumn of 1966 through the summer of 1968, witnessed a more unfettered form of activism. Political participation was left to one's own choice, frequently entailing dangers that outweighed any prospect of personal advancement. This shift from institutionalized activism to unfettered activism was accompanied by changes in the young people's conceptions of themselves, of the party and, later, of Mao himself. It became a watershed in their political socialization. By the close of these two years, their thinking had been radically altered.

PHASE I: INSTITUTIONALIZED ACTIVISM

When recalling what happened in those first several months of the Cultural Revolution, most of the interviewees remember themselves as 'naive'. They confess they were not quite sure what the political issues were. They talk of the excitement, confusion and rapidity with which half-comprehended events succeeded one another.

At first, the format of the new campaign had seemed little different from earlier nationwide campaigns. That May of 1966, urgent speeches were delivered by the school authorities, and newspaper editorials criticizing the Peking literary circle as anti-party were read and 'studied' in classes and meetings. Students were urged to write essays and big-character posters denouncing these obscure literary figures who had dared to pen historical allegories challenging Chairman Mao's wisdom. Normal school schedules were increasingly disrupted to allow full participation. As in all political campaigns, students were supposed to assert their activism. But, frustratingly, this entailed no more than transferring onto big-character posters a series of stereotyped editorials denouncing the chairman's enemies. The students none the less competed to churn out as many of these posters as they possibly could.

Events took an unexpected turn in early June when newspapers carried headlines about a poster written by a young philosophy professor attacking Peking University's party officials. When Mao publicly endorsed the poster, the message seemed clear to students throughout the country. Attacks were to be launched against 'bourgeois academic authorities', 'ghosts and demons' (mainly referring to people under attack for their class backgrounds)[1] and 'revisionists', who were accused of having wormed their way into the party in order to restore capitalism. All of these despicable categories had, till then, been mere abstract phraseology to students. But now they suddenly seemed to leap into human form. Every 'struggle campaign' had 'struggle targets'; in this one, the targets were to include some of their own teachers. Interviewees report how, as news spread of student attacks against teachers in Peking, their own secondary schools, in imitation, blossomed almost overnight with big-character posters denouncing teachers and sometimes even principals.[2] The students criticized their former mentors for anything that came to mind: from their teaching methods and laziness in labour to their deemphasis of politics and the thought of Mao Zedong, to their not allowing students to play enough soccer. 'As long as you were a teacher, you were in trouble', says one interviewee. Though teachers who had been unpopular generally were attacked most severely, the criticisms were so many and so diffuse that almost all teachers were exposed to some form of abuse.

Gradually students began focusing on specific complaints. Many of those of good-class background began attacking teachers for glorifying academics rather than redness; for being partial to the non-red-origin students; for placing undue stress upon examination results. The denunciations were still limited to the writing of big-character posters and criticism meetings (no violence was involved yet). Even so, the sudden outbursts against authority figures astonished the participants themselves, considering the prestigious position of teachers in Chinese schools. An interviewee recalls how the decorum vanished in his own classroom:

> As long as he was the classmaster he was always in control of the students. Psychologically you could feel he was controlling you. You were scared of him, more than other teachers, because it was he who wrote the evaluations on you. When we got there [the staff room] we were nervous, not knowing what to do or say. We had no guts. But a high-level cadre's son who was never scared of teachers just put out his hand and grabbed at our teacher's collar, yelling, 'You so-and-so! We're going to struggle against you now. Think about it carefully!' Oh, we were like puppies following behind, not knowing what to do. But he just walked this teacher back to the classroom: just by grabbing his collar. There'd been a mask separating us from the teachers, but after that, the whole mask was

ripped away. When we reached the classroom, the rest of the classmates were amazed to see us coming back like that. Immediately, their awe of the classmaster was gone. The teacher was shaking. He had never dreamt of this. He spoke with a trembling voice, no longer his former self.

In this rebellion against the authority of teachers, they genuinely believed they were acting in support of Mao, that hidden 'ghosts and demons' who wanted to attack the chairman were everywhere. The worldview they had internalized let them see things only in red and white: the revolution's pure good challenged by absolute evil. They were intent upon proving themselves as politically upright by exposing this hidden evil. Above all, they *needed* to prove themselves upright; they felt under intense pressure from their own peer group to be activist.

At that time, no one had thought that the Cultural Revolution would last two years. The campaign was expected to be short-lived and a golden opportunity to demonstrate activism. Among my own interviewees, two submitted applications to enter the League within the first few weeks.

But after the initial excitement had died away, when day after day they made the same criticisms and wrote the same big-character posters, a feeling of uneasiness and frustration set in. Despite all their efforts, they often could find no real fault with their teachers. But to show they were revolutionary, they still had to wrack their brains to conjure up 'reactionary' statements they could accuse teachers of once having uttered. They became quite proficient at this: grabbing hold of an ordinary sentence and twisting its meaning into an instance of political heresy. They were aware they were distorting the facts, but they saw little wrong in doing so. The most important thing was to find 'ghosts and demons'. The more severely one denounced the teachers, the more militantly one was supposed to be following the correct line; and thus, the more activist one was perceived to be. They were anxiously playing to their audience of classmates.

The rationale that they were struggling against the 'bourgeois black line' – though not quite knowing what it meant – and their eagerness to shine in their performance were conscious motivations encouraging them to 'catch up with the tide'. However, a quote from a middle-class interviewee who had been academically at the top of his class and who earlier had been troubled by the triviality of activism suggests how the attacks also relieved pent-up emotions:

For a long time the students had harboured a whole bellyful of concealed discontent. But when we acted we did something else – scolding the teachers. Because the whole society had a lot of slogans for us to employ in that way – 'anti-revisionism', 'anti-restoration of capitalism', etcetera. Actually these terms were just caps that were fitted onto many things . . . At that time, people's feelings were very complicated. Some wanted to do something for the country, but couldn't see what they could do. Your life wasn't in your own hands. For example, you wanted to study more so that you could contribute more. But there was no way . . . Although you wanted so much to do something for everybody, you weren't able to enter the league. On the contrary, that hodge-podge of people who'd engaged in all sorts of stupid schemes could get in. Anyway, many people could feel their initiative was stifled. I believe this was the thing people were most angry about.

We only have to look at the everyday atmosphere of classrooms, the strict discipline, the constant pressure to conform, the hypocrisy of the emulate Lei Feng campaign, the hierarchic peer-group structure, and the constant anxiety that one might have to settle in the countryside, and it becomes clear that these repressed dissatisfactions had only to be precipitated by a catalyst.[3] But the students were in no respect politically disenchanted. Indeed, they were so committed to the polity personified in the chairman, so ready and willing to act for the 'revolution', that their fervour had been awaiting an outlet. The two ingredients – dissatisfaction and dedication – became intermingled. The teachers had become vulnerable surrogates for everything that had been repressing the students and everything that had been preventing them from proving their loyalty and devotion. The zealous attacks thus were comprised of two contradictory elements: a yearning for self-liberation and a willingness to surrender themselves to a supreme authority figure.

This anarchistic period lasted only a few weeks. In June 1966, party cadre workteams were dispatched into all the educational institutions to put a halt to the chaos. On the grounds that the Cultural Revolution should be carried out systematically, the workteams of party officials narrowed the targets for attack to a group of teachers who largely were older and of bad-class background.[4] In some schools, 'cow-sheds' – makeshift prisons – were set up to house them. During the day, the targetted teachers were dragged out to do heavy or menial labour and to attend meetings in which they were denounced and beaten.

The function of the cadre workteams in a political campaign normally has been to keep it under strict controls. Based on the ideological rationale that 'class struggle' should always be waged against the former exploiting classes, workteams in previous campaigns had similarly dragged out people of bad class background for the masses to criticize. What was left unsaid was the strategic purpose – to drum up passions *under* the party leadership. This was what the Cultural Revolution workteams did the moment they took over the school's administration. To help steer the Cultural Revolution safely within the tracks of a 'class struggle' crusade, the workteams turned to the good-class students. In each classroom, Preparatory Committees for the Cultural Revolution were established, and red-class students were appointed to command them. The league members of non-red origin were cast into the background.

The bad-class students felt stigmatized as never before. Picking out bad-class teachers as ghosts and demons had only underlined their own precarious position. The new heightened play upon students' class origins portended even graver problems for them. Their main concern was to avoid trouble by conforming passively and staying unobtrusively in the shadows. They had little interest or ambition to be politically active.

The middle-class students, on the contrary, resented not being given a chance to prove their dedication. They had seen this campaign as a long-awaited opportunity. They found it tedious and frustrating to return to formal struggle meetings[5] in which they had no major part to play. Their dissatisfaction later would be articulated in the accusation that the workteams had suppressed the 'masses' revolutionary creative spirit'. One of the interviewees recalls:

The workteam organized orderly struggle meetings and discussions, but we were all tired of doing that every day – digging up dirt and making accusations against the 'ghosts and demons'. They entirely ran out of new things after a while. So the workteam organized study classes, to discuss why there was this feeling of having nothing more to write about [in big-character posters denouncing those teachers]. The conclusion was that our class feelings were not deep enough. They said that we should intensify our class feelings and never let up on the class enemies. They made you wrack your brains thinking up new counterrevolutionary statements and acts to tag teachers with. It was meaningless; the exercise had no passion to it. Of course, the red-class students were enjoying themselves very much. Every single thing was to their advantage. What they were doing was in reality sinister and perverted. The only thing they did was to dream up accusations to work on.

Uneasy and dissatisfied though they might be, the great majority of these middle-class youths were in no respect ready to rebel against the workteams. The authority of teachers and principals might have been broken, but the workteam remained sacred. It acted as a proxy of the party. To be anti-workteam was to be anti-party, and to be anti-party was counterrevolutionary.

But suddenly, in late July, a month after the workteams had moved into the schools, Mao ordered that they be withdrawn.[6] He accused the workteams of seeking to stifle the Cultural Revolution by diverting the 'spearhead downward' towards powerless targets. Mao was not opposed on general principles to a party-sponsored campaign of class struggle against bad-class people, but he wanted to give a new twist to the term. In a document known as the Sixteen Points,[7] Mao in early August 1966 singled out both 'bourgeois academic authorities' and 'power-holders in the party taking the capitalist road' as legitimate targets for class struggle. But who were these 'power-holders . . . taking the capitalist road'? And what exactly was this 'capitalist road'? Neither was specified. Point no. 16 of the directive provided the only definite and concrete instruction for action – 'The Thought of Mao Zedong must be upheld as a compass to the Cultural Revolution.' In short, anything or anybody regarded by Mao himself to be out of line with his own thought was 'capitalistic', was 'bourgeois', was 'revisionist'. But Mao at that time was not even spelling out precisely what his Thought entailed.

With the advantage of hindsight, knowing what happened after 1968 in the wake of the Cultural Revolution, when the Thought of Mao Zedong dominated policy-making, the meaning of the Thought of Mao Zedong becomes clearer. 'Capitalist-roaders' were those who envisaged a different strategy of development for the country, who advocated step-by-step modernization of the economy under a routinized bureaucracy. The very nature of their line required reliance more on the 'experts', i.e., those who had been branded 'bourgeois academic authorities'. Mao saw the two categories of targets – these party leaders and the 'academic authorities' – as going hand in hand.

The competition between the two development strategies was termed by Mao the 'struggle between the two lines'. This could be most clearly seen in the conflict over educational policy both before and after the Cultural Revolution. Whereas the 'capitalist line' favoured cultivation of 'experts' and when implemented tended to benefit children of the former bourgeoisie more, Mao's 'revolutionary line' favoured 'redness', which when carried through after the Cultural Revolution benefited those of red origin.[8]

To win his 'struggle between the two lines', Mao was prepared to shake up a political system allegedly permeated with 'power-holders taking the capitalist road' and 'reactionary bourgeois academic authorities' at each level of the party administrative bureaucracy. He needed the help of the 'masses'. And he was prepared to give the teenage generation, nurtured under socialism but never having experienced a revolution, a surrogate revolutionary experience. He would allow them to be his spear-carriers in a dramatic, tumultuous purge.

But what we today know of Mao's intent, and to whom he was referring, was not clear to the young people at the beginning of the Cultural Revolution. The rhetoric was couched in revolutionary clichés without clear definitions. What did 'proletarian culture' mean, for instance? Who could have known it would turn out to be the kind of culture that Jiang Qing was to impose for ten years? In practice, once the thought of Mao Zedong was accepted as dogma, what the phraseology meant was irrelevant.

In fact, the directives reaching the students were often so vaguely worded that they could be interpreted in whatever ways suited one's interests. On this rested some of the confusion of the Cultural Revolution. Each student group could claim support from Mao by selectively emphasizing different revolutionary clichés. The red-class youths focused their main attention on the 'ghosts and demons', i.e. the former bourgeoisie, and were reluctant to attack (or even defended) the 'power-holders taking the capitalist road', i.e. the representatives of the political establishment. When the Sixteen Points directive was announced, the non-red-class students, who did not identify as closely with the established order as the cadres' children, could contrarily interpret the major targets as 'power-holders'. In the schools, these would be the party secretaries and other party members. Mao repudiated neither interpretation; both fitted his design.

It was not coincidental that of all the clauses of the Sixteen Points, the one which interviewees of middle-class background took as their credo was Point 4:

In the Great Proletarian Cultural Revolution, it is the masses who must liberate themselves. We cannot do the things for them which they should do themselves.

We must trust the masses, rely on them, and respect their creative spirit.

These students felt they had as much claim to be considered among the 'masses' as the cadres' children. When Mao ordered the workteams to withdraw from all the schools, some of them wanted to believe Mao was giving them the go-ahead to assert themselves.

But they were quickly disappointed in their expectations. The workteams' activities had bolstered the red-class students' claims to superiority, and when the workteams quit the schools, they had left the red-class students in control. This transfer of power was dramatically legitimized on 18 August 1966, when Mao officiated at a mass rally attended by Peking students of red-class origins. Students from several of Peking's elite schools had banded together in a new, exclusively good-class organization they called the Red Guards, and at the rally Mao publicly gave the new group his blessing. Overnight, in Canton, similar Red Guard groups sprang up to replace the now-defunct Youth League.

The cadre children who headed these new groups denied the middle-class youths admittance and only grudgingly allowed those of worker-peasant background to join their ranks. No matter how perturbed they might feel at being barred from the doors of the new Red Guard groups, a majority of the middle-class students still hoped to accommodate themselves to the new order that Mao had endorsed. They rallied round and let themselves be formed by the new Red Guards into groups called Red Outer Circles, even though the name itself implied that the red-born students constituted the true vanguard. They hoped that through their proven activism they might be promoted to the privileged status of 'Red Guard'. They were still eager for official recognition.

Some middle-class students, though, found the new turn of events unacceptable. A few daring ones – and they had to be very daring – set up their own rival groups to challenge the Red Guards, contending that the main purpose of the Cultural Revolution was to storm the school Party Committees, not simply to attack 'ghosts and demons'. These 'minority factions', as they were called, came under severe attack from the Red Guards. Chang and Deng were both founders of minority groups in their own schools. Just as they would not submit docilely to the league before, they would not now bow to the Red Guards. Deng spoke caustically of those who had joined the Red Outer Circles as people willing to demean themselves by accepting 'second-class citizenship'.

Almost immediately after the Red Guards had been founded, a Destroy the Four Olds movement – to destroy 'old ideology, culture, habits and customs' – brought most of the students out into the streets under the command of the new Red Guards. They ransacked bad-class households and carted away furniture, books and other possessions that might be classified 'bourgeois' in nature. They humiliated and terrorized bad-class residents. The zealots were mainly red-class students eager to play up the issue of class. Middle-class interviewees talk of how they tagged along, under pressure to show their activism. But they were caught in a conundrum. Changing street names, sacking churches and humiliating fear-stricken bad-class people might be exciting; but they were bothered to see the symbols of 'bourgeois decadence' – vases, books, beautiful furniture, paintings – smashed and burned. Many of their own homes had at least a few of these possessions. The Four Olds movement was placing their own families in a more questionable status.

They were further perturbed when the cadre children began propagating a 'blood-line theory'. First enunciated in Peking by a university student of high-level cadre origins, its tenets were succinctly encapsulated in three rhythmic lines:

If the father's a hero, the son's a great fellow.
If the father's reactionary, the son's a rotten egg.
If the father's nondescript, the son's a fence-straddler.

Previously, no matter how the red classes' claims to an inherited 'revolutionary nature' were interpreted, the argument rested on the tenet of parental social influence. The new blood-line theory transformed and rigidified the notion of 'revolutionary nature' by ruling out the possibility of attaining revolutionary virtue by political activism and correct attitude. Only 'red' blood in one's veins was now to be recognized. Essentially, the cadres' children were redrawing the main line of cleavage in society by placing the sharpest social boundary between the good classes and the rest of the social groups. They thereby expected to reduce the number of people in society entitled to share in social privileges and, most importantly, to disqualify their chief competitors, the achievement-oriented professionals' children. The cadres' children could narrow even further the number of people entitled to claim privileges by relegating the workers' and peasants' children to the bottom of the good-class scale. In essence, they were attempting to build a caste-like structure based on hereditary principles. They were claiming for themselves – to borrow Weber's term – an 'hereditary charisma'.[9]

They insisted that each student's origins be reinspected, to ensure that each occupied a place in the new pecking-order no higher than deserved. In what was known as 'investigating into three generations', red-origin students went to the places of work of their classmates' parents and demanded access to the parents' dossiers. Even some of the working-class students were obliged by the cadres' children to go through the process of 'proving' the legitimacy and purity of their family backgrounds. Many children came to know for the first time exactly what even their grandparents had done long before Liberation. This fetishism of the 'blood-line theory' rested on the explicit assumption that there was a physiological heritability to one's disposition towards the polity.

The 'blood-line theory' became one of the justifications for the violence exercised in what the cadres' children themselves proudly titled the Red Terror. Maltreatment of bad-class 'ghost and demon' teachers became increasingly ferocious. In some schools, a small corps of good-class students was selected to keep guard of the cowsheds, which kept the abuse of teachers more or less under control. But in other schools, the situation degenerated into chaos. So long as you were of the red classes, you could do whatever you pleased with the 'ghosts and demons'. Chang describes the punishment meted out to such teachers at his own school. 'They painted the faces of the teachers and then in the playground made them walk around carrying big rocks. While the students beat drums and gongs, they were made to mumble: "I am a ghost and demon. I am a ghost and demon." And then came the beating.'

What was the emotional impetus behind this cruelty? The acount given by an interviewee who went to an elite key-point school, a

school which pushed hard on academic achievement, can help put the
problem into perspective:

> Because their grades were bad, the students of good-class back-
> ground had always felt under pressure from the teachers . . . They
> made the teachers memorize the Mao Quotations: 'Quotation No.
> x.y.z.!' Actually they themselves didn't know which was which.
> 'Do you know or not? No?' Then – whap – a slap. Again they'd
> yell: 'Memorize! Do you know the quotes or not?' – whap – Study!
> No? Okay, another whap. The teachers would plead: 'How could I
> memorize all that?' 'How come you pressured us like this before?'
> Then the teacher would say, 'Yes, I know I was wrong. I was
> wrong.' 'Ha. Wrong?' Another slap.

These red-origin children harboured a frustrated jealousy of the
non-red-origin students' academic superiority. Now that they could
assert their own superiority, based on their 'natural redness', they
took vengeance. They forced bad-class schoolmates to engage incessantly in self-confessions and denunciations of their parents, and at
times even beat them. Three of my interviewees had experienced
such humiliations, including one who was of middle-class origins. She
had half of her hair shaven off in what was called a 'yin-yang head', as
a conspicuous sign of her political damnation. A decade later, she
still fought back tears when recounting the incident.

The better the secondary school, the more violent the Red Terror
tended to be, for it was here that the children of high-level cadres
were concentrated in substantial numbers. Based on the logic of the
blood-line theory, they felt they had to show that they were the most
revolutionary of all the red-class young people, expressed through
the militancy of their class hatred. And banking on the superior
status and power of their parents, they did not give a second thought
to the consequences of their violence.

Here is an account of the extremism at one of the schools:

> During the period of the blood-line theory it was terrible. In one
> third-year junior high school class, the workers' and peasants' kids
> sat towards the front, and those of office-worker origins were made
> to sit in the rear. At the very front, some desks were piled up, like
> a pyramid. On the very top sat the son whose father was the most
> important cadre, then others in descending order. In front of them

was a bonfire, and silhouetted against it were the children of bad-class background. Whap! Whap! Those cadre kids came down in turns to beat them with belts. Some of the bad-class kids wet their pants. Wow, if they wet their pants the beating must have been horrifying. Both boys and girls were beaten in the same way. Yi – they sounded like ghosts shrieking! It was incredible.

This was a somewhat exceptional classroom. The Red Terror in Canton was relatively 'gentle' compared to Peking, where the top-ranking cadres' children were concentrated in greater numbers. There, the attacks upon bad-class householders reached the point that deaths from beatings became sufficiently common that the Party Central Committee had to pass a resolution to put a stop to the killings.[10]

In Hong Kong, a decade later, an interviewee of revolutionary-cadre parentage defended his participation in the Red Terror:

I don't think the whole blood-line theory should be discarded. Those who were most opposed to the theory weren't even welcomed by their own Red Flag faction. [The Red Flag faction was later to become the umbrella faction made up primarily of middle-class students.] They were usually small, common or very selfish people. I had no sympathy for them. They were only good with their mouths . . . Admittedly, as I wasn't a target I didn't feel the pressure. The targets of course felt it much more deeply . . . Actually, no matter whether it was the assailants or the victim, it wasn't an individual's affair. It was a policy from above . . . For all these years the party had been using the blood-line theory, though not so blatantly . . .

He had started with an argument based on 'class' bigotry and ended by unloading responsibility onto the system. The root of the extremism does seem to have lain with the programme of political socialization that the party had sponsored: the Manichean worldview, the fetishism as to the moral purity of the proletariat, the teachings that class feeling transcends all humanitarian feelings and that class enemies should never be shown sympathy, the profusion of warlike slogans, the incessant hammering that the reddest of the red classes were innately more revolutionary than the rest and should put their dedication to the test. When Mao sounded the alarm that the 'dictatorship of the proletariat' was under siege, that 'bourgeois academic authorities' were 'restoring capitalism', it was natural that in their defence of the system – simultaneously a defence of their own class interests – they competed to exhibit their hatred of the former exploiting classes as 'class enemies'.

Almost all the young people of whatever class background shared to some extent in these intolerant beliefs and authoritarian proclivities. In their eagerness to prove their political dedication, middle-class students also maltreated those they considered lesser beings. Both emotionally and intellectually, they believed they were justified. But many of them were deeply troubled by the Red Terror. Though normally they were spared physical abuse, most could not escape one or another form of humiliation. Yet, as we have noted, only a few daring middle-class students protested against either the blood-line theory or the Red Terror. It was not just fear of retaliation from the good-class Red Guards which stilled the tongues of the majority of the middle-class youths. They quite simply did not see any strong legitimate grounds to oppose the cadre children's ascendancy, since Mao seemingly had given them his support. The middle-class students were not yet sceptical of the national class line policy *per se* and felt they had to support all party doctrines in order to legitimize their own standing.

It was not until some months later, in February 1967, that they even saw an articulate counter-argument to the blood-line theory: a manifesto that originally had appeared in a Peking Red Guard newsletter, which referred to the blood-line as a 'new racist system'.[11] In certain respects, the parallel was apt. Some of the red-class students had proposed that bad-class people be separated physically from the better classes, as in a system of racial segregation. Students at one Peking high school had even advocated that they be dealt with by methods not dissimilar to the apartheid system in South Africa – e.g. to deny to them most of the urban services and to drive many of them out of the capital into the countryside.[12]

In the early autumn of 1966, suddenly, the blood-line theory and the cadre children's monopoly of the student leadership were repudiated by Mao and his supporters in the Central Committee. Mao at no time repudiated the idea of a class line *per se*. But for the time being, he wanted to see the 'spearhead' of the Cultural Revolution pointed at the 'capitalist-roaders' in the *party*; and the cadres' own children would be the last young people who could be expected to carry out such attacks. Mao's followers in the party leadership proclaimed that one's political devotion, not 'natural redness', defined the true revolutionary activist. All students who wanted to 'defend Chairman Mao' had the privilege and the duty to do so, irrespective of class origins.

PHASE II: UNFETTERED ACTIVISM

The establishment of the new Red Guard groups by the good-class students and the setting up of 'minority factions' by some of the middle-class students had been fledgling attempts by students to redefine political activism in their own terms. But freedom to act independently, especially for the non-red-class students, had been largely curtailed. Confined to a classroom setting and intimidated by the Red Terror, most of them felt even more constrained and stifled than they had earlier under the surveillance of league members.

Now, in the autumn of 1966, with the new pronouncements, they obtained the right to travel throughout China to 'exchange revolutionary experiences'. All organizations temporarily collapsed. Students swept out of the school grounds and scattered to all parts of the country. Some went to Peking to try to have a glimpse of their beloved Chairman Mao in person; some wanted to pay their respects at the historic revolutionary sites; others walked for a thousand miles or more to temper themselves by reliving the Long March. The experience of travel was exhilarating, but not so much because they were on pilgrimages to the historic sites or to catch sight of the beloved chairman. Rather, it was the feeling of release, of leaving behind the tensions of the past few months and the yoke of institutionalized peer-group pressure. They began communicating to friends feelings which they had never dared express in school. For the first time, they could act out their political activism without the guilty feeling that they were doing it for an ulterior motive.

When they returned to their hometowns in late 1966, many who before had been members of the Red Outer Circles abandoned the red-class Red Guard organizations in favour of the originally beleaguered 'minority factions' of the type Chang and Deng had founded. The more recent directives of the Cultural Revolution had vindicated their earlier position, that the main thrust of the movement was to pull down 'power-holders taking the capitalist road'. These expanding groups gradually merged to become what were known as the Rebel Faction Red Guards. The initial red-class Red Guards reformed into what were commonly known as the Conservative Red Guards or Loyalist Faction.

Whether one participated, and with which faction, was completely voluntary. There was no need to show off one's activism to win institutionalized approval any more, as all institutions had crumbled. It was the moment many of the more frustrated young people had been awaiting – a genuine 'revolution' in which to manifest their activism.

Class background provided a reliable indicator of factional alignment among the high school students, with the cadres' children overwhelmingly on one side and children of the middle-class intelligentsia on the other. The bad-class young people largely stayed at home. The further away they kept from the vortex of action, the safer they felt.

The stand of the worker-peasant children was, as a group, ambivalent. Officially, they were of the favoured 'revolutionary' classes in society. Yet they had, at the same time, been snubbed by the cadres' children. Economically, they were inferior to both the cadres' and middle-class children. Socially, because of their less successful academic records, they had commanded little prestige in the classroom. Dividing almost equally between the two factions, their choice depended much on personal circumstances. For example, it appears from interviews that those working-class students who were as adept in academic studies as their middle- and bad-class schoolmates felt less antagonistic towards these classmates and less need to promote the class line. They tended more often to defect from the Loyalists.

Moreover, in a number of the junior high schools in working-class neighbourhoods, the pre-Cultural Revolution splits had been principally along the lines of an activist minority versus a non-activist majority. In some of these classrooms, the good-class activist minority had dominated the early phases of the Cultural Revolution; and in the autumn of 1966, the majority took the opportunity to oppose them by joining the Rebels.

At the same time, as Table 1 indicates, not many middle-class students defected to the Loyalists. Hence, the class ranks of the Loyalists were relatively 'pure', whereas the Rebels' membership was of mixed class backgrounds. The Rebels accordingly were put on the defensive by accusations that they were harbouring impure elements: that they were dupes of 'rightists turning the sky upside down' or of 'class enemies seeking revenge'. To ward off such accusations, even the Rebel faction did not usually welcome people with bad-class backgrounds, still less allow them to hold important positions. Often, to boost the prestige of their groups, they adopted as their formal leaders people of impeccably red-class background, though real

TABLE 1 *Factional affiliation of Canton high school students*
in the Cultural Revolution

'Class' origin	No. of students	Rebel Red Guards %	Loyalist Red Guards %	Non-participants %
Revolutionary cadre	285	19	73	8
Working class	537	34	40	26
Non-intelligentsia middle class	302	40	10	50
Intelligentsia middle class	664	61	7	32
Bad class	399	36	4	60

SOURCE Questionnaire responses covering 50 classrooms; see Anita Chan, Stanley Rosen and Jonathan Unger, 'Students and Class Warfare: The Social Roots of the Red Guard Conflict in Canton', *China Quarterly*, 83 (September 1980) 440.

leadership might lie with the middle-class second-in-command. Even then, a disproportionately high percentage of Rebel Red Guard leaders came from middle-class homes.[13]

In general, each faction had a minority core of diehard members. The majority wavered in accordance with the favourability of the general political situation. The Rebels in particular witnessed this waxing and waning in their sizeable membership. It was not that any appreciable number went over to the opposite faction. But because the position of the Rebel faction was always more precarious, and the class status of its supporters less politically secure, in times of adversity large numbers of would-be adherents stood aloof.

For almost two years, these two major factions fought over a series of local arguments and charges and countercharges that to the foreign observer appeared almost arbitrary. The Rebels would seek any issues that attacked the seat of power, i.e. the real holders of power at different administrative and party levels. The Loyalists, on the other hand, tended to protect the leading party cadres, and directed the spearhead of attack towards lesser personnel in the same organizations.[14]

However, it should be borne in mind that it was *not* these political attacks which actually split the young people into two factions. The fighting over particular personalities and niggling local issues should be taken as surrogate manifestations of the fundamental 'contradictions' between the different groupings of students, predating the

Cultural Revolution. Otherwise we would easily be persuaded by what the official Chinese line, including Mao's, would have us and the Chinese believe: that it was unprincipled factionalism which caused the split into two Red Guard camps. We shall come back in much greater detail to this point, for on it hinges the reason as to why the Rebel Red Guards and Mao diverged further and further in the end.

The question remains as to why some interviewees, even years later when recounting their experiences as Red Guards, were unwilling to acknowledge that group or personal interest had played any part in the fighting. One reason was that many of the Red Guards had been intent upon demonstrating that contrary to the competitive activists of pre-Cultural Revolution classrooms, they did not *care* about personal interests. As the Cultural Revolution degenerated into armed violence between the two factions, the young people even welcomed the growing conflict as a means to prove their dedication. They had been granted an arena in which to emulate the revolutionary martyrs and war heroes, no longer confined to models of conformity and banality like Lei Feng or the other 'heroes of socialist construction.'

The ultimate form of dedication to the revolution, as we earlier observed, had always been posed in the storybook messages as death. When confronted with the possibility, some of these teenagers did not shrink from the final test; heroic disregard for death provided the grandest way to express their consuming need to prove genuine activism. Nowhere is this better illustrated than in the recollections of an interviewee who had fought as a Rebel in Guilin, a city in Guangxi province where bloody civil war erupted. His account portrays graphically the passionate, romantic attitude towards death that some students adopted:

My friends and I likened life to a box of matches. If you light the matches one by one they give off only a small flame. But if you set afire the whole box it gives off a flare far bigger, even though the quantity of matches is the same. We felt that to die a hero would be like burning the whole box of matches. So we thought that if there was a grand occasion for which we could die, then dying would be transformed into a happy thing . . . We talked about not leading a useless life. At that time we all felt the main thing was that if we grew old or whenever we were about to die, if we looked back at our lives no part of our lives should have passed away worthlessly. If we could have achieved that, then to die was all right. It was best not to die of sickness. The best way was when surging forward on a battlefield, dying in a big way, a worthwhile cause . . .

That's why, during the Cultural Revolution, so many people didn't take death to heart. They felt as if there was no time more timely than the Cultural Revolution to die. I myself felt like this, and many of my friends also. Talking about it now, it was really mad to look at death so lightly. But during the Cultural Revolution we thought it was for defending Chairman Mao. We regretted not having participated in all those big revolutionary events: such as the Long March, the anti-Japanese War, the War of Liberation. Those were the great days. As for us, we found our lives too mundane. Yes, we were said to be building up socialism, but that didn't conjure up in our minds the same grand image. That's why in the Cultural Revolution, when the warfare began, some of the young people talked about dying heroically. There were some I knew who were besieged in mountain caves by peasant militia. Every day, under siege and starving, they sang songs, songs like 'Thinking of Mao Zedong'. They were called upon to come out and surrender. But they steadfastly refused. In the end, all of them died of hunger in there – more than a dozen of them.

Of course, only the most romantically devoted were prepared to die like this. Many, as pointed out earlier, withdrew at times of adversity. Though to some of them the pre-Cultural Revolution activist behaviour had seemed petty and unworthy of themselves, they did not now let themselves be drawn into so extreme an effort to prove their genuine activism.

THE REBELS' CREDO

The Rebel teenagers brandished the slogan 'rely on the masses and believe in the masses' creative spirit' as Mao's 'most precious gift'. Yet independent thinking took time to mature. Throughout the Cultural Revolution, they looked to Mao, the Central Committee's Cultural Revolution Small Group and the Peking Red Guard Head-quarters for guidance and moral support. Many times, they took action only after Peking had initiated the first move or when some central leader had come out with a statement of support. Their mode of thinking was confined to what they took to be the framework of the thought of Mao. It was a time when Mao's thought had been raised to the level of religious dogma. But beyond that, political pressure required that they wave the Little Red Book to ward off attacks from the opposing faction and that they use appropriate Mao quotations to support their arguments. The result was a confused plethora of accusations and counter-accusations that each side was 'waving the red flag to oppose the red flag'. The Mao quotations, sayings and slogans were sometimes used correctly but sometimes out of context, and purposefully so, to bolster their own arguments. The Rebel leaders were only taking the initiative to rebel against immediate institutional controls, not yet fundamental party tenets.

As the Cultural Revolution fighting wore on, however, circumstances increasingly encouraged them to think issues through on their own and to come up with their own standpoints. Every time they were faced with a crisis, they had to use their own discretion. Instructions from the centre were often vaguely worded and even contradictory.[15] For one thing, there were divisions even within the Cultural Revolution Small Group of the Central Committee.[16] The directives were so confusing and came down from so many top leaders that in order to maintain a consistent line the young people found they had to fall back on their own interpretation of Mao's thinking and their own judgement.

At no other time had the young people been exposed to such an unrestrained atmosphere or such a free exchange of ideas. They related their feelings to each other without apprehensions of being reported to a league branch. People like Chang and Deng, who had always felt isolated, secured close friends during this period. They discussed political issues and strategies late into the night. They expounded their viewpoints in Red Guard newsletters. They attended incessant meetings of Red Guard groups, arguing and debating. Increasingly, as circumstances dictated, they unconsciously or deliberately accommodated Mao's thought to their own thinking, rather than the other way around.

While formulating and administering political activities for their spontaneously-formed Red Guard groups, they came to discover a very different kind of organizational democracy than what the league had claimed to offer. The idea of the Paris Commune-style of electoral system and organizational structure for mass organization, which was mentioned in the Sixteen Points Directive of August 1966, captured their imagination, and when running their own groups they transformed that imagination into practice. An interviewee recalls the emergence of mass-organization leaders, without any need for legitimization by higher authorities.

The candidates for leadership came out to debate. If you agreed to what someone said, then you accepted him as head . . . But when he had no viewpoint, then naturally you listened to someone else. A Rebel leader had to be very careful that he wasn't going against the masses. Even if the masses were wrong he had to submit to them a bit. If he angered the masses they told him to stand aside. It was all subtle, but the masses had the greatest power . . . If the masses supported you, fine. If they didn't, you were all alone, you looked stupid.

Such ideas were soon applied to the entire political structure of the state. As they pulled down 'capitalist-roaders' one after another, from work units to the provincial level and even to top Central Committee officials, uncovering the 'political dirt' of the established structure, they saw no reason why the Paris Commune style of election should not be applied to the higher echelons as well. The interviewee who was quoted above observes:

At that time I had this fantasy. I thought that those big shots should somehow only be up there in the same way as the heads of these mass organizations were. That meant that when the masses were dissatisfied with them, they could remove them from office. Officials normally kept their posts for the rest of their lives. If the masses had the power to remove them then they wouldn't dare do so many of the things which were against the interests of the masses . . . Ah, I realized what it meant for a country to have democracy. That was it!

Such feelings helped to fuel the January Seize Power, when Rebels in cities throughout China toppled Party Committees. Exhilaration was generated by news of the establishment of the Shanghai People's Commune. As early as 1967, a few of the Rebels were demanding a complete reorganization of China's political structure – which would, if implemented, have meant an end to the monolithic party system.

BREAKING AWAY FROM THE MAOIST PARADIGM

Some of the Rebels were beginning to adopt the belief that there had emerged in China's socialist society a new privileged elite composed of the families of the revolutionary-cadre youths: a stratum of 'red capitalists' and 'new-born bourgeoisie'.[17] This view was expounded with the greatest sophistication in the autumn of 1967 in one of the best-known Rebel Red Guard manifestos – 'Whither China?',[18] written by a Hunan high school student. These new ideas, very rapidly condemned by the leadership in Peking as an 'ultra-leftist trend of thought', none the less circulated widely among the Rebels. Previously accustomed to thinking in terms of two polarized forces, the evil KMT–capitalist–imperialist–anti-Communist force versus the revolutionary Maoist camp, the new mode of thinking was a threatening alternative to the paradigm this young generation of students had learned.

Mao had hinted at his concern with party bureaucracy in a paper listing twenty manifestations of bureaucratic behaviour.[19] But awareness of the problem of bureaucratization is not equivalent to claiming that there had already formed in society a self-perpetuating privileged 'new class'. Mao was not prepared radically to change the system of Leninist controls, which would have been required in order to dampen seriously the political power of the party bureaucrats. He sought only to give the political bureaucracy a series of shake-ups, in the form of many rectification campaigns that punctuated the years after Liberation. The largest of these was to be none other than the Cultural Revolution. The phrase he liked reiterating, '95% of the cadres are good or comparatively good', served indirectly to deny the existence of a privileged 'new class'.

In the chaos of the Cultural Revolution, the Rebel Red Guards had no time to ponder Mao's position. Misinterpreting the rhetorical political slogans, they were blind to the several fundamental points of divergence that were developing between Mao and themselves. Already, Mao had opposed in January 1967 the setting up of a Paris Commune style of political structure in the Shanghai People's Commune, on the grounds that 'if everything were changed into Communes, then what about the Party? . . . There must be a Party somehow; there must be a nucleus.'[20] Mao had ordered instead the formation of a Revolutionary Committee, to be based on a 'three-way alliance', i.e. an alliance composed of the army, former cadres and representatives from the new mass organizations. This implied little change in organizational structure. It would mean a comeback for the rehabilitated cadres and a gradual return to the old order. Mao was suggesting that he wanted the monolithic political structure, with a Leninist Party, to remain.

Yet my interviewees had continued to approve of the Paris Commune style of organizational structure. But they had little inkling of the concrete measures that might be taken to attain that form of government. There was no political programme, no long-term plan. In fact, after a 'seizure of power' (sometimes no more than snatching an official seal), the Rebels had great difficulty simply trying to keep the administrative organs functioning. Usually events had caught them before they were prepared.

By February 1967, the army was moving into the schools to force the students to 'carry on the revolution back in the classroom' and to agree on the 'three-in-one' Revolutionary Committees. The Rebels were suppressed; but only momentarily. The Cultural Revolution leadership, fearing a political shift towards the right, withdrew the military units in April.[21] But in the end, to bring the Cultural Revolution to a close, the military would again be used; and again Revolutionary Committees would be the chairman's prescription.

The young Rebels' hopes differed from Mao's stance towards the class line, too. When the army had temporarily moved into the schools in February/March 1967, the class line was revived. A short-lived Central Committee directive of February 1967 invited such a revival:

> Red Guard organizations should be reorganized, consolidated and developed during the movement. Red Guards should be formed mainly of revolutionary students born of families of labouring people (workers, peasants, soldiers, revolutionary cadres, and labourers engaged in other fields). Students who were not born of families of labouring people may also join the Red Guards providing they cherish deep feelings for Chairman Mao, have the proletarian revolutionary spirit and have consistently behaved themselves comparatively well politically and ideologically.[22]

What did this imply? It meant not only a reapplication of the class line but also a restructuring of the Red Guards along the same lines as the league. The autonomous Rebel Red Guard groups would be dissolved and the Red Guards of good-class origins placed under centralized control. For the Rebel Red Guards, especially those not 'of families of labouring people', it meant a return to the late spring of 1966 when party workteams had controlled the schools. The armymen coming into the schools in February 1967 rallied the Loyalists around them; the Rebels, and especially their leaders, were criticized, and some of the more important ones arrested. However, despite this setback, the Rebels were careful not to bring their dissatisfaction over 'class' out into the open.

A third difference between the Rebels' view and Mao's, as a logical corollary to the first two, was that Mao would not admit there were fundamental and major 'contradictions' splitting the Chinese student body into the two factions. Thus in the autumn of 1967, when Mao was anxious to call an end to the disorder, he issued a directive declaring, 'Within the ranks of the working class there is no fundamental clash of interests. There is still less reason to form two antagonistic factions within the working class under the dictatorship of the proletariat.'[23]

Under the weight of this directive, the two factions were again pressured unsuccessfully to form a single Red Guard organization. Persistence in fighting was denounced as 'unprincipled sectarian mentality'. But as we have earlier seen, the differences between the two factions were not merely 'sectarian' bickerings. Above and beyond the specific issues that came to be at stake, the factions' memberships closely reflected the pre-Cultural Revolution tensions in the classrooms – and, in particular, the tensions over the class line that had been exacerbated during the early phases of the Cultural Revolution. The two factions could not be brought together while these underlying tensions remained unreconciled. The middle-class Rebels could not be expected to accept docilely a humiliating status reminiscent of the summer of 1966.

There was a 'follow-closely faction' which adhered to whatever was the prevailing trend and continued to observe Mao's instructions without the slightest show of scepticism. There was the 'pragmatic faction', who saw the hopelessness of the situation and yielded when force was applied. But there were also the 'ultra-leftists' who saw defeat coming, but refused to yield. This is how one of my interviewees describes the compelling idealism which propelled them.

When our ideas were still fuzzy, the centre[24] had called on us in the Sixteen Points to 'believe in the masses, rely on the masses'. In the end, when we really came to realize that in a genuine socialist revolution this was the crucial point, suddenly the centre said they did not want this thing anymore! How could we then, because we had to obey the centre, give this thing up? We couldn't anymore. If we hadn't really come to experience it through a mass movement, perhaps we could. But after going through more than a year of this so-called revolutionary experience, when it had already been rooted in us, to tell us suddenly to change our direction, well, we couldn't do so anymore. At this point, everyone began to discover that he was a bit reactionary, reactionary by not listening to the centre. On the contrary, we expected the centre to direct us as it had earlier, in accordance with our aspirations, our hopes, our demands.

Disillusionment came gradually and painfully for those Rebels who were truly committed. Like the interviewee quoted here, they used the term 'reactionary' to describe their own unorthodox ideas, for within their frame of mind, thinking that was not congruent with Mao's was 'reactionary'. Even after the autumn of 1967, they had resisted the evidence that Mao was responsible for the Central Committee's decisions and preferred to believe that he was compromising merely under the pressure of the situation. They desperately needed this illusion to prop up their sagging morale.

However, by the end of 1967, once more under the control of the army in the schools, many of them had turned despondent, angry, bitter, perplexed and anxious. While representatives from both Red Guard factions sat with rehabilitated school officials at the negotiating table to form a Revolutionary Committee under the army's supervision, the rest of the students had to attend daily sessions to 'struggle against self, repudiate revisionism'. Many refused to turn up for school. Between the end of 1967 and the summer of 1968, several interviewees went on tours around the country. Others stayed on campus, but with an attitude of cynicism and passive compliance. They rebelled by feasting, drinking, smoking, succumbing to modes of behaviour which earlier in the Cultural Revolution they would have condemned as 'decadent'. The interviewee from Guilin, Guangxi Province, who had witnessed some of the bloodiest Red Guard warfare in China, recalls an especially traumatic sense of loss, disillusionment and depression:

Though I didn't, many others stole and broke things. Some would see a glass window, fling a stone at it and run. They just didn't know how to express their anger and disappointment. We saw a dog, surrounded it, and simply beat it up. It was really stupid. We purposely went swimming in winter. The water was freezing. It was so cold our skin became numbed, and when we got onto shore and put on our clothes again, we felt much better, that numbing sensation. Oh, we didn't know what the hell we were doing. We were just crazy. We felt changed. Sometimes we just roamed the streets. We just, well, didn't know what we were doing. We wanted to vent our anger on something, but we couldn't. We just

felt we had nothing any more, those ideals we had, those expectations and enthusiasm to serve mankind. These seemed so unreal. I
didn't know how to express my feelings at that time. That was why
when I later was sent to settle in the countryside I didn't want to
speak anymore. I felt I hated all people. Even if they were nice to
me, I found them a nuisance. There was no more meaning.

Though the Loyalists had gained the upper hand when the Revolutionary Committees were formed in the autumn of 1967, the situation
remained unstable. In the summer of 1968 armed struggle flared up
once more between the two factions. This was the last round. The
final crackdown came. The army moved in, the Rebel leaders were
arrested. Worker Propaganda Teams sent by Mao to take over the
educational institutions enforced a ceasefire.

A fierce campaign began throughout China. Known as the Cleansing of the Class Ranks Campaign, it was to bring the chaos of the
Cultural Revolution forcibly to a halt.[25] At school, students were
pressured to expose each other and to criticize those who had been
specially chosen by the army as campaign targets. The pressure to
perform as 'activists' once more was operative, but this time the
consequences were serious; an accusing finger could easily land a
classmate in jail. The weak-willed exposed their friends to secure
better conditions for themselves. Those whose class backgrounds
were bad but who had dared to rebel were the first to be picked out
for mass criticism. The 'ghosts and demons' – the bad-class teachers –
were forced again to undergo public humiliation.[26] The Cultural
Revolution ended much as it had begun.

In the autumn of 1968, the students were allotted job postings. The
assignments were yet another defeat for the Rebels. The class line
was invoked to determine their careers. Though the great majority of
students, Rebels and Loyalists alike, were told they would be settling
in the villages for life, a fair proportion of the cadres' children were
able to join the army or stay in the city.[27] Every one of my interviewees (including the one of revolutionary cadre class background)[28] had
to go to the countryside. Apart from easing urban unemployment
problems, sending the young people *en masse* into the countryside,
dispersing them geographically, served as a means to break up their
Red Guard organizational networks. Quite unlike the days when Ao
had gone, settlement in the countryside was seen by a great many of
the former Rebels as a punishment: that they had been 'shovelled
into the backyard'.

THE SAMPLE

Inasmuch as my sample of interviewees disproportionately included bright, highly motivated, middle-class students attending above-average schools, it is not surprising that they included a number of very active Rebels. Of the fourteen interviewees, half became Rebels; and every one of these seven was a leader at one level or another. Three of them became quite well known among the Rebels in Canton, in particular Deng and Chang, who emerged as first and second in command of a united front of the city's secondary school Rebel Red Guards.

There were four Loyalists among my interviewees. Two of these were Ao and Bai, and the third was the student of revolutionary-cadre parentage. The fourth was of middle-class background, but his father was a senior official in his own work unit and consequently had quite a high salary and enjoyed some social standing. The interviewee himself had always got on well with cadres' children, and when the Red Terror swept his school, he was protected as their protégé. His school being second rate, tucked away in the suburbs far from the centre of action, without large numbers of cadres' children, it was never an 'active' school in the Cultural Revolution. So, though a Loyalist, he did not seriously participate. He joined mainly because his friends did. He spent a great deal of time 'having fun', and as law and order broke down went on joyrides with his cadre-origin friends in stolen jeeps. There were times, however, when he sided with the Rebels over specific issues and even got involved in arguments with people of his own faction.

Three of the interviewees were members of the 'stand-aloof faction' – that is, non-participants – but all three were sympathizers of the Rebel faction. One of them was of capitalist background and another of 'rightist' family origins, and so had been targets of attack. Once left in peace, they carefully never got involved. The third was of middle-class background. Though officially a member of the Rebel faction in his school, he was of a serious, steady, unassuming and non-aggressive nature and had never cared to compete for the limelight. When the Cultural Revolution broke out, he remained once again in the background. He found the Red Terror, the Destroy the Four Olds, and finally the factional strife repulsive, which reinforced his decision to stay inactively on the sidelines. He recalls telling his best friend of his alarm at the 'fascistic' tenor of the Red Guards' fanaticism. But he remained politically concerned. At the end of the

Cultural Revolution, when the mood among most Rebels was one of intense dissatisfaction, he was eager to go to the countryside to build up socialism. After he left China, he was also one of the few I have met who conscientiously has remained on guard against being corrupted by a 'bourgeois' life-style and has persisted in living a life of 'proletarian' simplicity and self-discipline.

CHANG: THE REBELLIOUS ACTIVIST IN THE CULTURAL REVOLUTION

The qualities required of an activist during the upheavals of the Cultural Revolution were very different from those which made for an activist in times of stability. Those who, for example, had earlier gained their league memberships by whole-heartedly emulating Lei Feng had been rewarded for obeying the authorities, for adhering strictly to regulations, for dutifully carrying out policies issued from above, for not asserting independent thinking. But in the Cultural Revolution, a young person distinguished him- or herself for quite opposite qualities: for daring to go against authority, for a readiness to break rules and norms, and for a willingness to make independent, bold and quick decisions in a situation of local chaos, when directives from the Great Helmsman Mao were often ambiguous.

It is not entirely coincidental that none of the seven interviewees who came to be recognized leaders in the Rebel faction had been league members. One factor was applicable to all – they had not conformed sufficiently to be recruited. That Chang and Deng became leading Rebel activists, and Ao and Bai active Loyalists, owed much both to their personalities and to their different social statuses.

The preceding description of the development of the political thinking of the Rebel Red Guards applies well to Chang. Initially, he was as unaware as his peers of what the Cultural Revolution was all about. But Chang feels, at least in retrospect, that psychologically he was already in tune with and awaiting the coming events:

During that period [on the eve of the Cultural Revolution] a lot of cryptic condemnatory essays were published, and I read them avidly. I felt as though I was awaiting the arrival of a storm, though I had no idea what kind of storm it was going to be. I thought to myself: if this storm comes, perhaps I can liberate myself from this oppressiveness and inability to express myself. An upheaval would create a situation different from the style of life I was used to. My character was one of storms and I felt I would synchronize with a stormy situation. I began talking with classmates about the growing campaign, but they didn't have the same enthusiasm. My heart was filled with expectations, thinking IT will come, IT will come.

One Sunday evening, in the very early period of the Cultural Revolution, news spread to his school of upheavals at some of Canton's universities. Thus began the two years of chaos:

Our people got very excited. They began counting the number of universities that had rebelled. Then gradually they began criticizing our own school: the food's so bad, etc. They had never complained about anything before. Ha, ha, it was so funny. Hee, hee, they turned to criticizing the headmaster: how sickly he looks; he never takes part in labouring; when out in the fields, he stands around holding an umbrella. We seldom talked about him before. 'Eh, let's start swearing!' We started banging on tables and chairs. 'Let's write big-character posters.' We rushed in a body out of our classroom. The moment we were outside we realized other students in other classrooms were rushing out at the same time. The whole school was flooded with lights. It turned out the high-level cadres' children were already rebelling. In that one night, we must have written 10,000 big-character posters . . . Oh, the next morning when we emerged, we felt so incredibly happy. There was no one in charge of the school. The teachers were hiding away somewhere. Oh, that feeling of being so free. It was such a strange feeling. Such a change from all those years. In this society of Hong Kong you don't feel it. The whole of me was so free.

No other interviewee recalls a similarly intense emotion of liberation. But in this initial convulsive phase, Chang, like the others, did not know what he was after.

Soon a workteam arrived and took control. From his own interest, Chang was dissatisfied with the workteam's open emphasis on 'natural redness' and with the mounting attacks on bad-class teachers. Having one day by chance seen a slogan in a factory criticizing 'capitalist-roaders in the party', he became convinced the target of the Cultural Revolution ought not to be the 'ghost and demon' teachers, but the school party committee which the workteam was obviously protecting. He was not yet quite sure what was wrong with the school party committee, but it did not matter: 'its problems must be clarified'. He drafted a big-character poster attacking the work-team for not 'dragging out capitalist-roaders' and managed to convince several other middle-class students in his class to pledge their signatures to the poster. Already he was assuming the role of a leader:

> That very evening all the other students in the school came to attack us. Wow, they were like a mob, these people hypnotized by the workteam. They were hysterical, shouting and screaming at us. They wrote a big-character poster several storeys long: 'Whoever opposes the Party is against Chairman Mao.' The other people in my class dared not say anything. I stood firm. I knew if even I didn't, the whole group would collapse. So I answered all the questions fired at us. At that point, whoever was firm became the leader. The children of high-level cadres of course were on their side. At night they followed us wherever we went. It was really a period of white terror. I felt very isolated. But they didn't beat me up. Others who revolted in the beginning had a much more difficult time, a few in some other schools even committed suicide.[29]

With the announcement of the Sixteen Points Decision in August and the withdrawal of the workteam, Chang's prestige and credibility rose among his classmates. But the class line soon reasserted itself. The Red Guards were formed, and the Red Terror escalated. Chang, protected by most of his own classroom, was not a victim of the Terror. But he was struck with guilt and self-reproach at his own powerlessness to arrest the brutality.

> I began to feel something was wrong with the system. The way they treated the classmates of bad-class background, so primitive, uncivilized, shocked me. What shocked me more was that what seemed to be such a rational society could have such things, such barbarism which seemed somehow to coexist with our society symbiotically.

By now Chang was well recognized as the leader of a 'minority group' in the student body. In October, as the 'blood-line theory' crumbled, the group expanded in membership and he was elected to become his class's representative in the school-level Rebel faction. Asked to be first-in-command, he declined the honour, preferring to operate from a less prominent position. A number of times in the months to come, he was offered leading posts and each time he declined. He hated being tied down physically by administrative and organizational work and by programmes and discipline. As second-in-command, as a *de facto* rather than *de jure* leader, he could enjoy more individual freedom. Good at penning big-character posters and manifestos, known for quick decisions, he thrived in crisis situations, but not as an organization man.

Chang felt supremely grateful to Mao for allowing them this opportunity for self-expression, and in early 1967, when the waves of the 'January Seize Power' rippled across the country,

> I had great expectations that we were going to win, and easily. I was expecting a radical change in society. My worship for Mao Zedong reached a crescendo; but my worship for him was different from the other students. I was at the same time evaluating him. He represented to me the one who could and would bring about the great changes. I misinterpreted him.

At that time the 'great changes' he was expecting were not yet structural changes. The Paris Commune was still a vague idea. He was equating the changes to a collapse of all authorities (excluding Mao, of course) and, emotionally, as a self-liberating experience. 'After the "seize power" took place, I was certain that *that* was a true revolution. Not only in myself, but even in the people around me, I saw a great change. Even those people who had been lowly before were liberated by their own better side.'

Earlier I compared Chang's adolescent development with that of radical American student leaders. Here Chang himself has completed the comparison between them: above all else, a search for self-liberation and meaning in life by rebelling against established social constraints.[30]

Before he had time to consider the significance of the establishment of the Revolutionary Committees in place of the Shanghai People's Commune, the army control corps moved into the schools and factories to suppress the Rebels. Confidence wavered, and membership of the Rebel faction immediately dwindled. Chang, angry and disappointed at the weakness demonstrated by the Rebels, took the risk of joining a small militant group outside the school 'to carry on the revolution'.

In April the verdict against the Canton Rebel faction was reversed by Zhou Enlai. Once more the Rebel faction swelled in size. Antagonism between the two factions increased from sporadic confrontation to organized violence. Chang's school was one of several in which the factional fighting first broke out in full-scale warfare, both sides armed with daggers, spears, shields and armour, and each side initially occupying a separate part of the campus. The Loyalists, led by children of cadres and armymen, were armed with more sophisticated weapons. None the less, in the end, being fewer in number, they were driven off campus. Chang took part in military affairs, as well as frenziedly participating in all other Rebel activities. He prided himself at being good both with the pen and the sword, a dual accomplishment that he felt was well within the heroic tradition of Mao Zedong. Physically, he strained himself, with endless meetings and nights on end without sleep. The physical tempering which Chang had been practising paid off in a stamina that outlasted others. But he pushed himself beyond his own limits. During this period, he contracted attacks of headache and bouts of din in his ears which still trouble him today.

Not all participated in the violent struggle. Many went home when it began, not convinced of the worth of risking one's life. Chang had given much thought to life and death at ordinary times. He frankly admits he was frightened of death. But as an essential part of his self-cultivation, he had constantly tried to force himself to overcome his fears by studying biographies of heroic martyrs. He had consciously tried to put himself in a frame of mind of being willing to die for the revolution. Even after the Cultural Revolution he was still testing himself, and leapt into a river to save a drowning man in the heroic manner described in those many stories of revolutionary martyrs which his generation had been consuming for so many years:

This guy was drowning and yelling, and no one was willing to go to save him. It flashed across my mind that I might be dragged down by him too, because I didn't know how to save people in water. But I thought again: 'it seems this cowardice won't do. Man shouldn't be like this.' I hated those people standing on the shore yelling, but who wouldn't go in. I couldn't stand that. Besides, I . . . well . . . I would have felt awfully ashamed for the rest of my life. So I jumped in. It was very quick, a very quick decision. Afterwards I felt very content. At that instant my heart had been filled with courage. In the Cultural Revolution this kind of feeling had also emerged in physical combat. This could be said to be a righteous emotion.

The Cultural Revolution was a god-sent opportunity not only righteously to risk death but also to fulfil his fantasy of performing like the historical heroes to whom he had felt so emotionally akin as a student. Those who emulated Lei Feng could put into practice the Lei Feng virtues any time. Those who emulated great historical figures had to wait for the arrival of a period of momentous events. Both Chang and Deng, having become Rebel leaders, felt they were finally achieving 'great deeds' like their legendary revolutionary predecessors. They, too, were now pushing forward the wheel of history in dramatic fashion. In one battle involving several thousand students, which Chang excitedly describes at great length, he had broken enemy front lines at the head of a corps of shock-troops. The military tactics he had studied and dreamed about in reading Mao and Napoleon had been brought to reality. There is no way of telling whether he is exaggerating his own significance in a well-known Cultural Revolution episode in Canton, but the incident did give him the sense of having fulfilled his destiny.

In the autumn of 1967 the Red Guards were ordered to hand back stolen arms to the military. Whether to surrender and accept the formation of the Revolutionary Committees became an issue that split the Rebels. Chang initially advocated that his group stand with the 'ultra-left'. Were all their struggles to come to nought? But the more practical side of Chang realized that no alternative existed to laying down their arms; they could not countermand Chairman Mao's directives. He agreed reluctantly to represent the city-level secondary school Rebel organization at the negotiation table to designate the municipal Revolutionary Committee. At that same meeting the article 'Whither China?' was condemned. It was there that he read it for the first time. 'The moment I picked up that article it affected me, very deeply. I began to *question* the system. I realized there definitely was such an elite class.'

He was well aware that his faction would lose out when the Revolutionary Committee was formed at his own school. Without permission, he once more took off for a tour around the country. By now the most rational choice for any Rebel leader harbouring personal ambitions would have been to agree to compromise and then work to get oneself selected a member of the school Revolutionary Committee, with a prospect of becoming an official in later years. Contrarily, by not cooperating, one was treading a politically suicidal path. The situation was so unfavourable that no one could have held onto any illusion that continued resistance might, in the end, result in the amassing of more power. By leaving Canton, Chang was attempting to make a statement: his allegiance to the powers-that-be could not be bought.

By the time Chang returned to Canton in April 1968, a renewed equivocal stand by the Central Committee had aroused one last hope for the Rebels. After calling and propagandizing daily for the formation of the Revolutionary Committees throughout the country, the *People's Daily* had begun intermittently including articles favourable to the Rebels.[31] Rumours were circulating in Canton that Mao was under attack, and the last diehards of the Rebel groups, by now much dwindled in size compared to their heyday of a year before, formed a united front to launch what they took to be a final life-and-death struggle. Chang became second-in-command (Deng was commander-in-chief) of a 10 000-strong secondary school Rebel Red Guard united force. There were renewed clashes with the Loyalists and the robbing of arsenals. Chang explains why he persisted: 'My idea was that even if we lost we should lose with glory, that we shouldn't be the type to surrender with a loss of moral integrity. I just wouldn't admit defeat. I had to carry on to the very end, from the beginning to the very end.' As they foresaw, they were crushed by the army. For the first time, the Rebels were obliged privately to question Mao's tactics and political stand. Most of the adamant Rebel leaders had been arrested, including Deng. Chang by sheer luck was spared; the army corps commander dispatched to his school happened to be sympathetic to the Rebels and let him volunteer to settle in the countryside. Before Chang went, he too released his passion and anger in what he and his friends earlier had considered decadent behaviour: drinking, smoking, aimlessly stealing dogs and chickens. As if to mark the end of his political fervour, he 'even seriously considered falling in love'.

DENG: THE PRAGMATIC ACTIVIST IN THE CULTURAL REVOLUTION

In many respects, Chang's and Deng's characters have much in common when compared to Ao and Bai – a streak of rebelliousness, a desire for spontaneous self-expression, an unwillingness to conform, an unflinching private drive for physical tempering and testing. These qualities helped motor their rise to leadership. But there was a major difference between them – Chang was more idealistic, with his

'class' interests and personal interests subdued. From my own observations, supplemented by Deng's friends' comments about him and
evidence from the many episodes he describes from his own past
history, Deng was not the type to lay down body and soul for an
ideal. To be sure, he had ideals. But they were combined with an
underlying ambition which simultaneously pushed him to strive during the Cultural Revolution for social prestige and status.

Deng claims that, immediately before the Cultural Revolution, he
too was psychologically prepared. He was eager to grab the chance of
accomplishing something great, since he had 'excessive energy' and
'not many worldly worries'. Again like Chang, he pasted up a huge
couplet at the school's main entrance, sarcastically pointing out that
the workteam had been eating the people's rice without achieving
anything and that they should be ashamed and work harder in the
future. He acted, he recalls, mainly out of personal discontent at
having been slighted by the workteam for not having a good enough
class background.

He was not subjected to the same attacks or suppression that
Chang had to bear. But as the movement continued, he became more
and more annoyed at not being given the right to participate actively.
After the cadres' children formed their first Red Guard group and
forbade the rest even to take part in the Destroy the Four Olds, he
grew furious:

> They [he really means 'I'] were very eager to do something. You
> see, they were told the Cultural Revolution was a political test,
> related to one's future. How could one remain idle? One must find
> something to do. Ha, ha, it's just like now, I have to find some
> work before I can make a living. [At the time of the interview,
> Deng was facing unemployment and had been quite preoccupied
> with the problem.] So I thought to myself: 'What the hell was
> happening in the other schools?' So with another guy of better class
> background – mine was one degree lower than his – we went
> around the whole city, to a dozen schools to observe their move-
> ments, and when we returned from our survey we were determined
> to start our own combat platoon.

Deng draws a revealing parallel between the desperation of job-
hunting in Hong Kong and his fight for a right to participate in the
Cultural Revolution. He had viewed official activism as political
capital in a most literal sense; and his determination to set up a

separate group for the students of ordinary class background, as an alternative to the cadre children's Red Guard group, should be viewed in that context.

When he called a meeting to form the new platoon, his classmates of middle-class background, about twenty in all, responded enthusiastically. Then came the discussion on giving the group a name:

> When everyone tried to suggest a name for the organization, I came out and said: 'Hey, why so many flowery names. Now, though we're not qualified to join the Red Guards, our class backgrounds aren't that bad; because we belong to the "fence straddling" faction, we too can rise up to rebel. Let's call ourselves "Progress Upwards", meaning to strive for the best.' Some people didn't agree. But I said: 'As long as we're able to achieve something, that's enough. Let's leave it at that.'

Without further ado the group was named as Deng insisted. Thus, even the name of the group inherited Deng's orientation towards achievement. Since he was the one who initiated the alternative Red Guard group, he presumed and achieved the role of leader. His leadership style was fast emerging: down-to-earth, forceful, slightly autocratic.

One problem he faced after forming the corps was that he had read no more than the politics class assignments and was not even acquainted with much of Mao's works. Since some theoretical knowledge was necessary to 'run' the organization,

> when the Cultural Revolution came I buried myself in books to catch up. In the very beginning only me and another fellow wrote our group's stuff, but his pen was faster than mine by three times. Ha, ha, I didn't know what the hell I was writing, but the other fellow's arguments were very good. So I worked on myself to catch up.

This need to prove himself more capable than others provided impetus to his activism. Chang, too, had wanted to prove his capability, but what he had wanted most to be recognized was his revolutionary devotion.

Under the Red Terror the members of Deng's platoon quietly deserted, and only a few hard-core members stayed with him. Giving vent to his frustration, Deng wrote an essay, entitled 'Long Live the Fence-Straddling Faction' which he sent off in dozens of letters to other parts of the country. But he could not help being anxious when the good-class Red Guards forbade him to take part in the National Day celebrations. He could not yet detach himself from the norms of institutionalized activism. His paramount concern was to be given a fair chance to prove his activism and be recognized for it.

At the height of the Red Terror, Deng was not mistreated, merely humiliated. He was angry about this, but he did not seem to have been much disturbed by the cruelty around him. In fact he continued to abide by the class-line framework, as the episode of naming the platoon well illustrates. Implicit in his argument that they, the fence-straddling classes, had a right to show their revolutionary fervour was the notion that the bad-class students were unreliable and should be ignored.

Chang, on the contrary, was not envious of the red-class students nor contemptuous of bad-class schoolmates. He was able to ignore or place himself against the established norms of activist behaviour. He encountered greater repression than Deng for setting up a 'minority group', but this had only reinforced his own views.

At first, Deng could not grasp the main points of the Sixteen Points Directive. The only point he understood was the one about believing and relying on the masses:

At that time it wasn't so often that one looked into the very root of things. It was those more practical things, things which were useful to me, that I was more sensitive about. This clause: 'believe in the masses, rely on the masses' was practical, right? You the Preparatory Committee [the Committee monopolized by the good-class students which had been set up in the classrooms by the work-team], why should you forbid people to rebel, right? Believe in the masses, rely on the masses, why not rely on me? I'm one of the masses! So if you people do not trust the masses, I'll do so myself.

He had missed the major thrust, the point instructing the masses to drag out the 'power-holders in the party taking the capitalist road'. It was not until Peking students 'exchanging revolutionary experiences' came down and taught them how to read the editorials that he, with a few in his platoon, wrote a big-character poster denouncing the 'capitalist-roaders' in their school.

Immediately the several of them became targets of abuse. Every evening, groups of students descended on their rooms to challenge and yell at them. But as the political climate outside the school altered in the autumn of 1966 in ways favourable to those who had attacked the workteam, the tide gradually turned. Deng's 'minority group' expanded into the school's major Rebel group. The official leadership post was given to a student of high-level cadre background, a common tactic of Red Guard groups, as we have already seen. Deng was put in charge of general affairs and served as the *de facto* head.

The turbulent events of the 'January Seize Power', which had aroused such exhilaration in Chang, passed Deng by completely. He was absorbed in restructuring and strengthening his platoon, which was undergoing growing pains. The day-to-day chores of running the organization preoccupied him more than the ideological issues. That is why, understandably, when relating his Cultural Revolution experiences Deng talks mainly of strategies, tactics, organizational matters but little of his own ideological development.

When the armed struggles began, he accepted the turn towards violence as a logical outcome of the deep hostility between the two factions. When one could not win by reason, force became the last resort. He was not in charge of military affairs; but on the several occasions that he participated in armed combat his worry was not so much the possibility of dying but of being disabled.

With Deng, as with Chang, this attitude towards death did not arise from the pressures of battle. It was a product of long and deliberate cultivation. Dispassionate though he was as a teenager in school, he had been much preoccupied with the question of death. He had discovered that he had an abiding fear of death, but the official message was that revolutionary heroes die fearlessly and earn glory by doing so. And he wanted very much to be a hero. What if the opportunity to die arose and his feet gave way and he missed the chance of becoming a hero?

In senior high school, during a 'sweeping the grave' festival, Deng and his class had gone to pay tribute to the revolutionary martyrs at the monuments built on their behalf, and he had come away with the disturbed feeling that what was left of the revolutionary heroes were no more than photographs, engraved names and decorated graves. On the one hand, he wanted to be honoured as a hero; on the other, he was struck by the transient nature of such glory. It was more important to achieve something while still alive.

He made ambivalent preparations to face death. As an example of 'grabbing hold of opportunities to cultivate my courage' he relates the following incident:

Once in the 1960s, there was a typhoon, and I was asked to see a girl and boy classmate home. That boy wanted me to accompany him, so you can see what a weakling he was. On the way an electric pole toppled over in front of us, and I knew that with all the water the electricity might be conducted. So I told the two of them to walk carefully, and I walked in front. If electrocuted I would be the first. At this instant, another person passed in front of us and collapsed, electrocuted. Wow, at that split second I thought: 'If I threw myself forward to help him I would die with him, and to be this kind of hero is useless. I had better save the trouble.' Ha, ha, so it crossed my mind that I would instead call for help. People rushed out and helped push the electric pole away. An army jeep passed, and we called to the jeep to stop, to help save the man. But the jeep refused to stop. I rushed out onto the street, forced the jeep to halt and had them carry the man into the vehicle. I felt I had done very well. I was very clever, did not throw myself in and get needlessly electrocuted.

As he began the story, I had wrongly expected, as an example of his 'cultivation of courage', a valiant show of heroism of the kind Chang related. But that did not fit Deng's disposition. Two points surfaced when Deng was confronted with an opportunity for heroism. First, his quick wrestle with the question of whether to save the man indicated a sensitivity to the official teachings of self-sacrifice; and second, his step forward to stop the jeep provided an on-the-spot compromise solution to the dilemma. Deng normally managed to find a middle-of-the-road solution to many of the idealism-versus-realism contradictions. Be it in his physical tempering, choosing a career, emulating heroes or choosing whether to risk death, he managed to maintain both his integrity and half-passionate idealism on the one hand and his awareness of reality on the other.

So, too, in the closing stages of the Cultural Revolution, he was strongly against the formation of the Revolutionary Committees, but was no staunch ultra-leftist, which he considered foolhardy. Reading 'Whither China?', he had found the analysis supported his own subconscious dissatisfaction with the class line, but he thought that to propagate such a stand was untimely and dangerous. One should know the tactical advantage of compromising at the right moment. Having noted that the authors of the famous article had been jailed, he put up a submissive front; and as a Rebel leader with a mass base, he was elected into the school's Revolutionary Committee. During the day he passively attended the Revolutionary Committee meetings, but afterwards would go back to his own 'brothers in distress' to carouse unhappily in a shared mood of disillusionment. Having been a leader of some importance, he had to allow strategic considerations to override ultimate goals. He felt he had to participate in the Revolutionary Committee, but did so only to the minimum extent necessary. He could have established a more favourable official status by participating more fully, but he was not willing to forsake his friends and integrity. He enjoyed a position that allowed him to wield power, but he was not obsessed with it. He had yearned since a child for recognition, prestige and status, but felt himself vindicated so long as his capabilities had been fully expressed and recognized.

In the end, he was not able easily to strike the balance between idealism and pragmatism. In 1968 he revived his rebellious activities for the last time and took up responsibility with Chang to form the united front of Rebel student groups. Deng, like others, was under the illusion that Mao supported them; but more than that, the situation was such that Deng could not resist popular pressure. Having been a leader, he felt that any retreat that summer would betray his group's stand and his group's expectations for him. So, despite the imminence of defeat, Deng surrendered to a display of idealism. He managed to flee during the crackdown, but was arrested none the less.

BAI: THE PURIST ACTIVIST IN THE CULTURAL REVOLUTION

Bai's interpretation of the Cultural Revolution differed markedly from Chang's and Deng's. Three factors accounted for this: (1) the fact that he was a university student, and in particular at a university in the capital, Peking; (2) that he was older, more experienced and mature; and (3) that he had occupied a different social status, as an official activist.

The clear-cut split along class lines which so neatly divided the secondary school students into Rebel and Loyalist factions, the former attacking the Establishment and the latter protecting it, was not obvious at Bai's university.[32] The university students, having gained the honour of entry into institutes of higher learning, could expect a promising career, and thus undergraduates of whatever class background had not felt their opportunities threatened in the same way as the secondary school students. They had had little reason to feel hostilely competitive towards students of other class origins.

The labels Loyalist and Rebel in the universities of Peking only have meaning when applied to the initial stage of the Cultural Revolution, when a small minority rebelled against the university Party Committees. Being in the nation's capital, each faction soon established direct links with different Central Committee members and vehemently flung the pejorative label 'Royalist' at the opposing faction, claiming for itself the revolutionary title of 'Rebel'. Both factions at Bai's university not only were tied to members of the central leadership; the conflict between the student groups was so ideologically and politically ill-defined that by 1967 both the main factions, though deadly enemies, found themselves paradoxically belonging to the same Red Guard Headquarters. From Bai's description, their squabblings often seem to have been unprincipled and petty.[33] There may have been more to the infighting, but to comprehend it, more detailed and systematic research into the nature of university factionalism would be needed.

Since in the factional alignments at his own university Bai saw only the evil force of sectarianism at work, by the end of the Cultural Revolution he had interpreted the upheaval as merely a manipulation of the masses by power-holders involved in a power struggle. Canton high school Rebels like Chang and Deng, whose groups were not directly linked to the upper-level powers ploys, did not similarly see themselves as having been simply manipulated. Their activism being independent and spontaneous, they were willing to take responsibility for their actions.

The Cultural Revolution in the universities did not arrive as suddenly as with the secondary school students. The issues of revisionism, education and material incentives had been discussed, and with some theoretical understanding, in the months prior to the outbreak of the upheaval. But when the craze of writing big-character posters denouncing party literary figures erupted, the speed at which stereotyped posters toeing the official line were churned out was not much different from the secondary schools. Bai was contemptuous of this type of formalistic activism:

Putting up big-character posters was allotted as a duty: 'Okay, for these two periods today, no lessons and you all go to write big-character posters. Each one should hand in two.' And after that we put them up.

Q: So all big-character posters contained the same thing?

A: Yes, almost all the same. All the same. I very rarely wrote any.

Q: But you said it was required.

A: So I wrote just two lines.

Q: And some people wrote a lot?

A: Ah, yes, some wrote and wrote and then told the party branch: 'I've written ten big-character posters!' They were trying actively to get into the party. As for me, when you made me write, I wrote.

Q: So it was not very meaningful?

A: No, not at all meaningful. I didn't go to read them. They were mainly going after quantity. That was how the university reported up to the centre, claiming, say, that 'the whole school, in writing big-character posters condemning *The Three Family Village*, has written a total of 5556 posters!' That was how it worked. In the beginning I already saw it this way. That was why people composed black materials against me so early. At that time I was dissatisfied. It was controlled who should condemn this, who should denounce that. I said: 'Why not cut loose from these controls and allow all of us to condemn on our own?'

To bypass the restrictions, he became the first in his class to break with the classroom structure, by going from one department to the next before the concept of an 'exchange of experiences' was formally endorsed by the party centre.

But we should not confuse his frustration at the formalistic nature of the campaign with a search for self-expression. Basically Bai had no tendencies that were directly against authority or anti-Establishment, nor any aspirations to asert his own independence. During the phase of dragging out 'bourgeois academic authorities' he participated enthusiastically, digging out 'revisionist stuff' on professors, making trivialities into a matter of political line, in much the way the secondary school students did. But all the while he was aware of a contradiction:

We felt we must follow the general trend in accordance with the condemnations and criticisms from the centre. We accused the department head of opposing the thought of Mao Zedong, even though he hadn't, since we felt we ought to follow the fad. To go with the tide was a very important thing. I felt it was correct. But I wrote very few big-character posters. Why? Because somehow deep down I felt it was not correct.

Here, his 'party nature' and obedience to authority overrode his intellect and personal sense of right and wrong. Time and time again Bai talked of 'following the current', 'running after the trend', of being 'swept into the tide.' Bai's activism was essentially an effort to conform and to carry out the authorities' instructions as best he could. When he voiced any protests, it was, as usual, because he believed that people of his acquaintance were implementing the instructions in ways that fell short of the ideal.

Bai's reluctance to rebel against authority *per se* is illustrated by his defence of the various authorities at his university. When two junior members of the staff in his department instigated an attack on the department head, he was against it, because, he argued,

Peking University had a Lu Ping [the Party Secretary of Peking University under attack]; their university had bad luck. But our university was a political university. It was still very pure. The staff members were old cadres, veteran officials, the roots of the revolution. So when these teachers put up big-character posters against the department head, we felt those teachers should be criticized for breaking the rules: that is, big-character posters should not be made public. Even though there were problems, the posters should be put up indoors only. It did not matter whether the department head was revisionist or not. At that time the people's thinking was conservative, including me. I was conservative.

Whereas someone like Chang took the opportunity to attack the school's Party Secretary at all costs, whether he was revisionist or not, Bai defended the authorities, and similarly the reason did not matter. Being an official activist, part of the Establishment, Bai identified with the party. Still unaware that the main thrust of the Cultural Revolution was to attack power-holders, this seemed to him the most orthodox stand to take.

He did feel the workteam was restraining the students' initiative, but was not dissatisfied to the extent of challenging it. When a group of twenty to thirty high-level cadres' children, who had inside information on the direction in which Mao was pushing the Cultural Revolution, formed a Red Guard group to attack the university's Party Secretary, a majority of the students, Bai included, came out to protect the Party Secretary. A debate and confrontation erupted between this minority group[34] and some 90 per cent of the student body. By now the workteam had left and all Party branches on campus were in disarray. Bai, together with a few others, formed a liaison centre. 'In the first meeting we made clear its purpose: to unite the whole school, etc. But one point was bad [he began chuckling at his own mistake]: we advocated protecting the university cadres. This was wrong, yes, wrong.'

They were wrong only because the Party Central Committee later indicated it had been wrong to defend the Party Secretary. The definition of what was right and wrong came from the party, so that when the latter reversed itself, he and his colleagues had to follow suit. They discovered that by protecting the Party Secretary they were 'not catching up with the tide', and were labelled 'Royalist'. In no time, members of Bai's liaison centre deserted the 'capitalist-roader' they had been protecting, and the chief organizer of the liaison group had to make a self-criticism. Bai took this about-turn of the Royalists and of himself as natural, not as opportunism. To move with the tide was to him an ideological maxim, because it meant following the party. Now that Mao took precedence over the party, it became a matter of following Chairman Mao's revolutionary line.

Bai again ran after the tide over the issue of forming Red Guard groups. At that time, in the high schools of Peking the children of cadres were busily organizing themselves into elitist class-based Red Guard groups. There was resistance among university students to do likewise. Even many of the good-class students, as party and league members, were reluctant to disband the existing organizations. When a small group of high-level cadres' children did declare themselves 'Red Guards', there was strong opposition from Bai's liaison centre, which consisted of people of both good- and middle-class backgrounds. However, no sooner had Mao given the first grand reception to the Red Guards at Tien An Men than some members of the liaison group hurried to found their own Red Guard groups, thus once more reversing their stand. Bai, too, shifted his position and tried to join the Red Guards. But he was rejected for having 'unclarified historical problems', acquired during the Four Cleanups. He admits feeling snubbed, but managed to get in through connections. He was not in the least defensive nor embarrassed about his 180-degree turnabout in attitude.

Of the Red Terror, Bai relates that the blood-line theory attracted an audience only in the high schools, finding few followers at the university. University students, in particular those who had participated in carrying out the Four Cleanups campaign, had been enough in touch with real life, Bai says, not to uphold a rigid correlation between class background and revolutionary fervour. He himself recognized the fact, but at the same time Bai thought the first sentence of the saying 'if the father's a hero, the son's a good fellow' correct. What he had objected to was the emphasis on class background to the extent of turning all non-red-class people into enemies. He was critical only of the extremism of the blood-line theory. Hence,

> When during the period of the Great Link-up I went to Shanxi to organize Red Guards in the countryside, I used the same method: immediately gathering together the good background people. Even though some of the other young peasants were very active and had a very good relationship with me, because they were of middle-peasant stock I wouldn't let them in. They would have to wait a while and we would let them in only in the third recruitment.

Because of his social and political status, not only was his attitude towards the blood-line theory different from that of my middle-class secondary school interviewees, but so too was his comparative lack of humanitarian feeling even when faced with the violence and sadism practised against the bad classes:

> It was the beginning of the Cultural Revolution, in August or September, the first time we went travelling to exchange experiences. We were trying to take the train from Peking railway station, and we saw those secondary school students beating people, completely out of hand. Whap! Whap! They were whipping some former landlords and whatnot. Blood all over. That was the 'beating craze'. Wow, our group of people found it frightening to witness, because we university students were used to being genteel. So I quoted a passage of Lu Xun to my friends. I told them: This is only the beginning. If you're scared already how are we going to stage the movement later? Lu Xun had said: 'True fighters dare face the sorrows of humanity, and look unflinchingly at bloodshed.' We memorized that, and as we walked along I encouraged them.

He steeled himself to cultivate class feeling and to ward off feelings of empathy. There was no sympathy even when he heard that autumn that in some villages surrounding Peking the rural bad-category elements and all their male offspring were being massacred by the peasantry.[35] At that time, he was a leader of a small group, and a classmate had come to him to plead for protection after her rich-peasant parents were murdered in the pogrom. Bai agreed to look into the matter for her, but failed to do so. Amidst all the organizational chores he had to do, this one was not high on his agenda. In fact, 'I felt that the way the masses struggled against each other was inevitable. I thought that in a mass campaign, killing a few was nothing. No, I don't mean nothing. I mean I thought it inevitable.' In relating the incident, it was evident that his vantage point was that of a confirmed official-activist who justified all human or individual sufferings as inevitable episodes in man's great historical process, in this phase of the 'proletarian dictatorship'.

Consequently, Bai understood none of the complicated tensions that had built up among high school students of various class backgrounds. His insensitivity and lack of empathy for people who had never enjoyed a red status, together with his own disinterest in self-expression, has left him perplexed to this day as to why the secondary schools exploded.

Bai's perspective differed from some of the teenagers who became Rebels for another reason: in general, naïvety, idealism and spontaneity seem to have decreased with age. In Bai's own school, those who dared first to 'jump out', to rebel against authority, to go against the tide, or to form new organizations were often the first- and second-year university students.[36] Bai speaks of the senior undergraduates from personal experience:

> Senior students were conservative. They had a lot of worries, had seen enough to worry. They'd consider what would happen after graduation. What would be the party branch's evaluation of them? How about the chance of joining the party? What if at the end of the campaign they were declared rightists?

All students, be they university, senior or junior high school students, at the beginning of the movement saw the Cultural Revolution as an opportunity to prove their activism, as had been the case with many of the other campaigns pushed by school authorities. But it was the university students, mature students who had been working or had joined the Four Cleanups workteams, who were aware of the universal law of Chinese campaigns. Hence, our purist activist Bai, by now a fourth-year student, understood:

> We who studied economics and politics had always known that in *all* campaigns there was, in the last stage, a period of rectification. And a portion of those who'd jumped enthusiastically into the

campaign were bound to be cleaned off at the end. The Communist Party has always worked like this: 'Shoot down first the birds which fly in front.' That is to say, first get at the cadres, and afterwards balance things off by getting at the most outspoken of the masses. A law. Has been like this all the way through. We remembered the Anti-rightist Campaign of 1957. From the very beginning of the Cultural Revolution we already knew. In fact, many people warned those from our faction who were jumping out: 'Look, you're not going to have a good ending. Just wait and see.' And the reality proved to be so. In the Cultural Revolution, the scenario was first dragging out the power-holders, and in later days it was getting back at the students. It wasn't that we were unaware of the process of such a campaign. But we participated actively anyway because of the tide. It was impossible not to plunge in headlong like this.

As if his original prophesy that all campaigns followed a law and that the party always 'got back' at the masses were to be proven valid, the tide began to turn on Bai. He noticed that the classroom party branch was treating him with decided coolness and even animosity. Suspicious that black material had been collected on him, one night he broke into the party office and found a special dossier on himself. 'The moment I looked at my materials, my blood coagulated.' He was confronting a carefully compiled report of the everyday things he had done and said, twisted and distorted and transformed into a matter of political line, in very much the same way that he himself earlier had helped devise cases against professors and lecturers while 'collecting revisionist materials on the reactionary academic authorities'. His own experience in such affairs advised him that the report had been constructed to serve as 'a complete set of materials on an anti-party, anti-socialist, reactionary student'. His self-righteousness, his over-zealousness, and his refusal to fake petty activism had been turned against him. The report, if it were to accompany him for life, portended a bleak future.

Friends persuaded him to withdraw from Cultural Revolution activities. With such a file, no matter which faction he participated in and no matter what he did, at the end of the campaign these could be made to work against him. So together with a friend he applied for half a year's supply of food-ration coupons and a cash stipend to travel the country. But at the last moment he changed his mind. Though he had never held many illusions regarding the Cultural

Revolution, he had always been too devoted an activist to remove himself so easily from the scene of action. He describes his dilemma:

> We were swept into the tide. I was, after all, an activist. I knew that in the end others would brand us as phoney activists and would club us down. Not that we couldn't see this; we predicted it. But the tide was like a storm and swept you along. If you yourself didn't have strong enough will power to restrain yourself, you were carried into it by a need to participate with all the others.

He not only decided to stay. When a figure in the Central Committee opposed to Bai's own broader faction fell, Bai even helped organize a squad to travel to the official's provincial power-base to collect 'black materials' on him. In early 1967, in the midst of ransacking an office there, Bai was arrested by the public-security bureau. His premonition that in the end some of the masses who 'jumped out' would be 'cleared out' was realized, but ahead of schedule. For the greater part of the Cultural Revolution, two miserable years, Bai stayed behind bars. But he could keep track of political developments outside through waves of newly-arrested Red Guards. As the days wore on, the prison swelled in population until, by the latter half of 1968, in the final Cleansing of Class Ranks Campaign, the 9 × 6 foot cells, originally meant for three, were packed with up to seventeen inmates.

He kept himself mentally occupied to guard against self-pity. *Mao's Selected Works* was the only literature available apart from the national newspaper, and he took the opportunity to read over the *Works* several more times. Before, he had gone to Mao's work for spiritual guidance and for clues on how he should behave. Now, each time he read it he noticed increasingly the loopholes and inconsistencies in Mao's arguments.

Yet Bai retained a view of China's political system quite different from Rebels like Chang and Deng. He found no fault with the monolithic Leninist political structure as a whole. Whereas by the end of the Cultural Revolution, 'ultra-leftist' Rebels like Chang agreed with the basic tenets of the Sheng Wu Lian manifesto, that there had emerged in China a new bureaucratic class, when Bai first heard of the manifesto after his release from prison he unhesitatingly dismissed it as anarchistic. He continued to believe that China, once purged of a relative handful of corrupt bureaucratized officials, would be set on the right path again. He denied the existence of a new self-perpetuating privileged class; and if there was such a stratum, it would be, according to him, an objective necessity.

Neither had he questioned, as the Rebels did when they experienced it, the 'law of campaigns'. It was a time-tested party campaign technique: 'whether it was correct or not, it has to be like this'. It was beyond query for no other reason than that it was the party's normal practice. Someone like Bai, who had been accustomed to employing the party line as the arbiter of rights and wrongs, did not independently redefine these in terms of his own inner conscience.

Similarly, he continued dogmatically to believe in the necessity for continued severe 'struggle' against bad-class people. We cannot explain away this attitude as a case of insensitive ignorance regarding the problems that such people faced: for, a year after Bai's release from prison, his own class background was reclassified and he himself acquired a bad-class label. His university had carried out an elaborate investigation into his family history, collecting materials from as far away as the home village from which Bai's family had fled when he was a toddler. The upshot was that he was given the worst possible of family origins, that of 'tyrant landlord'. It was the most severe blow he had ever experienced. He henceforth would have to endure the humiliation and discrimination of a member of a 'dictated class'. Even so, he did not question the basic tenets of the class line or of class struggle. He felt his new status merely a personal misfortune, an anomaly, in a system that was basically correct. Contrary to Chang, who had never held a 'proletarian standpoint' and had subconsciously rejected the class line long before he could articulate intellectual objections to it, Bai continued unwaveringly to view Chinese society from the perspective of the political authorities.

AO: THE CONFORMING ACTIVIST IN THE CULTURAL REVOLUTION

Ao, though she bore a middle-class label, became a Loyalist. To understand why is to understand her experiences in the countryside in the two years before the Cultural Revolution erupted.

The village in which Ao and the other four dozen volunteers had settled in 1964 was trapped in a stark poverty of poor food, mud-walled housing and back-wrenching labour, where even a wheeled cart was considered too expensive and all loads were hoisted by shoulderpole. But rather than complain among themselves about the harsh conditions, that first year the young people were intent upon proving the sincerity and depth of their activist commitment.

The labour we'd had in school had been so light. Now we had to carry mud. Our shoulders and feet were all covered with sores, and our bones seemed to be disintegrating. The worst part was going barefoot. We had to temper ourselves to become like the peasants. There was a slogan: 'black skin, red heart, hard bones, iron soles'. We purposely didn't wear shoes and hobbled along until the skin got thick. We made ourselves eat pea leaves and turnip leaves, which even the peasants wouldn't eat. When we had only a bit of rice to eat we felt content and happy. Oh, we were so stupid then. Our thoughts were so red. We only thought of how to unite with the poor-and-lower-middle peasants, how to emulate the Red Army, how to temper ourselves to become revolutionary successors. We felt we had to be able to endure anything.

Luckily, the economically backward village needed their help and their skills of literacy and numeracy, and this gave them a sense of purpose. But the young people's initial sense of solidarity in facing hardships quickly crumbled.

Our relationships seemed sort of hypocritical. On the surface we were concerned with each other: when one of us had trouble everyone came to help. But all of them wanted to join the league. The will to progress was very strong. We had come to the countryside to perform in a revolutionary way, to prove that we obeyed the party, to prove that we were useful to the country. We came because we had this line of thinking, since no one had forced us to come. And once there, everyone wanted to advance, everyone competed to get into the league.

The same tensions as at school were played out in the countryside, but with heightened competitiveness and severity. Out of school, after all, one's 'political face' had an immediate repercussion on one's present, not merely future, career. Their self-interested jostling for recognition gradually eroded the original sense of altruism. The students came to realize that the number of posts that carried any weight or prestige was necessarily limited in a village of only a thousand people. The seven league members were monopolizing whatever positions were available to the young people. Ao, for example, simultaneously held five posts. This was on top of her eight hours or more of daily manual labour and the extra time she had to spend in heart-to-heart talks with ten league aspirants. The workload, both manual and mental, was so taxing that she found herself unable to fulfil all her duties. But she would not relinquish any of the posts. Younger than some who held no posts at all (there were senior high school graduates among the volunteers), less capable than some, and a girl (and a thin one at that, whose labour power could not match the boys), she became the target of some of the non-league members' complaints:

> So whenever it was time to elect five-good youths and it was my turn to be appraised, there were always so many criticisms against me, for this and for that: that I didn't care enough for the others, that I was proud . . . Anyway, as long as you had a high post and a greater responsibility than others and were in the limelight, they demanded more from you. Always such a lot of criticism. Everyone hoped to be better than the other. When the reporter came to interview us [because their group of youths had been publicized as a model to illustrate the great success of the new policy of sending educated urban youths to the countryside], of course the best [i.e. herself] should be chosen, right? For no reason, everyone boycotted me. I was left out in everything. I'd no share in being photographed, no chance to give a speech. I hid away and cried. Working so hard, and there was no result. Everyone wanted to be progressive. I advance. You advance. The competition among us was keen. Later the backward ones ganged up together to go against us, the progressive ones.

Q: Why did they become backward?

A: They said: 'Ah, we all came down to the countryside together, all of us sacrificing so much to leave the city. Now you people have become so very red, with so many responsibilities. For example, you, Ao, are in charge of the sessions in the village to study Mao's Thought and in charge of the village's cultural centre, and we have nothing to do.' So very naturally they became jealous of me.

Q: Why didn't you give them some responsibilities then?

A: Well, there was work for them to do such as reading the newspapers to the peasants and doing volunteer work as night-school tutors. I don't know why, but they just didn't like it.

When she talked about them being backward did she mean backward in labouring or backward in thought? 'I mean without a post they didn't like it. No, they weren't less active in labouring. They still laboured okay in the fields, but individually they had complaints.'

Yet Ao strenuously denies that she and other league members were purposely accruing all of the responsibilities and power. To do so would have amounted to acknowledging the criticism that she was not trying her best to help the others to progress. But she and her six colleagues in the league placed such harsh and testing demands on league applicants that at the close of two years there were only three new league members. The schism between the official and the unrecognized activists became more open and more antagonistic than normally found in classrooms.

By the second year, Ao discovered that she did not have to be bothered by criticisms from her own peer group of urban-educated youths, if she could instead build up her prestige among the peasants. The latter, after all, formed almost all of the village's population and power base. She could justify her new stance as the revolutionary behaviour of 'going deep among the masses; uniting with the poor-and-lower-middle peasants'. She was permitted by the Four Cleanups workteam in the village to take the minutes during workteam meetings and participate in collecting information on the peasants. She gained the important advantage of being in the know about village affairs, the kind of knowledge invaluable for establishing a footing at the lowest rung of the political hierarchy she aspired to climb. She graduated from this to become the village broadcaster. It was not a post officially endowed with power. But in addition to dutifully transmitting national political messages, the broadcaster informally held a modest influence in village politicking. Her public criticisms and commendations, daily blaring out through the loudspeakers, set the official norms for the peasants' behaviour. She was not yet formally a cadre, but she was undertaking an intensive on-the-job cadre training. Perhaps not overly optimistically, she dreamt of herself moving up the administrative ladder from village to commune, from commune to county, and onward.

Her haughtiness made her increasingly unpopular among her peers. As in school, she had not a single friend among them. Her best friends were her superiors, in this case middle-aged peasant cadres. She was painfully aware of the contradictory motives that had driven her since childhood: her admixture of genuine dedication to the socialist cause with barely concealed strivings for personal advancement. Others, too, wrestled with an internally contradictory world: Deng oscillating between dreams and pragmatism; Bai between purist strivings and realism. In Ao's case, her desires to enjoy a comradely spirit of group solidarity came up against her contempt for, and alienation from, her peers. She resented the wall that formed between her and the unrecognized activists, a wall which she herself had created. In the Cultural Revolution, her vexation at being isolated would turn into anger and in desire for revenge.

To a certain extent, Ao was shielded from the Cultural Revolution's turmoil. While the cities were convulsed in upheaval, the peasantry carried on their daily toil in the fields, a routine only intermittently punctuated by the ripples spread from the urban centres. Consequently, national events which are inscribed deeply in the minds of city youths like Chang and Deng and Bai did not become significant markers in Ao's memories.

Nor, unlike Rebels such as Chang and Deng, was the Cultural Revolution ever a watershed in Ao's ideological development. Her understanding of the Cultural Revolution was of a simple two-stage affair:

> In the beginning there was chaos; and then the Cleansing of the Class Ranks in 1968. In the peasants' language it was 'tying up the opening of the bag to catch bad people'. They said Chairman Mao was very clever, he let you jump and jump, observed who was good, who was bad, and then he pulled the strings of the bag to purify the classes. Yes, it was truly fantastic; such a mess and he still could tighten it up. The pressure of the regime became *much greater* than before. This is my impression: a period of chaos and then a period of tightened control.

I had the good fortune to interview in depth three of Ao's urban-educated colleagues from the village who had joined the opposition Rebel faction.[37] From them a fuller picture of the 'chaos' and 'tightened control' in the village can be reconstructed. One of them explained very simply why and how a Rebel group emerged among the youths. He divides the urban-educated youths into three categories: the 'aristocratic', the 'middle' and the 'lower'. The latter were those who had lost interest in competing to be activist in the village. The Rebels themselves had belonged to the 'middle' category, those 'who had no concrete posts in the village, but were active and hard-working'. Only one of the initial dozen was a league member. The situation here was therefore similar to the secondary school phenomenon – the frustrated and more rebellious of the unrecognized activists of middle-class family origins forming the backbone of the Rebel faction.

As news of the upheavals in Canton spread, some of these youths had gone back to their former schools and returned with new ideas about the Cultural Revolution – that it sanctioned rebelling against the authorities. Earlier, at the commune market town, the commune-level authorities had been organizing attacks against a few selected 'ghost and demon' teachers, in exactly the way that Party Secretaries in the urban schools and universities had encouraged students to attack teachers with problematic histories. The youths returning from Canton with their new ideas put up a big-character poster in the market town attacking the commune party leadership. They demanded that the spirit of the Cultural Revolution be spontaneous, from the bottom up, not organized from the top downwards. Like the early Rebels in the urban schools, they made much of the phrase in the Sixteen Point Directive about relying and believing in the masses, and equated all power-holders with capitalist-roaders. As the campaign developed, their targets were widened and lowered to include village cadres and the village's Four Cleanups workteam, all of whom they attacked for authoritarian work styles. They felt no qualms about criticizing the adults who had slighted them. Through their attacks, they hoped to show that they themselves, and not the workteams or the cadres or their more successful peers, were the true followers of Chairman Mao.

Within weeks, a second Red Guard group confined to red-class youths was formed in the village by the local cadres.[38] Since the recruitment policy of this group was based on the class line, even Ao, despite the strategic posts she held in the village, was denied entry. Having no aspirations to join the Rebels, she helped form a small third group that played a role similar to the urban Red Outer Circles. Ao defends her choice of allegiance in interesting terms:

Those intelligentsia [in the commune market town] without real power considered themselves as belonging to the Flag Faction [the Canton Rebel faction]. If I were in Canton, I too was bound to have been of the Flag Faction. After all, my class background wasn't too good; and in Canton the Loyalists bullied us people of non-red class background . . . Folks said we were following the conservatives, the Loyalist faction. Actually we were just being practical: just like if I were in Canton, I would have been in the Flag Faction, because I would have been among the oppressed.

The Rebel Red Guards found themselves in an isolated position in the village. Their attacks had angered the grassroots leadership; some of their peers, like Ao, found their own positions threatened by the attacks; and the peasants were angry with the Rebels for taking off from work, for running off to 'exchange revolutionary experiences', and for stirring up trouble by attacking cadres. The villagers were perplexed by all this talk about 'revolution', about 'seizing power' and 'dragging power-holders out'. One of the peasants told them, 'Go ahead and run around boiling up a riceless gruel. We'll go dig out private plots.' The young people's 'revolution' seemed frivolous to them. To a great extent, Ao looked at the Rebels from the peasants' perspective. She still speaks disdainfully of the Rebels.

They emphasized only small things and pushed aside important things. *We* concentrated on how to mobilize the peasants, how to educate them, how to spur them to heighten their enthusiasm for production. *They* just talked about who in the country was this and that, all those trivialities. We didn't have time to pay attention to them. I don't know what the hell they were doing. I don't understand them. The thing was, they didn't have any concrete power. They only jumped up and down. Concrete power to get real things done was all on our side.

It was during this period that she was catapulted into a position at the centre of village power. The cadres had become angry that, just as the Four Cleanups campaign had subsided, they had been faced with this new wave of attacks. Most walked away from their posts. This was the kind of disruption in the countryside that the Party Central Committee was anxious to avoid. To ward off a decline in grain production, Peking issued directives to the countryside to 'grasp revolution and promote production', with the emphasis upon 'promote production'. Ao, as a supporter and surrogate of the village's most powerful personages, used her positions as village propagandist and Mao study leader to step into the vacuum created by the cadres' resignations, to restore a semblance of stability to the village. To her, that was the substance of 'revolution'.

I was in the countryside all the time [as opposed to running around 'exchanging revolutionary experiences']. We listened to Chairman Mao: to grasp revolution and promote production, to persist in carrying on the revolution in our own locality. We read the news-paper, listened to the radio and studied the directives . . . We followed every 'battle strategy' they asked us to follow. They told us to investigate the power-holders, so we went to investigate the power-holders; they told us to form the revolutionary alliance so we formed the alliance; they told us to grasp hold of spring planting, so we grasped hold of the production; they asked us to establish the revolutionary committee, so we went to look into it; they asked us to criticize the party and to build up the party, so we went to criticize the party members; they told us to clean up the class ranks, so we went to catch the bad guys.

Throughout, her lack of independent analysis was part and parcel of her desire and urge to conform. One of the Rebel youths observes:

She knew only how to recite the newspaper. Oh, she used all her might to recite the newspaper! But I'm sure she didn't understand what the hell was said in the newspapers. She wasn't concerned about national affairs. In her broadcasts, she just accused this villager of not labouring hard enough, and that person of doing sloppy weeding. I recollect her as always just reciting that news-paper and furiously digging in the fields. She didn't care about the great events of the Cultural Revolution that were going on around her. We didn't understand her and she didn't understand us.

By 1967, the urban-youth Rebels in the village had begun to lose heart about their prospects in the countryside. Influenced by ideas circulating among urban-educated youths from outside, they began debating among themselves whether it might not be more effective and more ideologically correct to 'return to the cities to rebel'. They began questioning whether the down-to-the-village programme had been Mao's revolutionary plan or Liu Shaoqi's revisionist line. They used both these grounds to justify their earlier unspoken desires to leave the countryside. Recalls one of the village's young Rebels:

At that time in Canton, a lot of small Red Guard pamphlets began appearing which put together all of Liu Shaoqi's speeches con-cerning the sending down of educated youths. So we thought this must be Liu's policy. We had been sent down to the countryside and told we would become the driving force of the countryside, but this wasn't true. We began to question whether we should be down there. Does the countryside really need us? We wanted to go back to Canton to make our problems known to society. We wanted to see whether it was Liu's line. Even after a year in Canton, and even when we were finally forced to come back to the village in 1968, we still thought it was Liu's line. It was not until November 1968, when the documents made the truth very clear, that we finally gave up hope.

Well over half of the urban youths in the village had gone back to the city. Some participated actively in Rebel groups, some merely idled away their time at their parents' homes, and some took the opportunity to find part-time employment. But they were exposed, even if marginally, to the experience of 'great democracy', of free discussion and criticism of policies. Some even felt it allowable to express privately their distrust of Lin Biao, as having ulterior motives in building up the Mao cult.

If anything, the defection and flight of the other urban youths improved Ao's standing, as someone who could be trusted to stand by the interests of the village. By the end of the Cultural Revolution, she had been selected to the honorary position of vice-chairman of the county Poor and Lower-middle Peasants' Association. She saw herself as having reached the pinnacle of glory and honour, finally recognized as having succeeded in 'uniting with the poor-and-lower-middle peasants.'

At the Cultural Revolution's close, law and order was restored to the countryside through Bai's predicted period of 'getting the masses'. In the Cleansing of the Class Ranks campaign of autumn 1968, the 'strings of the bag got pulled'. Ao found her power augmented as a village prosecutor, responsible for interrogating suspects and collecting incriminating materials. In all, three categories of people in her village were to be attacked: (1) bad-class peasants and their relatives, targetted for class struggle; (2) a local cadre and a few of his friends, who had lost out earlier in a village power struggle and were now to have their defeat confirmed; and (3) the leaders among the Rebel youths who had gone off to the city and had now been forced back to the countryside.[39] A total of seventeen people were thrown into a makeshift village jail for various lengths of time, a figure equivalent to 3 per cent of the adult village population.[40] In building cases against these targets, Ao learned the arts of interrogation, how to threaten, coax, apply psychological pressure and play suspects off one against the other.

Ao was more dedicated and persevering in this role than she need have been. The earlier antagonism between the official activists like Ao, who had stayed in the village and risen, and the unrecognized activists who had unsuccessfully attacked the village *status quo*, could now be played out once more on terms advantageous to Ao; and Ao made full use of the opportunity. But beyond that, Ao's passion for the campaign grew out of her own political convictions and attitudes. She brought charges against several of the urban youths for having jokingly said to friends in Canton that Mao was fat or for having said that Lin Biao had a 'sly look'. Having herself helped build up the Mao cult in the village and having come religiously to believe in what she preached, Ao genuinely regarded such remarks as blasphemy.

Her feelings here were complex. She had been frightened that she herself could hold such subversive thoughts:

Let me tell you something more. You see, during the Cultural Revolution there were a lot of photographs. The thought 'Chairman Mao looks like a pig' occasionally flashed across my mind. I had to push away that thought. It was the same with Lin Biao. It flashed across my mind that he looked like a dog with a wagging tail. Oh, I was scared of myself. You see, we often went on propaganda tours and slept together, and I often talked in my sleep. I was afraid that such a thought would leak out and other people would overhear it. I knew a lot of people were caught for counterrevolutionary activities based on evidence like this. I feared being thrown in prison, so every morning when I woke up I asked the people around whether I had said anything in my dreams during the night.

Afraid and ashamed that her own thoughts were sacriligious, she was convinced that others who openly expressed such ideas must be guilty of conscious and purposeful subversion.

In the Cleansing of the Class Ranks, two-thirds of the victims in the village were bad-class targets, and here Ao tried to act with the heartlessness of a cultivated class feeling. Unlike Bai, who earlier had learned in the Four Cleanups campaign to be less rigid in associating class background with personal character, Ao's beliefs had been strengthened by her residence in the countryside. She subscribed fully to the fear that the rural bad-class households were constantly seeking 'class revenge', that by their 'class nature' some could be expected, say, to try poisoning the village wells. This fear was derived in part from the logical deduction that, having been singled out as targets in all campaigns, they *ought* to have felt vengeful. But this realization only encouraged her to 'cultivate' a stronger hatred towards them. When she discovered that she herself perhaps did not love the chairman from the marrow of her bones (for, she questioned, why else would she have such impure thoughts about his photographs?), she was fearful that she might be incapable of cultivating a true proletarian worldview, that she was trapped in an impure middle-class ambivalence. She had to be sure not to let any of the humanitarian feelings she detected in herself get the better of her 'class feelings'. This became a secret predicament. When confronted with brutality in the Cleansing of Class Ranks treatment of bad-class targets:

Of course I thought the accused were in the wrong, but when I saw people beating people I was scared. I said to myself: 'Ah, luckily I'm holding the pen. If not, I'll be in a difficult situation.' If I was told to curse at and beat those people, and if I refused, that wouldn't befit my status. Because I was an activist, in struggling against class enemies I would have had to show that I was decisive, merciless. Yet, at the same time that I knew the accused were wrong, I couldn't make myself hate them. As for beating them up, maybe I wouldn't be able to make myself do it. So I congratulated myself that I was holding the pen and didn't have to come out to perform. But I was scared of this kind of thinking, because it showed that my class stand wasn't sturdy enough, my will to struggle not strong enough, that I didn't perform like a proletarian, or a bolshevik, was not up to the standard of a Communist Party member. We not of the proletarian class were often reminded to self-consciously change our thoughts, to stand entirely on the side of the masses. We had to examine privately our own errors. So I felt guilty. But of course, I dared not tell anybody.

The Cultural Revolution had become a process of disenchantment for most of my interviewees. But not so with Ao. On the contrary, because of the sociopolitical position she had occupied in the Cultural Revolution and its aftermath, her identification with the polity was reinforced and her efforts to steel herself intensified.

SELF-DELUSION

We have seen that, whereas a successful official activist like Ao remained staunchly committed to political orthodoxy, the Cultural Revolution became a political experience of a very different kind for a majority of my interviewees. The long period of 'unfettered' activism, following the disintegration of the red-class Red Guards' monopoly of power in late 1966, had provided them with a chance to express themselves freely. Frustrated with the hypocrisy and oppressiveness of their years in school, they relished the new independence of speech and action. Their perceptions of themselves and of the Chinese political arena changed apace. By the end of the two years of turmoil, they had begun to reshape their confused individual frustrations into focused group interests, increasingly at odds with what they had been taught at school. These sharp shifts in belief away from the political lessons of childhood will be the subject of the next chapter.

What interests us here is that the Cultural Revolution, like a double-edged sword, had been cutting in opposite directions at the young people's beliefs and emotions. The conflict not only fostered unorthodox attitudes and perspectives; it also brought to the fore, especially in the first few months of the turmoil, an exaggerated, frightening form of activist behaviour characterized by strong authoritarian proclivities. Nonconformists like Chang and Deng were not so strongly affected. But a majority of Canton's high school students behaved unconscionably those first months; and to the extent that some did not, it often was because they were not permitted to by their classmates of better family origins. The initial uprisings against teachers, as well as the Destroy the Four Olds movement and the Red Terror, in rhetoric claimed a yearning for revolutionary purity, but in essence became frenzied drives to persecute the weak, the helpless and stigmatized. Good-class students beat up bad-class people without qualms of conscience. Middle-class students, though themselves relegated to a vulnerable and humiliating second-class status, assisted in persecuting bad-class teachers and schoolmates.

What drove most of China's urban teenagers to these brutal extremes? A great part of the answer lies in the political education they had absorbed: the black-and-white Manichean worldview of Maoist teachings; the militancy and lack of compassion that they were supposed to exhibit when confronting the people's enemies; the pernicious class-line prejudice that was taught; all atop the frustrations, dissatisfactions and mutual hostility that had infested the tense pre-Cultural Revolution activist contest.[41]

During the initial months of Cultural Revolution conflict (what I earlier characterized as the period of 'institutionalized activism'), there was, moreover, a strong 'herd' effect: they acted in a crowd as they might not have as individuals. Their perspective was outer directed: taking cues from their peers as to what was right and wrong; looking towards the vague directives of a charismatic leader to validate their behaviour; anxious to conform and to be orthodox, and under pressures during that summer of 1966 to be militant; eager to retain or augment whatever scrap of status they possessed; happy to turn against a scapegoated out-group so that they themselves could lay stronger claims to being in-group.

They had possessed a high capacity for self-deception. This applies to the majority of the young people in the initial phases of the Cultural Revolution. They were able to sublimate their less noble impulses – their self-interested calculations and frustrated passions – deceiving themselves in the belief that they were dedicated to a charismatic leader and a greater cause without ulterior motives. Unwilling to shoulder responsibility for their own actions, my interviewees insist even today that they had been 'blinded', 'hoodwinked', 'cheated' or 'used'. These phrases should be taken as more than mere excuses or figures of speech. Often, they were indeed unaware of their own motives. They had lost touch, as it were, with their inner selves. It was not until they were released from the confines of the school campuses in the autumn of 1966 that some of them took the first tentative steps to shake off the dogmatism and authoritarianism that had characterized their classrooms.

Even though the views and attitudes of such teenagers had been substantially altered by the end of the Cultural Revolution warfare, none of my interviewees, not even Chang, had yet escaped the emotional pull of the political milieu in which they had been raised. They remained committed to much of the worldview they had been taught, their mode of thought still heavily framed by their childhood political socialization. In the words of several interviewees, they had not yet 'awakened'.

5 Political Desocialization: The Cultural Revolution's Aftermath

'During the Cultural Revolution, it was action, action, action all the time', one of the ex-Rebels recalls, 'There was no time to think.' But once driven back into the classroom and then almost immediately into the countryside (or, for some, into jail), there was ample time and a lot to think about. The two years of whirlwind involvement in the Cultural Revolution had been a jumble of emotional experiences; of events one after another, without being prepared for them; of constant immediate reactions to new political situations. Now that their 'revolutionary passion' had been spent, they could sit back and 'synthesize the experiences'.

Before the Cultural Revolution, young volunteers in the country-side like Ao had been prepared to withstand hardships. Though the idealism and enthusiasm of many of those earlier volunteers had worn thin when reality had not measured up to expectations and propaganda, few of those who were sent down to the villages after the Cultural Revolution felt even the initial idealism. The official slogans no longer emphasized the 'glory' of constructing socialism, but rather the need humbly to go down 'to receive re-education from the poor-and-lower-middle peasants'. Some youths were willing to go; but some were simply resigned to the fact that their generation had no other choice; and some went with much reluctance, or anger, or with a vengeful determination to refuse to labour.

The circumstances in which they found themselves in the country-side only unsettled them further. The sudden influx of a massive new wave of young people into already overcrowded villages aroused the peasantry's resentment. A lot of the youths were met by inadequate housing and discriminatory wage practices. As they grew older they faced bleak prospects of ever being able to afford to marry and have children.[1]

The government programmes of the early 1970s, which were officially dubbed the 'new-born things of the Cultural Revolution', were yet an added source of discontent, especially for the former middle-class Rebels. As seen in the previous chapter, when they had expressed support for 'Chairman Mao's revolutionary line' in the early months of the Cultural Revolution, they had ignored what the promised reforms meant in practice. It had never been clear to them that the 'proletarian educational reforms' would mean condemnation of studious students as 'white experts' or that class background almost entirely was to replace academic proficiency as the criterion for higher education. In the few years that followed, they saw a profound decline in the quality of education and a 'wind of going in the backdoor' through family connections in the recruitments to university.[2] The new school system was not what they had rebelled for. They had, moreover, misinterpreted Mao's notion of 'revisionism' and 'proletarian culture'. They had thought Mao supported breaking loose from institutional constraints, as in the experience of 'great democracy' in the Cultural Revolution. Yet never had the cultural field been more sterile or ideological control so tight as in the 1970s. They had helped Mao attack Liu Shaoqi's 'revisionist' line of material incentives; but in the countryside, in touch with the peasants' reality, they discovered it was Liu's line which many of the peasants preferred. Some of my interviewees became convinced that only by loosening the economic controls over the villages and easing the reins on the peasants' private endeavours could incentives to increase production be raised.

A series of political campaigns added to these young people's growing sense of distrust in the central authorities. In the Cleansing of the Class Ranks campaign of 1968–9, the young Rebels of Guangdong's villages and state farms, much as in Ao's village, were suppressed and the local 'cowsheds' filled. In the Lin Biao-sponsored Three Loyalties campaign of 1969, Mao worship adopted the trappings of a revivalist religious movement. Each household was required to intone words of thanksgiving before each meal;[3] 'morning and evening reports' were solemnized in front of a Mao bust or photograph; and villagers were called upon almost nightly to participate in 'Loyalty Dances' and 'Loyalty Songs.' The crudity with which the personality cult was pushed edged many of the young people towards their first open expressions of cynicism. The astounding news of the fall of Lin Biao in 1971 provided fuel for this cynicism. As one interviewee observed, 'We felt that if even the person who had raised highest the Quotations of Mao Zedong had toppled, who else could still put the Quotations on a pedestal?'

As a political rift in the party's upper echelons became increasingly apparent – Mao and the 'Shanghai leftists' versus Zhou Enlai's more moderate wing – the former Rebels found that their political views were closer to those of the 'Zhou moderates' whom they had attacked in the Cultural Revolution.[4] They wanted, among other things, to see a basic premise of Mao's teachings repudiated – the emphasis on 'class struggle'. Deng's observation is representative of most of my interviewees:

Mao said that there must be class struggle. But our understanding of class struggle wasn't the same as his. At that time we thought it should be struggle between the upper stratum and the lower stratum, not aimed at the landlord class. That class had disintegrated long ago, with its power permanently overturned . . . but the authorities kept propping up artificially a situation of confrontation with these old landlords.

Once their scepticism regarding Mao's programme was brought to consciousness, these young people had to look for a new theoretical base to take the place of Mao's teachings. It was a period of 'ideological flux' and one of voracious reading. The more intellectual of them pored through works by Marx and Lenin. Notably, they still held to the Marxist–Leninist paradigm. Indeed, this search for a yardstick against which Mao could be measured brought most of my interviewees to read Marxist classics for the first time.

They also read with eagerness any underground literature they could lay hands on. Ironically, it often was the very genre of literature that some of them, in the heat of the Destroy the Four Olds, had confiscated or burnt as 'bourgeois'. Their readings went hand in hand with heated debates. The policy of sending most of their generation to settle in the countryside had broken up the city-wide Rebel Red Guard network, but by dispatching them to the villages in clusters of classmates, friendship groups often remained intact. Some of these organized themselves into study groups, to facilitate the free exchange of ideas to which they had become accustomed in the days of the Cultural Revolution. Increasingly, they came to believe that the dogma they had embraced had betrayed them; increasingly, they were open to ideas of other political and philosophical persuasions. Interviewees who had joined study groups reported no concrete plans to engage in renewed political upheavals; but they had held vague hopes that the political climate would eventually turn in their favour and they would be able to revive their organizations.[5] Within a few more years, they were abandoning their illusion.

They found it no easy task to exercise independent thinking. The power of the party bureaucracy had survived the Red Guard assault, and its grip on the life of the ordinary people was restrictive and often heavy-handed. To make one's life easier, or to climb the mobility ladder, it was still best to go along with the system, outwardly enthusiastic. But whereas activist conformity before 1966 often had been practised with conscious idealism and subconscious self-interest, now it was performed blatantly for personal gain. The majority were willing passively to accommodate to the circumstances, simply to stay out of trouble. But a number went further, actively manipulating the political situation to their own advantage. Derisively they were known as the 'two-faced faction' or the 'wind faction'. They swayed in whichever direction the political wind was blowing, and for most of the decade of the 1970s the direction had been highly unpredictable. They were the phoney activists, who cynically knew that the best way to get ahead – more specifically, the best way to get out of the countryside – was to submit to the erratically changing political demands of the authorities and to ensure that others did likewise.

Discouraged and unwilling to demean themselves through phoney activism, fair numbers of the young people who had settled in the rural districts along Guangdong's border with Hong Kong quietly began crossing over the border to the British colony.[6] Their decision was precipitated by a frustrated, self-interested unwillingness to remain stuck in an economically backward countryside with little likelihood of a return to urban life. But for those who had once felt genuinely devoted, the flight to Hong Kong might never have been contemplated had they not first lost faith in the political system. Brought up to believe passionately in the exaggerated glory of Mao's polity, when they saw reality fall far short of the ideal, their disillusionment had to it a heightened bitterness and cynicism. They felt there was nothing they could do either for themselves *or* for the country.

POLITICAL DESOCIALIZATION

Had we ended our story of the political socialization processes in China at an earlier point in time, say in the mid-1960s, it would have been a tale of the system's relative success. The intensive political education of the children had paid off in a passionate political commitment at the command of the party and/or the charismatic leader. In short, our study would have been generally in accord with most studies of political socialization: a success story, despite the seeds of modest discontent that had been sown. Had we ended our story there, we would have committed an error of a tale half told.

Ted Tapper is one of the few scholars who has questioned the basic assumptions that have flawed most studies of political socialization. The messages that children learn, Tapper contends, are not, as generally assumed, always consistent with the social and economic realities they later encounter as adults. In capitalist democracies, for example, the polity does not work towards equal opportunities for all people despite the rhetoric, and this ultimately undermines the lessons taught.[7] The large number of American empirical studies of school children in the 1950s, which consistently assumed that children's positive attitudes towards the polity would remain basically unchanged through life, were proven wrong; the same generation who as children had held romantic images of political figures became, in the late 1960s and early 1970s, rebelliously anti-Establishment.[8]

Why then does so much of the work in the West on political socialization continue to be grounded in the same erroneous assumptions as thirty years ago? Tapper explains, not without a tone of sarcasm, that most of the projects still centre on the political attitudes of seven- to fourteen-year-olds because of the school children's availability in large concentrations for research surveys. It is this, Tapper suggests, which has prompted the convenient theoretical assumption that this phase of life is the most crucial to political socialization.[9] A more important stage, Tapper asserts, comes when an individual begins to assume his adult role: 'It is not that he may encounter new socialization experiences in the sense that he has previously, but rather what has already been learnt is now going to be put to the test in situations over which he has little control.'[10]

The political socialization of Chinese young people, as charted in this study, bears out Tapper's assertions. In China, just as in Tapper's critique, the authorities were responsible for inconsistencies in the schools' teachings and for the disjunctures between the messages and the practical realities the young people would be facing. The ideology that was preached, tied to rigid organizational frameworks and to a past era, was riddled with questions and internal contradictions that, once grasped by young people, could not readily be answered. In the course of growing up, if the young people had had any doubts in the system, these had been ill-defined and often self-suppressed. But once the stage of pubescent idealism had passed, the gap between ideals and reality could seem very wide. We have observed in this and the prior chapter that encounters with real life, away from the school environment, did put what had been learned in Chinese schools very much to the test. As Tapper observes, successful socialization at an early age did not guarantee a lifelong positive political orientation.

Socialization studies remain inadequate if they do not acknowledge that, as the other side of the coin, there can be oversocialization,[11] desocialization[12] and adult resocialization.[13] 'Oversocialization', defined as the realization by a socialized individual of the gap between reality and ideals and a consequent refusal to regard the reality as acceptable, has vital explanatory value for our study of 'desocialization'. Keniston's analysis of American anti-war radicals utilized these twin concepts of over- and desocialization to account for the driving force that ignited the anti-war, anti-Establishment movement. Our young Chinese activists similarly did not start on the path to desocialization until the gap between reality and ideal had become too wide to bridge. In both cases, desocialization was triggered by great political upheavals which jostled youths away from the orthodox conceptions of their country's sociopolitical system: in the case of America the Vietnam War, and in China the Cultural Revolution. The origin and nature of the two movements were very different, but both upsurges became crucial 'liberating' experiences for the young people in both countries: upheavals that exposed the inconsistencies of their political systems. It was at such a moment of realization that they passed into and through the state of 'oversocialization'. The same values and norms once expounded by the authorities would be used by young people in both societies as a yardstick to measure the actual performance of the authorities and the system, and these would be found wanting. The system, the polity, the government and the reified symbols of authority would lose legitimacy.[14]

A question arises: did the Chinese young people's desocialization and rejection of the legitimacy of political authority in any sense alter their personal dispositions and values? We shall examine this, using the four case studies. By so doing, we shall also gain further insights into the relationship between personality and political activism.

CHANG

As the Cultural Revolution drew to a close, the young people in Canton had reacted in one of three ways to their predicament. Some, as we have noted, had resigned themselves to their lot; their main concern was to maintain a low profile so as to stay out of trouble. Others had turned unashamedly to self-seeking pursuits. Still others had remained concerned with national affairs and the betterment of society, not just their own circumstances. Chang belonged to this latter type.

When the campaign to force young people to the countryside gathered momentum in the autumn of 1968, Chang was offered a choice: to go to a state farm under military control on Hainan Island, or to a Guangdong village. He rejected both options, fearing an intolerably regimented life in a state farm and the possibility of supervision and detention in a Guangdong village for having been a Rebel leader. As a way out, he and a dozen acquaintances applied to settle in a very impoverished district in central China. Permission was granted. His very choice of a physically harsh destination, he says, was an indication that he did not feel totally defeated:

> I wanted to go to the countryside. I still wanted to go have a look at other places, see about their Rebel factions, see more about the countryside in the north, in order to understand China more. I wanted to live there for a long period. Why? Because I still had some political passion left, and the most basic problems in China lie in the countryside.

There was an even more idealistic reason:

> Influenced by the deeds of the previous revolutionary martyrs, I felt that a person should go to these hard and difficult places to temper oneself. Mainly it was for cultivating my will power. I had to reestablish my purpose of life, and so I felt I had to go steel up my will power.

This became the most rigorous and frenetic period in his history of physical tempering. He bathed in snow; pushed himself in manual labour beyond his physical limits till the droning in his ears became so loud that he was kept awake at night; forced himself to read Marxist literature after a day's exhausting labour, to the point that sometimes he did not have more than a few hours of sleep at night. The diet in this poor region of China barely reached subsistence level. He felt his health giving way but made no attempt to augment his food intake by tending a private plot after work, because 'reading was much more important'. His austerity was respected by the peasants, and he became the village's Mao study counsellor.

He remembers the two years as fruitful to his intellectual development. Stimulation came from discussions with his mates from Canton and contact with Rebel workers of the nearest city. He began to place into a theoretical perspective the unarticulated dissatisfactions he had felt at school, the distorted behaviour of teenagers during the Cultural Revolution, Mao's ultimate moves to crush the Rebels – seeing all these as the results of a totalitarian system attempting to strangle individual personality development.

In 1970, a large industrial city in the region was recruiting rusticated youths for its expanding industries. Several members of Chang's group left for the city, disappointed that their original plan to form a tightly-knit underground group had faded with time and beginning to find peasant life too hard. But Chang did not volunteer to go. He had no desire to be subjected to regimented factory life under the scrutiny of a party and league cell. He had already experienced that as a student. He 'wanted to be free' and preferred to stay a peasant, even though life in the village was tough. That same year there was a flood, and for several months the villagers had to subsist on grain mixed with husks.

Chang applied to resettle in the Guangdong countryside, hoping that closer to his own roots he could reestablish an underground Rebel network. In Guangdong, he still laboured hard in the fields, still intent on tempering himself through gruelling labour. His performance was so impressive, he claims, that the villagers wanted to elect him an agricultural production team leader. But he was not interested in taking up this responsibility, because he was trying to devote all his spare time to his political activities and intellectual pursuits.

His attempt to revive a Rebel core among his friends was a failure. Morale was low. Already the 'wind of escape' to Hong Kong was absorbing his friends' attention and energies. Frustrated, Chang began helping them in their efforts to seek new lives abroad. Many left for the sole purpose of bettering their own futures. A small number left with the idealistic aim of carrying on the 'struggle' from outside. Chang appears to have been among them. He decided to go after an intense month-long struggle with his conscience:

> I began to think: inside China there's really nothing more that I could do. I had wanted to organize something, but failed. So I thought: why not go out to organize? See whether it could have even a tiny effect on China. In addition, I felt I must understand things outside. I'd been reading and reading Marx and Lenin, and more and more I felt as if I were at a dead-end in it. It seemed as if there was no longer any new nourishment in life. If you look at China's history of the last hundred years, the new thinking all came from the outside, from the early reformers through Sun Yatsen, to the Communist ideology itself. I thought about it for a month. The main difficulty was that I loved China. In future might I have a chance to come back? On the one hand, I might not be able to return; on the other if I wanted to learn more things and somehow be able to contribute anything to China, I *must* venture out.

When I first met Chang in 1971, shortly after he had arrived in Hong Kong, he was agitating against 'the Chinese bureaucratic system' and ploughing through Erich Fromm. In succession, he made common cause with the major local New Left youth group, then two local Trotskyist groups, and finally joined with a group of ex-Rebel Red Guards to set up a 'human rights' group dedicated to 'Chinese socialist democracy'. He continues to think in terms of an international Marxist movement and was one of the very few young people from China who has shown a concern for the conditions of the Hong Kong working class.

In the mid-1970s, his life-style was unregulated and irresponsibly undisciplined. He persistently borrowed money from all his friends, and rarely repaid any. He was oblivious to night and day and paid scant attention to his health. During the year he was interviewed, he finally did bow to realities and took up a steady job as a door-to-door salesman, all the while continuing with his human rights activities. In such a job, at least, he did not have to tolerate a regulated nine-to-five office job. He still had great confidence in his intellectual capabilities and expressed aspirations to attend university. He wanted to go abroad to broaden his horizons. He had a premonition, he said, that someone 'passionate' like himself would surely have a short life span, and that he must quickly make a contribution to the revolution on a theoretical level before it was too late.

The strain of 'individual heroism' was still with him. But it was clear his talk would remain no more than an aspiration. He had not made the slightest preparations to go abroad. He had not conjured up the patience to begin learning a foreign language. He seems bound to Hong Kong, for once he leaves, the umbilical cord with China will be cut, and the continuing dream he has of participating in China's future will be shattered.

When I saw him again in 1978, three years after our interviews, he was still undisciplined, wilfully unemployed, still living on his friends and borrowed money, still active politically. On the one hand, he prides himself in the life-style he has adopted, asserting he can best express his personality through an unregulated life; on the other hand, he realizes, and in fact has made many resolutions, that he should exert more self-control. It is as if his inability to discipline himself is a rebellious overreaction to the overly controlled life he had to lead in China.

DENG

Deng was jailed for almost two years, largely in solitary confinement. During the first months, he felt perplexed and confused, not quite sure why Mao had ceased supporting the Rebels and why he should have ended up in a cell. Though normally dispassionate, in solitary confinement Deng experienced moments of emotional outburst. He had never been committed heart and soul to the Mao cult, as someone like Ao had been, but in his anger and desperation he developed a love–hate relationship with the chairman.

On National Day I got up early and faced north, sort of in a trance. When the early morning guard came he yelled at me: 'Lie down! Don't stand up!' So I said: 'Why not? I'm only expressing my loyalty to Chairman Mao.' I came to think, perhaps naively, does Chairman Mao know things are like this? I felt a sense of hatred rising in my heart.

That evening we had to do our 'evening reporting'. [During the

'Three-Loyalties Campaign' prisoners twice a day had to stand at attention to chant aloud their crimes in front of Mao's photo.] Suddenly it was as if there were a force driving me forward to tear down Mao's photo. I kept still, trying to control myself. I stood there like this for a long time. I realized that if I tore it down I couldn't just say that the wind blew it away.

Deng's anger was that of a son disowned by his beloved parents. The same anguish was felt by another interviewee, who had been imprisoned for two years for having joined a radical Marxist study group in 1969. He was deeply shaken when forbidden by a guard to address the latter as 'comrade'. It made him feel totally discarded by the political system he still felt emotionally part of.

Deng passed through several periods of bitterness and anger during his two years of imprisonment. He came to the conclusion that to accommodate himself to his political circumstances he would have to assume a cynically couldn't-care-less attitude. He began to play at using the system to mock the system:

When I was about to be let out of prison, I played games with them. They told me, 'Now that you're out, don't be influenced by anarchistic thoughts anymore. The situation is still complex outside.' I just listened. They continued: 'Other than the newspapers and party publications, don't listen or believe in anything else.']

So I said: 'Yes, yes.' And then I asked with disbelief in my voice: 'But what kind of complex situation can there possibly still be?'

'Oh, no', they said; 'it's still very complex outside. Very chaotic.'

I said, 'I don't believe it. The Ninth Party Congress has already been held. The country's situation is excellent. No, I don't believe you.'

'You don't believe?', they said, 'Out there, in this and that region there are still armed struggles going on.'

I persisted and said, 'No, I don't believe it. The party paper has not said so.' Ha, this made them mad. I frequently liked to talk nonsense like this with them.

Deng denies his alienation sprang predominantly from a sense of having been personally wronged or having personally 'lost out'. He likes to picture his departure from China as resulting from a philosophical disillusionment. But on several occasions he has indicated regret: if he had been less active during the Cultural Revolution and had gone home to study English like some of those of the 'stand-aloof faction', he would now have a better headstart in Hong Kong; or if he had been less rebellious at the end of the Cultural Revolution, he would probably now be a puppet sitting in some low-level administrative office. He indirectly but repeatedly blames himself for impracticality, for having allowed his passions and his desires for Rebel peer-group approval to have got the better of his common sense in the Cultural Revolution.

As if he had a right to claim vengeance for having been wronged, in China he came to reject not only the political values but also the social ethics he had been taught. On a bus he would not practice the Lei Feng virtue of giving up his seat even for a pregnant woman carrying a baby, 'for who the hell knows which faction she once belonged to'.

On release from prison he was sent to a state farm, where he spent most of his time stealing away from work. Those who laboured diligently were, he felt, fools. The idea of leaving for Hong Kong was conceived 'naturally', without internal struggle. When he pondered the decision, it was on whether his life was worth risking in return for an unknown future. Like others, he read widely during this period, but not in the manner of Chang's frantic search for new ideals. Deng left because he calculated that, politically and economically, he had no future in China. If he had had the opportunity to transfer from the countryside to an urban job, he would not have taken the risk of a long swim to the Crown Colony.

In Hong Kong, he accepted easily the individualistic values of a capitalist society, with self-enrichment his dominant goal. He had no contempt for Hong Kong workers and was content to work temporarily as a dockhand. But he dreamed of becoming a capitalist one day. Within the year, he was aspiring to go to the United States, which he saw as providing a wider arena of opportunities.

Publicly, Deng dismissed as unrealistic fools those like Chang who were still politically concerned. But his feelings were actually divided. Once, he privately confided to me his uneasiness and shame at being so uninvolved. The year before he emigrated to America, he changed course and spent his days writing a series of articles on the bureaucratic system in China, with an appeal for socialist democracy. In his struggle between self-advancement and ideals, he apparently took this as a last political act and testament.

BAI

Once released from prison, Bai was sent back to the university to wait 'under surveillance by the masses', while a new dossier on him was compiled. Assigned finally to Canton, he was permitted before he left to read a summary of the file. Among other things, it had stamped him with the revised class origin of 'bully landlord':

> Wow, I was shocked. And in the file it said that, because of the 'mistakes' I had made, they were expelling me from the league. I was really pissed off. First, I couldn't understand that crap about my class origin. It said I had hidden my class origin. That accusation was serious. It stays with you for the rest of your life. And it accused me of being a 'bad leader' in the Cultural Revolution; said I was a conservative in the movement. Not even one thing was good about me, not even one! I told them I personally rejected this appraisal. Could it be possible that in the Cultural Revolution I had done nothing good, all bad?

Bai was accompanied to Canton by two teachers who carried with them 'a huge basketful of my files'. He was to await an assignment to settle in the countryside. For two nights he was sleepless and on the third day sought out a friend to discuss with him the idea of escaping to Hong Kong. It was surprising that he had arrived at such a decision so quickly, considering that he had not been living in Canton and that the 'wind of escape' had barely begun to surface even among Canton's young people. Bai leapt at the stratagem precisely because he had been a cadre involved in directing 'class struggle' against bad-class elements:

> I already thought of leaving. Why? Though I knew nothing of what it was like outside and there was no place for me to rest my feet out there, I realized that here in China, carrying a 'bully landlord' family label, every minute I would be an object of discrimination and a repeated target for struggle. No matter which unit I went to, be it farm or factory, I would still be a bad element. With this class background, the whole of my life I'd be doomed. So I thought, there's no more hope. Even drifting to some foreign place, anything at all, would be better.

Bai, who had once prided himself as more selfless than his peers or superiors, was now quick to think exclusively of his prospects. There is no doubt that he had once been genuine in his dedication and selflessness, but this had gone hand-in-hand with a smooth-sailing upward mobility which had not necessitated direct conscious pursuit of personal gains. He had been selfless and successful at one and the same time: and in a sense, each had reinforced the other. Once his mobility was obstructed, however, the sense of personal loss for Bai was enormous, more than that suffered by people like Chang and Deng who had never received much approval from the political establishment.

We have observed how Bai had differed from the Rebels in being basically uncritical of the political structure's premises. Now, despite being relegated to a bad-class status, he still did not doubt the fundamental tenets of the class-line policy. When his plans to escape fell through and he was sent to settle in a village, there initially was some confusion as to whether 'class origins' could be counted against the sent-down youths. Thus, he thought again – this time unrealistically – of trying to fulfil his long-term ambition of building up a village into a model. He went about the notion as if he were still a Four Cleanups workteam cadre:

> When I first went there I devised a class-dossier notebook. I put down in it all the dozen-plus households in the production team, and from the moment I got there I groped for the facts: the names, class backgrounds, ages, number of children, factional alignments, who complained about whom, etc. I accumulated these investigation materials so that I could have a grasp of the village's situation of class struggle and factional struggle.

He was using the same frame of reference and the same techniques that he had learned in the Four Cleanups campaign – to employ 'class struggle' as a tool for political leadership. In two months, though, his prospects were thwarted and his last hopes dashed. The brigade party branch secretary lined up the dozen urban youths in front of the peasants, publicly exposed their dossiers, and reminded the peasants that 'good people are not sent down; people sent down cannot be good'. Henceforth Bai could only befriend peasants who were stigmatized as bad class and former cadres who had been politically disgraced in the recent campaigns. He made preparations for his escape. It took him eight attempts before he finally reached Hong Kong.

Once in Hong Kong, Bai demonstrated no propensity for entrepreneurship. When I first met him he was working as a restaurant waiter. Having been a university student and considering himself an intellectual, he hoped, though, to find an opportunity to do research and write on China. Ideologically, he was groping confusedly for a belief to fill the emotional and political void that his rupture with the Communist Youth League and party had created. For a few months he enthusiastically attended the revivalist meetings of a Protestant religious sect, while denying he believed in their god; it was the 'concern and love those believers have for each other' which attracted him. Later, he twice tried to form tight-knit political groups. In each effort, it was as if he were trying to recapture the spirit of collective solidarity and the sense of a higher purpose which he had cherished as a league member in secondary school. He hoped that his little groups would become eventually like a centralized party, with himself as leader. The two groups foundered when Bai tried to act in ways that the others considered 'manipulative' or 'dictatorial'. To this very day, he says that it is only through a tightly organized party with a well-defined ideological stance that 'you can get things done'.

One year after our interviews, Bai astonished his friends by embarking on a speaking tour of Taiwan as an 'Anti-Communist Warrior'. After his return to Hong Kong, he organized a magazine with pro-Taiwan and anti-Communist views. He had been brought up with a sharply Manichean view of the world; there were the 'good guys', the glorious Chinese Communist Party, and the 'bad guys', the Guomindang. Today he simply reverses the labels. His rationalization for this about-turn in attitude is that in the 1950s and even the 1960s the Communists were strong, the country's economy was improving and social cohesion strengthening, but in the Cultural Revolution and its aftermath the Communists had exposed their weaknesses. So it is legitimate to desert a cause that ultimately proved faulty, in preference for a worthier cause. There seems to be an urge in Bai forever to attach himself to a crusade.

AO

In the Cleansing of the Class Ranks campaign of 1968–9, as we have observed, Ao had played an active prosecuting role. But after the campaign had subsided, Ao discovered that her political prospects had not been improved by the effort. Class background continued to count enormously in cadre selections. She was disgruntled but not in any sense disillusioned. She would have continued to suppress and deny her dissatisfactions had not a new group of fifty youths arrived from the city. The new settlers had experienced the Cultural Revolution's 'great democracy' and had brought with them critical minds and a sense of rebelliousness. Among them was Ao's own younger sister. Initially Ao put up a strong resistance to the newcomer's influence.

> Once my sister and I had a big fight. I mean literally a fist fight. She criticized Mao in front of me. I got so mad. I was scared. I didn't dare hear such stuff. I forbade her to speak. If it should be heard by anybody, she could have been charged with being an active counterrevolutionary. So I threatened her, that I would call the poor and lower-middle peasants to teach her a lesson. She got scared, swung at me and we started slugging each other.

Having zealously served as a 'proletarian dictator' over the bad elements, she was terrified of being made a target of that 'dictatorship' – just as Bai had been sensitive to the ramifications of being stigmatized, having once stigmatized others. But the general atmosphere in the countryside was changing rapidly. Whereas before she had led the peasants in singing the praises of Vice-Chairman Lin Biao, after 1971 she had to contradict herself by preaching his evils. Several years earlier, she might have accomplished this task with a militant zest, but now her trust in the party was wavering. Now that her housemates and audience included the new cohort of youths from the city, she found the integrity of what she was doing placed in doubt:

> The new arrivals were like a large stone thrown into our little pond. I was influenced by them. I found them knowledgeable. When I talked to my younger sister I felt embarrassed at my meagre knowledge. They read a lot of books on politics and economics, a lot of novels, including foreign novels. We all began reading these books. We began using our brains and looked at problems using the method of one divides into two just as Mao Zédong says. I used to be worried over a whole lot of trivialities, such as not stepping on someone's toes, but not them. They were only concerned with big things. My thoughts were very orthodox, I strongly believed in the government, everything that was in the

newspaper. They were like this too before the Cultural Revolution. After the Cultural Revolution their thoughts changed. They asked 'why?' about everything. I just carried out whatever work I was told to do. They weren't afraid to rebel. They hadn't come to the countryside to cultivate poor and lower-middle peasants' feelings. They dared to question the whole system. I felt inferior. But they were unstable, changing their minds all the time. I was tenacious. They talked big, but when it came down to doing things they weren't any good. I concentrated my attention in pulling carts, never looking around; they only looked around without pulling carts.

The catalyst which led Ao finally to abandon her activist role altogether was a campaign to force the youths who had settled in the counties bordering Hong Kong to resettle in a jungle-covered wilderness region of Hainan Island that was being pioneered through state farms managed by the army. In her village, the urban youths were put under intense pressure to sign up to go 'voluntarily'. But when the village leaders tried to get Ao to volunteer as the 'model' for others, she resisted furiously. 'Even if you raise a dog for ten years you don't kick it away like that. I felt, am I more worthless than a dog in their eyes? I decided I don't want to work for these bastards any more.' In the end, the Guangdong authorities retracted the policy of forcing youths to Hainan. But in Ao's village, a residue of ill feelings lingered on both sides. Ao had demonstrated finally that she could not 'stand the test', could not go wherever the party wanted her to go. She gave up tempering herself. She 'didn't give a damn any more'.

After her younger sister swam to Hong Kong in 1972, Ao's political standing in the village was further eroded. During the next two years, more than half a dozen other urban youths made the same illegal escape to Hong Kong. Though she was still wary of Hong Kong's 'degenerate' capitalist society and the dangers involved in the escape, she finally began privately practising long-distance swimming. Ironically, her father, whom she had for so many years despised as 'backward', tried to dissuade her from leaving and to continue 'serving the people'. He told her that socialism was far better than capitalism, despite the many problems the country was facing and his own terrible troubles in the Cultural Revolution. Ao departed for Hong Kong one morning without saying goodbye.

She had taken the political system very personally – and in the end had taken rejection by it personally too. She thought of it as having discarded her, as having used her as an 'expendable tool'. She now regrets that she had 'wasted' ten years in the countryside. When she heard of Mao's death, she was beside herself with joy, as if it were Mao Zedong himself who had been personally responsible for her obstructed career. At the same time, she does not consider herself responsible for those of her own actions of which she now disapproves. In describing her prosecution of former friends in the Cleansing of the Class Ranks campaign, she refers to herself in retrospect as 'blind', 'asleep' and a 'tool'. To a certain extent she is correct, because, like other interviewees who have used those terms, she had always merely conformed to the norms and values without applying her own independent judgement.

Ao set out to study English the moment she reached Hong Kong. She wasted no time in making known her determination to climb the social ladder. She chose the academic route as a means to social acceptance; to Ao the content of what she studied did not matter, so long as one day a university degree would bring her the status and 'glory' that were awarded to education by Chinese tradition. The drive with which she memorized social science lecture notes conjures up images of how she had memorized reading primers in her childhood.

To make a living, she had to take up blue-collar jobs. Bai and Deng, among others, had accepted such 'menial' jobs good humouredly. Not Ao. She found such work demeaning and humiliating, and resented it. The 'proletarian class feelings' that she had once cultivated had evaporated into thin air.

In her frustration, she was aware of certain changes in herself.

In the countryside I tempered myself in not fearing hardship. I struggled not to quarrel with people. I controlled myself so as not to be the type of person who can only stand praise but not criticism, the type who only looks after their own interests. I was good. People said I later changed, that I became backward. Sure, I changed! [Said in a tone of voice suggesting she was justified.] You go ask my sister. I wasn't this fierce before. Ha. Before I was quite nice; I dared not be too fierce; I was approachable. I've become fierce only after coming to Hong Kong. Before there was an aim, a higher purpose to my life. I feel as if I'm letting myself go.

In China, under activist peer pressure and self-imposed restraints, she had managed to dampen the expression of her personal drives and weaknesses and to put up a show of concern for others. But there was no necessity any longer to do so. She 'let herself go'. If she complained that in Hong Kong there was no meaning in life, in part it was because she regarded Hong Kong as a stepping-stone from China to the United States. She had no immediate social milieu to identify with.

Three years later she emigrated to America. The last time I saw her she was sewing in a garment factory in Chinatown and simultaneously preparing to enter university part-time. She seemed to be adjusting to America easily. She felt the 'land of opportunity' was offering her the chance to attain a respectable place in the white-collar middle class. She has discovered a niche in the world where she feels she can play a role with a higher purpose. She told me she wanted to fight for the rights of the Chinese minority in America. She has built a scenario of becoming an intermediate-level community leader. It would be a role to which she is already accustomed, as propagandist, organizer and organization-woman. But for Ao it would in no way be a politically radical course. Much as she had earlier, in her yearnings for respectability and eminence, adhered to the party, so too she now sees the role she can play in Chinatown as a means to sustain a respectable Chinese identity, a means to become a cadre of the Chinese–American Establishment. Ao remains Ao.

6 Political Socialization and the Authoritarian Personality in China

On one level this study has considered how four young people of fundamentally different dispositions became political activists, the problems and difficulties they faced, and how and why as adults they personally became politically disaffected – desocialized – and left for Hong Kong.

On a more general level, this has also been a study of the processes the Chinese state employed to socialize young people. The book has examined the school environment that was created; the resultant mass conflict that followed; and lastly – what we shall specifically be addressing in this chapter – the influence of all this upon the personality structure of a generation of Chinese urban youths.

THE AUTHORITARIAN PERSONALITY

It will be shown that there was a link between the young people's political socialization and the development of what has been called the 'authoritarian personality'. Such a personality structure, as defined by Erich Fromm, 'admires authority and tends to submit to it, but at the same time . . . wants to be an authority himself and have others submit to him'.[1]

The 'authoritarian personality' occupies an important place in the social science literature on the relationship between personality and politics. In the many attempts to classify personality structures and to establish correlations with people's political orientation, no other concept has been more widely tested, debated and redebated.[2] In studying modern China, where the political system demands an unusual degree of submission to authority, the authoritarian personality thesis warrants particularly close examination.

Scholars such as Erich Fromm and Wilhelm Reich originated the concept of the authoritarian personality in their writings of the 1930s and 1940s.[3] Combining a Marxist framework with Freudian psycho-analysis, their general concern had been the alienation of man from himself and society in a period of history of increasing concentration of power in the hands of the state. Disturbed particularly by the rise of totalitarian states in Nazi Germany and Stalinist Russia, they were seeking answers to the frightening puzzle of the hold of such regimes on men's loyalties.

In the late 1940s, their conceptualization of an authoritarian per-sonality was subjected to rigorous empirical testing by a group of scholars in Berkeley headed by Theodore Adorno.[4] (Adorno, like Fromm, was a senior member of the humanist Marxist Frankfurt School of thinkers.) An underlying assumption of Adorno's 'Ber-keley project', as it is now usually called, was that the authoritarian personality was a latent character structure that could be present among people of any nationality, not only in countries experiencing authoritarian convulsions.[5] In the case of America, it was argued, a set of particular anti-democratic political attitudes found support among citizens of a specific type of authoritarian psychological make-up. The Berkeley project concentrated on perfecting a ques-tionnaire that could be used cross-culturally for identifying individ-uals with this latent 'authoritarian personality', regardless of the ideological content of their overt beliefs. (See Table 2 for a list of the underlying attitudes that the Berkeley project found were prominent among authoritarians.) Adorno's questionnaire results showed that high scorers in a test of one of the traits tended also to be high scorers in the other traits: that an 'authoritarian personality' comprised a syndrome of psychological traits.[6]

One assumption of the various studies on the authoritarian person-ality was that, given the right social, economic, political and historical conditions, increasing numbers of people can come to possess an authoritarian personality until it becomes a society's predominant personality structure: what Fromm calls the people's 'social charac-ter'. This term 'social character' stands in contradistinction to the 'individual character' by which people belonging to that same society differ from each other. Fromm has elaborated on the close fit be-tween a social system and its social character:

The members of the society and/or the various classes or status groups within it have to behave in such a way as to be able to function in the sense required by the social system. It is the function of the social character to shape the energies of the members of society in such a way that their behavior is not a matter of conscious decision as to whether or not to follow the social pattern, but one of wanting to act as they have to act and at the same time finding gratification in acting according to the requirements of the culture. [7]

This is not to say that all members of a social group will share equally in the attributes of the prevailing social character. A minority will be deviants; some others will adhere to the traits especially closely. In particular, Fromm posits that 'the leaders in any given group will often be those whose individual character is a particularly intense and complete manifestation of the social character – if not of the whole society at least of a powerful class within it'.[8]

An authoritarian personality structure that Adorno's Berkeley project perceived on an individual level in social systems like postwar America can become an authoritarian 'social character' in social systems which actively encourage it. In this century an authoritarian 'social character' had been encouraged, as examples, in prewar Germany, Russia and Japan. In most respects these political systems were very different. But all three governments, each in their own ways, sought from their young people strong and whole-hearted submission to a charismatic leader, party or government. The political authorities imposed strict discipline to ensure obeisance to the higher cause. People were encouraged to yearn for the experience of immersing their separate selves in a solidary group. In all these national movements, an urge existed to single out either weaklings or 'enemies of the state' as outsiders beyond the pale. People were advised to be constantly and vigilantly on the look-out for potential traitors. A Manichean worldview prevailed. A single-mindedness was encouraged, and an unwillingness to evaluate people as individuals but rather always in terms of rigid categorizations laid down in the ideology. In conforming to the goals of the higher political authorities, adherents had to cultivate a strong sense of self-denial as proof of their devotion. At the same time, they could strive to partake in the glory and power of the higher authority by themselves serving as an authority over, and saviour of, those lower in the political order than themselves.[9]

After the unconditional surrender of Germany and Japan at the end of the Second World War and the death of Stalin in Russia, however, the authoritarian social character that had characterized all three nations rapidly dissipated. The authoritarian social characters of these three nations, in brief, had been products of particular historical circumstances that had arisen and then evaporated over the course of a few decades.

Our brief description here of the authoritarian personality and the authoritarian 'social character' provides several propositions that will serve as points of reference for our discussion of the personality structure of the Red Guard generation in China. These propositions are:

1. Because of sociological and situational constraints, an authoritarian personality does not necessarily always manifest itself in overt behaviour.
2. But it is possible to identify individuals with an authoritarian personality structure through an analysis of latent attitudes that reveal a clear syndrome of psychological traits.
3. Given the right social, economic, political and historical conditions, more people in a social system can come to possess an authoritarian personality, leading to the formation of an authoritarian 'social character'.
4. Not all members of the group will possess this social character to the same degree.[10] Those who have adapted most successfully to the prevailing social environment will possess it to a greater degree than others.
5. Given political and social stimulation, the authoritarian 'social character' can be manifested in extreme forms of authoritarian behaviour, supported by most of the social group.
6. The authoritarian social character is not found only in particular races or nations, nor is it a permanent feature once formed. As the conditions instigating it change, so does the social character.[11]

In the pages which follow we shall see how the Chinese situation falls within the parameters of these propositions.

CHINESE ACTIVISM AND THE AUTHORITARIAN PERSONALITY: A CASE OF NATIONAL CHARACTER OR SOCIAL CHARACTER?

China under Mao was neither fascist nor Stalinist. To attach such labels to China would be to simplify and unfairly distort a very

TABLE 2 *Comparing the traits of the authoritarian personality* and the Chinese political activist*

Traits of the authoritarian personality, as identified by the Berkeley Project	Qualities of the ideal Chinese political activist	Observable behaviour of the activist
a. *Conventionalism*: rigid adherence to conventional values.	Adherence to Marxism–Leninism and Mao Zedong's thought.	Dogmatic interpretation of the ideology propagated by the party.
b. *Authoritarian submission*: Submissive, uncritical attitude towards idealized moral authorities of the in-group.	Obedience to Mao and the party.	Uncritical submission to Mao, the party, league and school authorities.
c. *Authoritarian aggression*: tendency to be on the lookout for, and to reject, condemn and punish people who violate the conventional values.	Constant struggle against 'bourgeois thoughts' and 'bourgeois behaviour'.	Condemn and punish all who adopt unsanctioned values and behaviour. Insistence upon rigid conformity.
d. *Anti-intraception*: opposition to the subjective, imaginative, the tender-minded.	Struggle against 'individualism' and 'humanism'.	Suppression of others' spontaneous and creative activities.
e. *Stereotyping*: the disposition to think in rigid categories.	Belief in 'class nature'; denial of 'human nature'.	Stereotyping people by 'class background', not judging them as individuals.
f. *Power and 'Toughness'*: preoccupation with the strong–weak, dominant–submissive, leader–follower dimension. Identification with power figures, exaggerated assertion of strength and toughness.	Physical tempering, self-cultivation, emulation of socialist war heroes, belief in the omnipotence of Mao's thought.	Extreme forms of physical tempering and self-cultivation. Worship of Mao; assertions of devotion by humiliating, degrading and beating up those who purportedly oppose him.

	Constant vigilance against internal and external 'class enemies'.	A war psychology. Beliefs concerning the dangers of hidden 'class enemies'.
g. *Projectivity*: the disposition to believe that wild and dangerous things go on in the world.		
h. *Superstition*: the belief in mystical determinants of the individual's fate.	Not applicable.	Not applicable.
i. *Destructiveness and aggression*: general hostility, vilification of the human.	Not applicable.	Not applicable.
j. *Sex*: exaggerated concern with sexual 'goings-on'.	Not applicable.	Not applicable.

* The traits of the authoritarian personality are listed in Adorno et al., *The Authoritarian Personality*, p. 228. The definitions have had to be modified slightly because Adorno's scale was constructed with the intention of measuring rightist authoritarianism in the United States. Several of the traits applicable to this American study – superstition, destructiveness, cynicism and exaggerated sexual concerns – do not readily apply here.

complex national state of affairs. But it is also plain that the Chinese polity's effort to 'cultivate' a generation of moralistic, conscientious, devoutly committed political activists had played a major role in promoting authoritarian proclivities. We need not belabour this point. Table 2 presents the most salient of the variables that form the syndrome of the authoritarian personality, as listed by the Berkeley project (column 1). In parallel columns are listed the attributes which the Chinese government ascribed to the ideal political activist (column 2) and the mind-set that we have observed among committed official activists (column 3). The parallels between the 'authoritarian personality' syndrome and the Chinese activist's attitudinal traits are strong and obvious.

It behooves us to explore the origins of the Chinese activists' authoritarianism. Was it the result, when last came to last, of their experiences at school? Or, more fundamentally, is there something inherently authoritarian in the Chinese character that predated the new system of political socialization and was merely reflected in the school system's methods of socialization? In other words, is there an element of cultural determinism in the nurturance of authoritarianism among a people? Or conversely, should outbursts of extreme forms of authoritarianism be ascribed to comparatively transitory political and social conditions, as prevailed in the decade immediately prior to the Cultural Revolution?

Lucian Pye and Richard Solomon, two well-known writers on China, have attempted to explain both Chinese politics and the personality traits of modern-day Chinese almost entirely in terms of the legacy of Chinese culture and a traditionally authoritarian family structure.[12] I would include both of them in what is called the 'national character' school of writing, which postulates, first, that the people of a given nation share fundamental personality characteristics that endure through history; and second, that child-rearing practices are mainly responsible for transmitting this psychopolitical makeup from one generation to the next. Solomon, in his lengthy book *Mao's Revolution and the Chinese Political Culture*, argues, for example, that the father/son relationship in China has always been authoritarian – and he assumes political ramifications. He posits that child-rearing practices in the earliest years of childhood are permissive and nurturant, but once the toddler reaches the age of 5 or 6 he is subjected to strict paternal discipline and forced to restrain all aggressive behaviour. These contradictory socialization practices, according to Solomon, have molded an 'oral' Chinese personality which is ambivalent towards authority: at once dependent upon and hostile towards the patriarch. This psychological predisposition, Solomon argues, also traditionally produced an ambivalent feeling towards political authorities. He further contends that this culturally-bound personality type persisted after the Chinese Communist Party attained power; that Mao Zedong, an 'anal' personality in an oral society, was determined to transform Chinese political culture by encouraging the Chinese to rebel against authority figures. The younger generation, for reasons not well explained in Solomon's schema, responded to Mao's call, culminating in the Red Guard movement of the Cultural Revolution.

Solomon's theories have been widely lauded and just as sharply criticized.[13] We need not examine here his worst excesses (for example, his 'pop' Freudian thesis about a Chinese 'oral' personality and an 'anal' Mao). Rather, let us focus on Solomon's (and Lucian Pye's) most reasonable assumption: that the makeup of the Chinese personality, imparted through the ages by way of Chinese child-nurturing practices, cogently explains mass political behaviour in post-1949 China.

This kind of 'old wine in new bottles' explanation is inadequate because it ignores the very complex developments in China of the past thirty years. Among other things, it neglects all the evidence presented in this book. What we have witnessed in some detail, especially in the stories of Ao and Bai, were the ways in which the authoritarian personality characteristics of the young political activists were closely linked to a new system of political socialization that centred in the schools.

We have seen that it was in the schools, not at home, that the young people learned to perceive the world in Manichean terms, a teaching quite contrary to the 'golden mean' (*zhongyong*) of Confucianism. It was at school, not at home, that the perfect good of a party and its chairman became posed against the insidious evils of hidden enemies and bad-class outcasts. It was at school that the students learned to desire to enter a non-familial solidarity group, the league, and once inside, to strive religiously to abide by its rigid credo and discipline. It was the schooling, not so much the families, that promoted such strong intolerance of unconventionality; it was the schooling, not the families, that instilled an emotional need to prove the sincerity and depth of one's political devotion.

The saliency of this school-learned socialization, as against the influence of the home, was not at all unique to China. When Fromm,

Reich and Marcuse examined the genesis of German fascism, they focused on the decline of the family as a socialization agent and on the displacement of parental authority by state authority.[14] Under a very different political system, Russia, a similar phenomenon developed. Zevedi Barbu has observed that in the Soviet Union, where the state took over from the family many of the socialization functions, the emotionality of the child was focused on the state. Party leaders and the party itself became powerful objects for love.[15] In postindustrial democratic systems a parallel trend has emerged. With the decline of the father as an authority figure in the family, the young seek authority surrogates from the peer group and mass culture. This new social character David Riesman calls the 'other-directed' man.[16]

China is still far from being an industrial society with a technologically sophisticated mass communications system. But the pervasive presence and influence of a highly centralized education system and well-organized mass communications network were effective in creating a mass culture after Liberation, at least in the urban areas. The emulate Lei Feng craze, which swept the length and breadth of the Chinese urban school system, is just one such example. The state's influence on value formation and behaviour was penetrating and profound. When questioning interviewees on their relationships with their families, it became clear, particularly with former political activists, that the family had receded in the shaping of values, displaced partially by children's emotional orientation towards the state, party, Mao and the model heroes.[17] Almost invariably, interviewees had regarded their parents as 'behind the times' and 'politically backward'. Ao's relationship with her family was only an extreme case, not at all an isolated one.

THE DIFFERENTIAL RESULTS OF POLITICAL SOCIALIZATION

To state that the family had declined in importance as an agent of socialization is not to imply that a state-sponsored socialization system was capable of simply mass-producing young people's attitudes or characters or that a specific authoritarian 'social character' accurately described all successfully socialized children. We have seen in our four case studies that there is a richness and diversity to the human personality that defies any such notion. Not all those who were successfully socialized and became activist became the same kind of activists. Not all activists possessed the same degree of authoritarian traits. Their individual characters, for one thing, did not all stem from a single mould: quite obviously, the contrary emotional needs that Ao and Chang had possessed as pre-school-aged children could not possibly be traced to the same Chinese 'national character'.

We have seen, moreover, that more than just their initial personality traits had an impact on the emotional and political development of interviewees. In the evidence presented in this study, we have observed, in particular two other factors that strongly affected the success of different individuals' political socialization and their tendencies towards authoritarianism: (1) the institutional position occupied by a young person at school; and (2) his or her class label.

Political Institutions and Role-playing

Our discussion of childhood socialization in Chapter 2 brought out clearly that whatever the dispositions various children brought with them to school, their orientations towards authority interacted with and were further strongly shaped by their classroom experiences. Certain traits of a child's personality were reinforced, others were repressed. Children who readily adapted themselves to the activist role, like Ao and Bai, were rewarded for it and in turn sought enthusiastically to support the official values. As Erich Fromm would have put it, activists like Ao and Bai found gratification in acting in the ways that they were expected to act.

In the process they were being habituated to playing certain social roles in preparation for playing equivalent roles as adults. The differential rewards that were distributed through the political socialization mechanisms served not only to reinforce conformity to the desired traits; they also served to sort children into different hierarchic roles. Through this, the political socialization processes acted as a screening device for the distribution of resources and power in a stratified society.[18] Some children learned the qualities and bearing desired of the middle and lower ranks of leaders; others learned the roles of active followers, habituated to being lower on the sociopolitical scale: the role of a cadre as against the role of the 'masses'.

The qualities that were sought and rewarded were those that served to maintain a structurally stable and routinized Leninist state. A Chang or a Deng might well have been rewarded for their individualistic, forceful, rebellious traits in the pre-Liberation era, when personal resourcefulness was an asset in the revolution against the pre-Liberation *status quo*. But the road to political success and party membership rapidly altered once the revolutionary wars had been won. After 1949, as the party became a regularized political bureaucracy, someone like Ao became more suitable for recruitment. The political socialization processes in primary school and high school were based on that very premise.

The precautionary screening procedures for admission to the league were intended to ensure that aspirants were suitable, first, to submit to organizational discipline (e.g. 'leaning close to the league') and, second, to act as 'vanguard' leaders for their peers. In turn, once accepted into the league, these dual roles of the activist reinforced traits in his or her original personality which were already compatible with the organizational demands and, in addition, encouraged new emotional needs and behaviour patterns. Both Ao and Bai acquired in the league the self-image that they were vested with a mission to shepherd and manoeuvre the rest of their peer group. Similarly, interviewees who were not league members have remarked that classmates who had just joined the league tended to turn with discomforting alacrity from the posture of a humble learner to that of a self-righteous spiritual mentor.

This playing of a 'role' in China was more than a sociological abstraction. Role-playing involved literal play-acting: a conscious assumption of the mannerisms and ways of speaking appropriate to the activist status and role. With this role-playing and the initial tendencies of the personality reinforcing each other in an upward spiral, it was not unusual that children who began as student officers in primary school later became league members. Ao, who learned to play the role of an official activist when very young, continued playing the same role in various stages of her life. This role-playing seems to have placed an actor in the disposition to be successfully socialized. As members of the vanguard league organization, youths were assigned exemplary roles, and under this pressure they tried hard to surpass others in their submission to authority, in keeping organizational discipline, in standing alert against the sabotage of 'class enemies', and in showing themselves extreme in the practice of self-cultivation and tempering.

This did not, of course, exclude a youth from beginning to play the role of an official activist at a later stage. Bai, for instance, did not hold a formal leadership position until he entered the league as a teenager. It was instructive to observe the rapid effect of his subsequent role-playing on his hitherto latent proclivities to organizational loyalty and authoritarianism.

But for Chang and Deng, the fact that they had not played roles of official activists early in life worked against their chances of recruitment to be official activists. This, in turn, influenced their subsequent attitudes and behaviour. Unrecognized activists tended to be less fully integrated into the processes of political socialization than official activists. Their modes of behaviour and personality traits differed accordingly.

Official activists acquired a group interest in the process of playing their roles. They came to identify with the political establishment, having been vested with considerable power by it. When the Cultural Revolution broke out, they tended initially to react in accordance with this group interest, by defending the party committees. League members who were excluded from joining the original good-class Red Guards tended to join the Red Outer Circle, and later on, for the same reason, few league members became important Rebel leaders. Having been accustomed to playing a compliant role towards authority and having identified themselves as adjuncts to authority, official activists were not potential rebels. Unrecognized activists, on the other hand, had no self-image as agents of the political establishment. Confinement to an uncomfortably peripheral role provided them with greater potential to act in ways that undermined the *status quo*.

The principal distinction between the official activists and their peers, seen quite clearly among my fourteen interviewees, was that the league members tended to exhibit stronger traits of authoritarianism than the non-members. Their watchdog role, the stringent organizational discipline they adhered to in the hierarchical climate of the league, and their need to present themselves to others as role-models of an authoritarian belief-system, all served to propel league members to adopt traits which characterize the authoritarian personality.

It is, of course, impossible to disaggregate the proclivities towards authoritarianism which they brought with them to school and the reinforcing tendencies that were aroused and 'nurtured' in them during the course of their political socialization. But these teenagers did absorb with differential success, and in different ways, what was taught to them by the structured environment in which they grew up. Let us, for example, briefly take Bai, who became self-righteously authoritarian. He devoted himself religiously to the party, even if he quite often disobeyed party members who were his superiors. In secondary school, he exhibited intolerant righteousness in dictating to classmates how they should behave. He subsequently developed an image of himself as the saviour who could change a backward village into a national model. Later, just as self-righteously, he has been the 'anti-Communist warrior'. He did not judge people as they were, but placed them into rigid categories as he was taught to do, and continues to do so despite his efforts to conceal this trait during interviews. His sense of right and wrong derived mostly from an external set of rules – rules shaped by a Manichean worldview. His political world was made up of two forces, the Communist and the Guomindang, and he would adhere to whichever of these two poles he thought embodied the 'righteous wind' and oppose the one representing the 'evil wind'. So much had Bai adjusted to the perspectives and needs that he was taught that they appeared to have entered into his personality, to the extent that when transplanted into a completely different social milieu like Hong Kong, where no similar demands were imposed on him, most of Bai's traits have remained quite stable. But at the same time, once the social pressures on him were relaxed, there was less compulsiveness in his authoritarian righteousness. Not only has he stopped keeping a diary, a habit all other interviewees have also let lapse. He at times even gives way to taking small advantages; as if to make up for his once deprived diet, he can become a bit of a glutton at friends' wedding receptions.

Ao also strongly exhibited authoritarian traits. Like others among my interviewees, she could be self-disciplined and ascetic, religiously so. Yet she was anxiously aware of her inability always to repress those elements of her personality which were disapproved of by the authorities. She is basically a very individualistic person without much collective inclination. She managed to overcome this deficiency with conscious effort, for the main drive which made Ao adjust well to the character that was wanted of her was her need to conform to the dictates of external authority. Fear of being shamed, a craving of her superiors' approval and for formal peer-group respect – all of which the school system nurtured and reinforced – led her to conform unswervingly. She succeeded, for example, in 'cultivating' an uncompromising Manichean view. She was more extreme than Bai in a paranoia about 'class enemies' and more aggressive and ruthless in suppressing the stigmatized minority of society.

Yet once she was immersed in a new milieu outside China, she could easily change course, seeking to conform to the norms of the new social environment. Seeing no reward to be gained by adhering to previous social norms, she let surface what she had earlier considered to be her failings. She no longer puts on the airs of a selfless person, but has taken on the views and rhetoric of an individualist, chasing after social recognition in the new society with undiminished compulsion. Though many of her most fundamental personality traits remain unchanged, she has brought to the fore certain of her traits of personality and has deemphasized or suppressed others.

Inside China, the behaviour of both Ao and Bai had been very similar in several respects. Both of them had held dogmatically to a red-and-black worldview in which good and evil were determined by the party leadership. Both of them had been willing to condemn and punish anyone who held to unsanctioned values or unconventional behaviour. Both showed rigidly unfeeling prejudice towards people categorized as 'class enemies', regarding them as contemptibly beyond the pale. Both yearned for the security of immersing their separate identities in a solidary group. Both Ao and Bai had sought to partake of the glory and power of those highest in authority by themselves serving as an authority over their peers. In short, both of them fit the classic characteristics of an authoritarian personality.

Chang and Deng would, I think, have ranked low compared to Ao and Bai had they been tested in 1966 on the 'authoritarian personality' scale. They had held to many of the ideals taught in the schools but, being neither official activists nor conformist followers, they were always in the anomalous position of outsiders. The differences in attitude between themselves and Ao and Bai were partly a reflection of the distance in political status that separated them. They did not emotionally surrender themselves to the party but instead, partly in self-defence against the social milieu they had been cast into, built up an inner resistance to being bound by organizational discipline. They sometimes went against the prescribed norms, refusing to be part of the crowd, in a struggle to maintain their individuality. As Rebel leaders during the Cultural Revolution, they did relish in their own ways the possession of power and the opportunity to dominate, seen especially in Deng's autocratic leadership style. But the urge to free themselves from social and organizational bonds seems to have motivated them as strongly or more strongly than any desires to control others' thinking and behaviour.

Neither of them had expressed any inclinations, either, to discriminate against the stigmatized members of society. They did not possess a Manichean perspective and were considerably more receptive to unorthodox ideas. They based their judgements of people and events more on their own feelings – unlike Bai, who measured them rigidly against the rules of an ideology, or Ao, who did so with an anxiety to gain the authorities' approval.

It was in their rigorous and diligent physical tempering and self-cultivation that Chang and Deng came closest to the personality characteristics desired by the party. But by no means were their practices aimed at bending their own characters to accommodate to the demands of the activist personality: in fact, quite the opposite, for their efforts had strong overtones of 'individualistic heroism'. And even these efforts at self-cultivation collapsed after they came to Hong Kong. In a milieu where self-discipline was encouraged, Chang could be a zealous ascetic, but once the pressure was removed, he could be one of the most undisciplined of people.

Yet even interviewees who, like Chang and Deng, did not have initial proclivities towards authoritarianism, tended to exhibit some degree of authoritarian behaviour as teenagers. The social and political pressures in the classroom, as we have seen, were sufficiently strong. Students less independent and less rebellious than Chang and Deng could not escape being conformists, sincere conformists, and as such, they temporarily exhibited authoritarian attitudes and behaviour.

In the early to mid-1960s, as the thought of Mao became transformed into dogma, the students increasingly were under pressure to conform rigidly and unquestioningly to political orthodoxy. In this peer-group competition, the Communist Youth League branches, as guardians of correct behaviour, tightly supervised the students and rewarded activist exertion. Anxious to get into the league and, through that, into higher education, few young people dared raise objections even when the emulate Lei Feng campaign went beyond rational proportions. Students found themselves, consciously or unconsciously, playing a role that was in accord with the competitive pressures of the peer group. All signs of spontaneity were suppressed for fear they would dangerously grow to undermine the dogma and the discipline. Unconventional behaviour was condemned by the peer group, at the 'level of political principle'.

Authoritarianism still had not been manifested in extreme form, but the props for this had been set in place by the students' experiences. The Cultural Revolution provided the conditions for extremism to come to the fore. Mao's appeal to the young people to 'defend his revolutionary line' brought to a fevered pitch the young people's submissiveness to an idolized moral authority. It promoted their Manichean rigidity; their 'war' psychology; their preoccupation with 'toughness'; their intolerance of any violators of the credos they had been taught; their competitive needs to be in-group. In short, their behaviour reflected in extreme form each of the major variables of the 'authoritarian personality' as tested by the Berkeley project.

Notably, the young people's beliefs and needs found full expression only when institutional structures crumbled and the political system's normal constraints against extreme authoritarianism disappeared. Sometimes there was a rational basis for their attacks against authority, as in the vengeance wreaked against overly restrictive or blatantly partial teachers. But more often than not, the violence was a product of prejudice, authoritarian intolerance, fear and peer-group pressure. All these elements promoted aggressively conformist actions. As Bai said, it was like being caught up in a strong current.[19] The first few months of the Cultural Revolution saw profoundly disturbing manifestations of an authoritarian 'social character'.

Class Categories

The writings on social character, we noted earlier, posit that even though most members of a given social group will share in a given social character, they will do so differentially. We have just observed the validity of this proposition: urban Chinese students of the 1960s who had been placed in activist leadership positions tended to exhibit authoritarian personality traits to a greater degree than their politically less successful peers. In a parallel fashion, as we shall now see, children whose class interests were served by the political teachings of the state tended to adhere more firmly to a belief system that favoured them. Like successful activism, class labels provided a good index of different students' authoritarianism.

The word 'class', as used in China, quite obviously was very dissimilar to Marx's original definition of the term. According to Marx, classes arise and are sustained by differences in the private ownership of the means of production. In China after Liberation, relations to the means of production had been restructured by nationalization and collectivization. This engendered the emergence of a new social structure. Similar structural changes had occurred in the Soviet Union. But there, in little more than a decade after the October Revolution, class struggle was declared to have ended, and in fact the party began to emphasize the classlessness of Russian society.[20] Yet the Chinese Communist Party insisted, with increasing rigour, upon retaining the old categorization of classes, artificially superimposing it upon a new and radically different social order. The party, including Mao, saw the revival of 'class hatred' as a means to keep alive the people's gratitude to the party and their adherence to the party's demands.[21] For their part, the renewed stress on ascriptive labelling in the 1960s was welcomed by the 'good classes' who benefited from it. But for middle-class interviewees, the policy had had disturbing consequences. They found themselves boxed in by artificial labels that *a priori* ascribed their political reliability. They were made to live under the shadow of the economic relationships of the *ancien regime*.

The use of obsolete class categories to define social relationships helped veil in people's minds the emergence of the new social realities. Unlike the pre-revolutionary society, where social stratification was a result of differential control of the private means of production, the new patterns of stratification were a product of differential power relations. As a consequence of the Leninist one-party system, a new elite stratum had been formed at each level of the political hierarchy, much like Djilas's 'new class'. Mao was personally opposed to the rise of these elite strata, but he could not undo the power relationships that shaped these strata without relinquishing the Leninist concept of party control. Mao's response to the paradox had been to launch mass movements and rectification campaigns against corrupt cadres as individuals, while simultaneously upholding the basic Leninist beliefs that provided the party bureaucrats with power and status as a group.

Throughout the 1960s, the officialdom and their children had sought to defend, extend and perpetuate their privileged status by wedding the protective Leninist concept of party leadership to the 'class line'. In the pre-Cultural Revolution classrooms, the cadres' children were seeking, in precisely this fashion, to inherit privileges on the basis of a Brahmanic red-class superiority. Their demand was that only young people with the proper caste credentials, i.e. themselves, should be allowed to assume leadership roles.

Such an extreme play upon the caste idea of 'class' did not dominate the schools until the early months of the Cultural Revolution. But even earlier, the class labels had provided the children with different statuses in the classroom, and with different self-images and different strategies for coping.

The youths from middle-class homes, believing they had a chance in the new society, largely accepted the views that were taught them in school about 'class'; Ao and Bai are prime examples of this. It was not just because their feelings and consciousness had been success-fully conditioned by a notion of class struggle that was divorced from the present realities. They had, beyond this, their own pragmatic reasons to accept such a perception. As members of a 'class' category that could 'be united with', the middle-class students enjoyed clear advantages over the bad-class children, and found it in their own interests to draw a very clear and prejudiced distinction between themselves and the bad-class households. Yet a great many of these middle-class students, precisely because of their insecure political statuses, were not *as* strongly prejudiced against the stigmatized class categories as were their red-class schoolmates. They themselves, after all, would be penalized by any strengthened emphasis on 'class hatred' and the class line. One of my interviewees had an apt description for their predicament: 'We, too, carried on our backs a "class" burden.'

The stigmatized bad-class youths grew up feeling socially inferior, sometimes even bitter, often refusing to be socialized into sincerely playing an active political role. Instead of being 'won over to the revolutionary side', they were 'lost' to their reactionary parents.

The good-class group of young people, encouraged by the official extolments, were amenable to the schools' concerted efforts at politi-cal socialization. But the privileged social positions and sense of superiority of the children of revolutionary-cadre parentage created certain difficulties. Though they were the most likely to defend the *status quo*, they were, at the same time, the least submissive to the adult authority figures at their schools. They had their own griev-ances, moreover. They felt insecure in their second-rate academic performance compared with the children of the professional middle classes. As a response to feeling at once insecure and innately superior, their tendency to trample on the weak, as in the Cultural Revolution, was the strongest.

The working-class-labelled children often had been raised, at home as well as at school, to hold feelings of gratitude towards the party. But at the same time, and unlike the revolutionary-cadre youths, they did not normally feel that the new society owed them positions of leadership and dominance.

Having observed the differing circumstances of the students of different class backgrounds, we may pursue the question of which of these groups of students had patterns of behaviour that were most or least congruent with the 'authoritarian personality'. Bad-class children, who were not given the chance even to show their devotion to the polity, demonstrated little authoritarian behaviour either before or during the Cultural Revolution: whether they, too, had any strong potential for authoritarianism is difficult to tell. The cadres' children, at the height of the 'blood-line theory' and the Red Terror, engaged in the most extreme and violent forms of authoritarian behaviour. The working-class and middle-class children showed more modest inclinations, even when they held the opportunity. Generally, the better the class background, the more extreme were the manifestations of authoritarian behaviour.

But even while we note this, we cannot help but observe that the various groups of students (except, perhaps, the bad-class cohort) shared to varying degrees in a 'social character' common to their generation. Authoritarian behaviour became the norm during these months for the middle-class 'second-class citizenry', too. Most of them were as submissive to the Mao cult as the red-class activists; most of them were as intolerant of unconventional thinking or behaviour; and most of them enthusiastically joined in harassing bad-class teachers. Only one middle-class interviewee other than Chang had felt horrified by the activities around them.

Let me reiterate here that I am not arguing that the extreme, violently authoritarian behaviour that erupted among the students was the result of any deliberate process of political socialization on the part of the party. What the party leadership had had in mind was the molding of a moralistic albeit somewhat authoritarian citizenry of a type we described in earlier chapters. But the model society Mao had in mind could not be willed from the top by a few social engineers. History took its own course of development. New social relationships and social tensions had developed, and ideology could be twisted to people's own self-interests. The antagonisms among the student population, and the rising tensions in the schools over this question of 'class', had been exacerbated by the students' worsening chances of either getting into a university or securing a job. Coming together, during these same years, with the students' increasingly frenetic efforts to be doctrinaire activists, the authoritarian 'social character' of this generation was becoming aggravated well beyond what the teachings and role-playing of the political socialization processes encouraged. In the Cultural Revolution, in a manner that apparently came as a bewildering surprise to party leaders, these extreme authoritarian traits surfaced in full force.[22]

AUTHORITARIANISM AND DESOCIALIZATION

We have seen in these pages how institutionalized role-playing and the tense question of class combined to influence a young person's attitudes towards authority and conformity. We have seen, too, how and why an authoritarian social character was formed among the generation of young people who were high school students in China during the 1960s. But in the chapter on the Cultural Revolution's aftermath, we saw also that the attitudes and belief systems of my fourteen interviewees had altered by the 1970s.

Erich Fromm, in his writings on the development and change of personality and social character, speaks to this point:

> The fact that certain character orientations, generally those adaptive to the child's environment, become dominant does not mean that the others simply disappear or are irretrievably lost by repression . . . When circumstances do change in a significant way, the child and even later the adult has the possibility of bringing forth orientations which have been latent, and which are more suited to meeting the new circumstances. This process of change is a complicated one. The initial character system will not disappear, but it will be partly replaced by, partly blended with, a new character structure which may not be radically different from the original one, but sufficiently so to create a very different set of motivating character traits . . . That the early adopted character structure seems to remain dominant in most people throughout their lives is due less to the fact that it is rigid and incapable of modification than to the mutually reinforcing relationship between character and environment.[23]

This is precisely the type of character change that occurred among my fourteen interviewees. We have seen that the young people's conformity to authoritarian traits had been sustained only under particular circumstances. Once these conditions were relaxed, different sets of individual proclivities superseded those that had been encouraged and held in place by the school milieu. It is possible that certain behavioural dispositions which we have linked to the 'authoritarian personality' would have lain dormant had they not been activated. In circumstances where they no longer were reinforced by social environment and political belief, these tended to fade. In examining China under Mao, we have seen 'desocialization' as well as socialization.

NEWER GENERATIONS

In this study we have looked at the childhood, adolescent and adult experiences of several people, but all from a single generation. This first post-Liberation generation is now in its thirties. From all evidence, including the recent published reports from China, it seems still to be a troubled generation.

A yet younger generation has still to be socialized. And with this younger generation, the authorities are now employing some of the same methods they had used with that earlier generation. In 1977 a new campaign to 'Learn from Comrade Lei Feng' was launched with much fanfare.[24] As of the mid-1980s, the model hero is still the party's 'docile tool'. The gap between rhetoric and reality and between ideals and interests is to be bridged once again through unswerving faith in the party and activist conformity.

Yet this younger generation, almost all of whom had not even entered primary school until after the Cultural Revolution had subsided in 1969, is markedly different from the generation we have studied. The Cultural Revolution had decisively marked off the first generation from succeeding ones. To many of my interviewees, the several years they spent as teenagers in the turmoil of the Cultural Revolution had represented a watershed in their lives. From youths who throughout their childhoods and early teenage years had known only a single 'truth', they were suddenly confronted with the realities of a complex conflict-riven polity. Those convulsive years shook them out of teenage dreams of activist idealism. The side-effects and ripples of these same tumultuous years caught up with the second generation while still young children, and they do not seem to share the first teenage generation's innocent idealism. Off-hand comments from my interviewees about their younger siblings and their nephews and nieces alert us to the limits to which we can generalize. Interviewees often marvel with nostalgia at the good old days of '*our* revolutionary passion', with a certain scorn towards their younger relatives. They talk despairingly about the younger generation's lack of revolutionary consciousness, of their overwhelming concern for personal career, of their attachment to materialism, of their disrespect for teachers.

What we have examined here, in short, is the tale of only a single generation, unlike those that come before or after. Our discussion has belonged to a period of modern China's history that undoubtedly cannot be resurrected. The particular climate that encouraged the development of the authoritarian 'social character' no longer prevails. The 1980s are not the 1960s; and the children of Deng are not the children of Mao.

Notes and References

CHAPTER 1

1. Political socialization means the internalization by individuals of the particular system of political values that is imparted by their polity.
2. I have had access, too, to Stanley Rosen's and Jonathan Unger's transcripts of interviews with another four dozen young people from the Red Guard generation. I am indebted to Professors Rosen and Unger for sharing their materials with me.
3. *Selected Works of Mao Tse-tung*, vol. 1 (Peking: Foreign Language Press, 1965) p. 16.

CHAPTER 2

1. John Emerson, *Administrative and Technical Manpower in the People's Republic of China*, International Population Report no. 72 (Washington, DC: US Department of Commerce, 1973) p. 95.
2. Much of the argumentation had been borrowed wholesale from the Soviet Union. Especially in the early 1950s, almost all theoretical articles on psychology and pedagogy contained long passages of translations and frequent citations from Russian sources.
3. Zhang Tengxiao, 'Critique of "Understanding Children is an Important Condition for Becoming a Good Teacher" ', *People's Education*, vol. 1, no. 1 (1950) 53–6; Wu Yanyin, 'Discussions on the Characteristics of Traditional Primary Education', *People's Education*, vol. 1, no. 3 (1950) 22–4; Mo Xin, *The Road to New Education* (*Xin Jiaoyu de Daolu*) (Peking: Everybody's Bookstore, 1949); Xu Han, *An Introduction to the Teaching of Disciplinary Education to Primary School Pupils* (*Xiaoxue Ertong Jilu Jiaoyu Jingyan Jieshao*) (Canton: Huanan People's Publishing Co., 1953).
4. Guo Lin, 'This is How We Cultivate Children's Creativity', *People's Education*, vol. 1, no. 2 (1950) 51–2.
5. The tracts argued against the notion that men are born with great differences in intelligence which remain unchanged throughout life. Chinese journals were pointing out that children in capitalist countries showed differences in intelligence simply because such societies were class societies. (On this see Donald J. Munro, *The Concept of Man in*

226

Contemporary China (Ann Arbor: University of Michigan Press, 1977);·
Psychology Textbook for Teachers Colleges, p. 89; and Zhang Tengxiao,
'Critique', pp. 53–6.)

6. E.g., Zhang Tengxiao, 'Where Lies the Reactionary Nature of Pragmatic Pedagogy?', *People's Education* (May 1955) 28; Zhang Jian, 'Criticize the Ridiculous Discussions on School Education in Dewey's Theory of Pragmatic Education', *People's Education* (July 1955) 23; Editorial, ' "Lively Education" and the New Democratic Education Are Basically Incompatible', *People's Education* (Feb 1953) 19; Wang Tie, 'Criticizing Dewey's Theory that Education Transcends Economics and Politics', *People's Education* (Aug 1955) 34–5.

7. Deweyism had been influential in China ever since Dewey's widely popular lecture tour of China in 1919–20, at a time when Chinese intellectuals had been hungry for new approaches to China's problems. Spearheaded by Western-educated disciples such as Hu Shi, Deweyite educational theory had dominated classes at the teacher-training colleges and the departments of education at universities during the three decades up to 1949. (See Barry Keenan, *The Dewey Experiment in China* (Cambridge: Harvard East Asian Monograph 81, 1977) pp. 1–51. Robert W. Clopton and Ou Tsuin-Chen, trans. and eds, *John Dewey's Lectures in China, 1919–1920* (Honolulu: University of Hawaii Press, 1972) pp. 1–28; Li Bingde, 'Cleanse the Influence of "Pragmatic Education" from Our Country's Educational Arena', *People's Education* (Feb 1956) 53–6; Chen Yousong, 'Examining the Reactionary Influence of Hu Shi in Education and its Influence on Myself', *People's Education* (Jan 1955) 32–5; Liu Songtao, 'Criticize the Reactionary Educational Thoughts of Hu Shi', *People's Education* (May 1955) 31–5.)

8. E.g. Zhang Jian, 'Criticize the Ridiculous Discussions'.

9. Dewey's principles had been a reaction against a rapidly industrializing American society at the beginning of this century, where a system of universal education was evolving that was not designed to encourage individual thinking. On Dewey's writings, see Oscar Handlin, *John Dewey's Challenge to Education* (New York: Harper & Row, 1959); George Dykhuizen, *The Life and Mind of John Dewey* (Southern Illinois University Press, 1973); and Arthur G. Wirth, *John Dewey as Educator: His Design for Work in Education, 1894–1904* (New York: John Wiley, 1966).

10. John Dewey, 'My Pedagogic Creed', in Martin S. Dworkin, *Dewey on Education: Selections with an Introduction and Notes* (New York: William Byrd Press, 1959) pp. 19–32. Also see John Dewey and Evelyn Dewey, *Schools of Tomorrow* (New York: E. P. Dutton, 1915).

11. George Dykhuizen, *Life and Mind of Dewey*, pp. 235–9. On Dewey's own discussion of Soviet education see John Dewey, *Impressions of Soviet Russia and the Revolutionary World: Mexico – China – Turkey* (New York: New Republic Publisher, 1929).

12. John Dewey, 'My Pedagogic Creed', p. 28.

13. John Dewey, 'The School and Society', in Martin S. Dworkin, *Dewey on Education*, p. 40.

14. Dewey himself noticed the major difference on this point between his

own educational theory and that of the Soviet's. John Dewey, *Impressions of Soviet Russia and the Revolutionary World*, pp. 101–2.

15. Interviewees report having made match boxes and featherdusters, sorting out metal from industrial wastes, etc., when they were in primary school.

16. William Kessen (ed), *Childhood in China* (New Haven: Yale University Press, 1975) p. 32.

17. Liu Anzhi, 'Criticizing *New Primary School Art Education* and *New Art and New Art Education*', *People's Education* (March 1952) 50–1.

18. A delegation of American child psychologists to China in the mid-1970s was astonished to see the nearly bare walls of nurseries and primary schools. William Kessen, *Childhood in China*, p. 82.

19. Oscar Handlin, *John Dewey's Challenge to Education*, pp. 36–7. For a Chinese criticism of Dewey on this point, see Zhang Jian, 'Criticize the Ridiculous Discussions', p. 25.

20. So, too, do moral messages permeate Taiwanese and Hong Kong primers. For a selection of readings from pre-Cultural Revolution Chinese schools, see Charles Ridley, Paul Godwin and Dennis Doolin, *The Making of a Model Citizen in China* (Stanford: The Hoover Institute Press, 1971). See also the journal *Chinese Education* (White Plains, New York), Summer 1977, for a selection of primer readings from the mid-1970s.

21. This contradiction was pointed up in 1956 in a series of dissident articles that castigated official practices for strangling children's independent thinking abilities, creativity and personality development. Zhang Lingguang, 'A Discussion of the Educational Issues Concerning the Cultivation of Students' All-round Development', *People's Education* (Aug 1956) 48; plus several editorials in *People's Education*: 'What is the Central Point of the Debate?', *People's Education* (Sept 1956) 7–8; 'Abstract of Letters Concerning the Debate Over the Question of All-round Development', *People's Education* (Nov 1956) 19–22; and 'Teachers Speaking on the Internal Contradictions of Educational Work', *People's Education* (Jan 1957) 6–8. This debate occurred during the brief period in 1956 of 'blooming and contending' in academic circles. On this, see Maurice Meisner, *Mao's China* (New York: Free Press, 1977) pp. 167–203.

22. 'The Work Experience of Shanghai's Children's Palace', *People's Education* (June 1956) 52.

23. Ibid., pp. 48–50.

24. Ibid., p. 50.

25. 'Educated youth' is the Chinese phrase for urban young people who were sent to the countryside to settle as ordinary peasants.

26. Students at that time were divided by the teachers into study groups containing several children who were to sit together to do their homework.

27. In contrast, an interviewee who was reasonably good in his studies but who lacked Ao's ambitions and aggressive nature never possessed the willpower to drive himself into the limelight by outdoing others in activism. He recalls:

When reading about those models in the magazine *Young Pioneers* I'd feel very envious, but I also thought that to become like them was extremely, extremely difficult. I never tried my best. Perhaps my self-control was not strong enough . . . Some of them did not sleep for several days and nights in a row to finish doing some piece of work. I would feel great respect for them, but I myself couldn't be like that. I felt sort of sad . . . I never tried my best. I was thinking that these acts were only very small things, that I'd do something greater in future. Perhaps this was only for comforting myself.

28. Most urban elementary school teachers were female.
29. David Easton and Jack Dennis, 'The Child's Image of Government', in Edward S. Greenberg (ed), *Political Socialization* (New York: Atherton Press, 1970) p. 53. Also see Fred Greenstein, 'Children and Politics', in the same book, p. 57.
30. In this there exists a similarity between Bai's orphanage and the kibbutz primary school studied by Melford E. Spiro, *Children of the Kibbutz* (Cambridge, Mass: Harvard University Press, 1958) p. 263.
31. In the kibbutz, a somewhat similar situation exists. Though the children there carry their own family identification, it is the policy of the kibbutz to treat all children strictly as social equals. Again the kibbutz and orphanage were akin, and unlike the ordinary Chinese primary schools.
32. Cantonese neighbourhoods in the 1950s continued to bear strongly the social imprint of pre-Liberation residential patterns. So, too, did the primary and high school systems. Poor and overcrowded working-class neighbourhoods tended to have an undue share of the ill-equipped and poorly-staffed schools. For a detailed explanation of the geographical distribution of the different types of schools and neighbourhoods in Canton, see Stanley Rosen, *Red Guard Factionalism and the Cultural Revolution in Guangzhou (Canton)* (Boulder: Westview Press, 1982) pp. 60–6.

CHAPTER 3

1. These documents were collectively known as the 'Nine Criticisms', published between 1963 and 1964 and serialized by the Foreign Language Press in Peking as *Comment on the Open Letters of the Central Committee of the CPSU*.
2. *China Youth (Zhongguo Qingnian)*, no. 13 (July 1963) 2.
3. For details see Martin K. Whyte, *Small Groups and Political Rituals in China* (Berkeley: University of California Press, 1974) ch. 6.
4. The league branch, if big, would also be subdivided into discussion small groups.
5. Peasants classed as 'poor and lower middle peasants' were categorized as such during the time of Liberation, and the label has no connection with their present economic status.
6. This was not the case at the less reputable senior high schools, where

most of the students had despaired of ever getting accepted by a university. Here, there was little activist activity. In fact, most of the students at such high schools preferred to stay outside the Youth League, in the belief that membership would place them under heavier pressure to volunteer to settle in the countryside when they graduated.

7. For other analyses of model emulation see Mary Sheridan, 'The Emulation of Heroes', *China Quarterly*, no. 33 (Jan–March 1968) 47–72; and Donald Munro, *The Concept of Man in Contemporary China* (Ann Arbor: University of Michigan Press, 1977) ch. 6.

8. One good collection of stories about this kind of hero is *Stories of Young Heroes*, vol. 1 (in Chinese) (Peking: China Youth Press, 1964).

9. *Excerpts from Lei Feng's Diary* (in Chinese) (Peking: China Youth Press, 1964).

10. Ibid., pp. 46–7.

11. Ibid., pp. 16–17.

12. *Stories of Young Heroes*, vol. 2 (in Chinese) (Peking: China Youth Press, 1965) p. 24.

13. *Excerpts from Lei Feng's Diary*, p. 57.

14. Ibid., p. 77.

15. *Stories of Young Heroes*, vol. 2.

16. Ibid., p. 96.

17. See *Long Live the Thought of Mao Zedong*, 1969 (in Chinese), reprinted by the Institute of International Relations, Taiwan, pp. 500–4.

18. Self-cultivation, a traditional element of Confucian training, meant the remoulding and disciplining of one's character through daily introspection. This practice of self-analysis was supposed to help adolescents attain a disciplined 'consciousness' (*zijue*) of themselves. They were to push themselves to master their own emotions and spontaneous urges and to impose stringent demands upon themselves.

    Liu Shaoqi's book *How to be a Good Communist* (Peking: Foreign Language Press, 1951), which until the Cultural Revolution was regarded as the Communist Party members' handbook, referred explicitly several times to self-cultivation and tempering as traditional practices in Confucianism (pp. 18–19, 23). (On these links, also see David S. Nivison, 'Communist Ethics and Chinese Tradition', *Journal of Asian Studies*, vol. 16, no. 1 (Nov 1956).) In Liu Shaoqi's book, of which 12 million copies had been distributed to party members, the purposes and methods of self-cultivation and tempering were dealt with in great detail. Though the book was criticized vehemently in official publications during the Cultural Revolution, these criticisms derived from the fact that Liu Shaoqi himself was under attack; the criticisms did not seek to invalidate or negate the core of Liu Shaoqi's premises, which were in line with the party's *continued* conceptualization of self-cultivation. (For a lengthy official criticism of Liu's book, see *People's Daily*, 21 July 1971.)

19. That year 11 000 youths from Canton went to the countryside, of whom 1000 were high school graduates. The other 10 000 were unemployed young people from the city, known generally as 'social youths'. Radio

Canton, 19 Nov 1964, in *News from Chinese Provincial Stations* (British government).

20. In the practice of tempering, the young people were supposed to place themselves deliberately in situations where they would have to pit themselves against physical difficulties in order to forge a greater willpower, perseverance and self-control. They were to 'test' themselves: to exert their physical capabilities to the utmost so as to steel their spiritual fortitude. China's leaders repeatedly propounded upon the benefits of such tempering. They themselves had achieved the revolution in this manner; the Long March was perceived as a symbol of the miraculous results that could be gained from surmounting extremely arduous difficulties. Tempering was to have a similar toughening and purifying effect on the new generation. Activists were to view the harshest physical aspects of settlement in the countryside in a positive light: as an opportunity to improve themselves through tempering.

21. If it had not been for her mistake, her chances of going to senior high school were high: because (1) her academic work, though not extraordinary, was above average; (2) her class background, though not red, was not bad; (3) she was a league member.

22. See Ezra Vogel, 'Preserving Order in the Cities', in John Wilson Lewis (ed), *The City in Communist China* (Palo Alto: Stanford University Press, 1971) p. 79.

23. Lei Feng, too, had been criticized for being subjective, as he noted in his diary. *Excerpts from Lei Feng's Diary*, p. 50.

24. Later, as the Mao cult built up, scribbling comments that marred the pages of Mao's works was considered disrespectful to the great leader. Illustrating the seriousness of this, Bai has described the anxiety he felt when he could not retrieve a marked-up volume of Mao's *Selected Works* which he had lent out casually to someone.

25. *Long Live Mao Tse-tung's Thought*, pp. 526–31, 548–61, 567–72, 624–9.

26. *The Youthful Revolutionary Activities of Comrade Mao Zedong* (Peking: China Youth Press, 1957) pp. 25–44. Note the use of 'comrade' in the book title, a more familiar and egalitarian form of address than 'Chairman' or 'Great leader', in the days before the Mao cult was launched.

27. On this campaign, see Chan, Madsen and Unger, *Chen Village*, chs 2 and 3.

28. Liu Shaoqi, 'How to be a Good Communist', in *Collected Works of Liu Shao-chi: Before 1944* (Hong Kong: Union Research Institute, 1969) pp. 250–3.

29. When they entered the university all 30 students in the class passed stringent medical examinations. In their second year, the school took stock and uncovered four cases of liver problems, seven cases of tuberculosis, ten to twenty cases of stomach ailments and a dozen cases of nervous exhaustion. The school moreover had to prescribe spectacles for half the class.

30. The 'Four Cleanups' referred to the cleaning up of accounts, granaries, properties and workpoints. For an analysis of the campaign, see Rich-

ard Baum and Frederick Teiwes, *Ssu-Ching: The Socialist Education Movement of 1962–66* (Berkeley: Center for Chinese Studies, University of California, 1968); and Chan, Madsen and Unger, *Chen Village*, chs 2 and 3. The description given by Bai of the way the campaign was carried out in his workteam is in accord with the analyses of both books.

31. *Long Live the Thought of Mao Zedong*, p. 549.
32. Chan, Madsen and Unger, *Chen Village*, ch. 2.
33. *Selected Works of Mao Tse-tung*, vol. 1 (1965) pp. 23–62.
34. This kind of arbitrary cruel treatment was more frequently found in the lower-level 'dictatorship organs'. The kind of detention station for vagrants Bai described was called a *shourongsuo*. In this case, many of the guards were once tramps themselves, who had stayed and been offered this work.
35. Kenneth Keniston, *Young Radicals – Notes on Committed Youths* (New York: Harvest Books, 1968) p. 78.
36. Ibid., pp. 78–81.
37. Li Rui, *The Youthful Revolutionary Activities of Comrade Mao Zedong* (in Chinese) (Peking: China Youth Press, 1957) pp. 33–6.
38. 'Research in Physical Exercises' (written in 1917 and carried in *New Youth*, 3rd vol., no. 2) in *Mao Zedong's Works* (in Chinese), vol. 1 (Tokyo) pp. 131–47.
39. Kenneth Keniston, *Young Radicals*, p. 84.
40. In the 1957 Anti-rightist Campaign, many intellectuals who had been encouraged by the authorities to criticize the party by speaking up in the Hundred Flowers Campaign were branded rightists for having done so. Though rightists were classed as of 'the people', they were also one of the five-bad elements and were socially ostracized as if they were 'class enemies'. In China 'class enemies', even if they were not imprisoned, were looked upon as dangerous, deserving the 'surveillance of the masses'. This former headmistress appears to have been in that situation.
41. It was not accidental that the very first Red Guard group was formed by high-level cadre children at the most elitist high school in Peking. It was from this high school that the Red Guard movement spread to other parts of the city and country. See William Hinton, *Hundred Day War: The Cultural Revolution in Tsinghua University* (New York: Monthly Review Press, 1972) p. 63.
42. For a good description of the bad-class students see David Raddock, *Political Behavior of Adolescents in China – The Cultural Revolution in Kwangchow* (Tucson: University of Arizona Press, 1977).

CHAPTER 4

1. In Chinese myths, 'cow ghosts and snake demons' connote hideously inhuman creatures of diabolical power.
2. In schools where there were large numbers of high-level cadres' children, these students were the first to rebel. Probably they got wind through their parents' social circle that rebelling was encouraged by Mao himself, with no risk involved.

3. It is interesting to note that the same chaotic situation resulting from a profusion of personal grievances occurred in Peking University as well, as recorded by a French student who was studying there at that time: 'Many of the students at first seemed to lack a theoretical basis for their attacks on Lu P'ing [Party Committee Secretary of the university], and they acted largely in the context of their somewhat mechanical "official lives". But in the days that followed a change began to occur. Their "official" political lives gradually began to become integrated with their private lives as, lacking theoretical notions, they found they had to talk in very personal terms about their lives under the old administration. Students described their feelings of oppression and intimidation. Some of the girls' speeches were like "Greek tragedies": swept up by their emotions, crying and tearing out their hair, they related how miserable they had been.' In Victor Nee, *The Cultural Revolution at Peking University* (New York: Monthly Review Press, 1969) p. 60.

4. Age and bad-class background tended to coincide. Older teachers had received a pre-Liberation education and therefore were deemed more bourgeois. They also tended personally to come from less acceptable class backgrounds than younger teachers. Moreover, a large number of older teachers had 'historical' problems, having joined Guomindang (KMT) mass organizations in their youth.

5. Struggle meetings in China were more serious than criticism meetings. In the latter, the target was merely denounced publicly. In struggle meetings, the target was screamed at from the floor in unison, even spat on and beaten.

6. *Long Live the Thought of Mao Zedong*, pp. 643–50.

7. 'Decision of the Party Central Committee Concerning the Great Proletarian Cultural Revolution' (adopted on 8 August 1966), in *Current Background*, no. 852 (6 May 1968) 9–15.

8. Jonathan Unger, *Education Under Mao* (New York: Columbia University Press, 1982) chs 7 and 10.

9. Max Weber, *Economy and Society: An Outline of Interpretative Sociology*, ed. by Guenther Roth and Claus Wittich (Berkeley: University of California Press, 1978) pp. 248–54.

10. *Current Background*, no. 852, p. 55. Mao personally referred to the problem in *Long Live the Thought of Mao Zedong*, p. 664.

11. 'Origin Theory', *High School Revolutionary News*, 2 Feb 1967, p. 3; translated in Gordon White, *Class and Class Origin*, pp. 71–93. Within a few months, nearly one million copies of the article were reproduced by students and circulated. The author of it was executed in 1970 for opposing some of the radical leaders who came to power in the Cultural Revolution. For details see *Guang Ming Ribao*, 21 July 1980, p. 1 and a report by the author's sister, Yu Luojin, 'A Fairy Tale in Winter', *Dang Dai*, no. 3 (Sept 1980) 58–107.

12. Gordon White, *Class and Class Origin*, pp. 45–6.

13. See Stanley Rosen, 'Comments on "Radical Students in Kwangtung during the Cultural Revolution" ', *China Quarterly*, no. 70 (June 1977) 395–6.

14. Hong Yung Lee, *The Politics of the Chinese Cultural Revolution*

(Berkeley: University of California Press, 1978) pp. 312–22. Also Hong Yung Lee, *China Quarterly*, no. 64 (Dec 1975) 645–55. Also see his reply to Stanley Rosen's comments in *China Quarterly*, no. 70 (June 1977) 399–406.

15. A case in point is that in the spring of 1967 after the chaotic 'Seize Power', Mao ordered the army to move into the schools to 'support the left' and directed that 'when genuine proletarian leftists ask the army for help, the army should send out troops to support them positively' (*Current Background*, no. 852, p. 49). But which group was the 'genuine left'? It was not specified. Both sides could solicit support from the army. In Canton the army ended up supporting the Loyalists and suppressing the Rebels. It was not until April 1967 that the army was criticized by the Central Committee for being too harsh on the 'masses'. This incident suggests the vague and inconsistent nature of the central directives. 'Order of the Military Commission of the CCP Central Committee', *Current Background*, no. 852, pp. 115–16.

16. For example, in August 1967 Jiang Qing suggested an 'attack on a handful (of erroneous power-holders) in the army'. After the Rebels accordingly robbed arsenals and attacked conservative 'power-holders' in the army, it was the army which was sent into schools to supervise the formation of the Big Alliance, forcing the two opposing factions to compromise. Similarly, several members of the Central Committee Cultural Revolution Small Group were dismissed as 'ultra-leftist' at the end of 1967. Under such circumstances Rebel Red Guards found it increasingly difficult to follow closely the centre's instructions, since the leadership of the Cultural Revolution was itself fraught with disagreements.

17. Milovan Djilas was unknown to the young people, but their critique implied a recognition of a 'new class' in socialism as defined by Djilas: 'The new class may be said to be made up of those who have special privileges and economic preference because of the administrative monopoly they hold'. Milovan Djilas, *The New Class* (New York: Praeger, 1957) p. 39.

18. This article is generally referred to as the Sheng-wu-lian article. Sheng-wu-lien is short for Hunan Province Proletarian Revolutionary Great Alliance Committee. A translation of the article is found in Klaus Mehnert, *Peking and the New Left: at Home and Abroad*, China Research Monograph No. 4 (Berkeley: Center of Chinese Studies, 1969).

19. 'Chairman Mao Discusses Twenty Manifestations of Bureaucracy' (date unknown), *Translations on Communist China*, no. 90 (*JPRS*, 49826, 12 Feb 1970) pp. 40–3.

20. *Miscellany of Mao Tse-tung's Thought* (1949–68), Part 1, *JPRS*, 61269, 20 Feb 1974, pp. 451–5. There is nothing on record of what Mao had said on this issue in his own words. His opinion was related publicly by Zhang Chunqiao.

21. 'Order of the Military Commission of the Party Central Committee' (6 April 1967), in *Current Background*, no. 852 (6 May 1968) pp. 115–16.

22. 'Party Central Committee Opinion on the Great Proletarian Cultural

Revolution in Middle Schools' (19 Feb 1967), *Current Background*, no. 852 (6 May 1968) pp. 87–8.

23. *Long Live the Thought of Mao Zedong*, p. 681.

24. The 'centre' was the short form used for the Central Committee of the Chinese Communist Party. Throughout the Cultural Revolution Mao succeeded in maintaining his control over it. All Central Committee directives coming down at that time were equated with Mao's orders.

25. 'A Summary of the Proceedings of the 13th Plenum of the Peking Municipal Revolutionary Committee' outlined the course the campaign was to take; in *SCMP*, no. 4225 (25 July 1968) pp. 11–14. See also Anita Chan, Richard Madsen and Jonathan Unger, *Chen Village*, ch. 5.

26. To acquire a feeling of this period read Hinton, *Hundred Day War*, ch. 22.

27. Statistics showing this are contained in Anita Chan, Stanley Rosen and Jonathan Unger, 'Students and Class Warfare: the Social Roots of the Red Guard Movement in Canton', *China Quarterly*, no. 83 (Sept 1980) 445.

28. His parents, like so many cadres, had got into trouble and were sent to a May 7 cadre school.

29. As Chang notes, here and there in other schools one found similar strong and rebellious characters. One of the top national Red Guard leaders, Kuai Dafu of Qinghua University, began his leadership role in the Cultural Revolution by similarly opposing a workteam. (See William Hinton, *Hundred Day War*, pp. 43–68.)

30. The contents of the political system that were rejected by the radical American student leaders and by Chang were of course very different. The parallel lies in the commitment to effect social change and the search for an alternative and better world. K. Keniston, *Young Radicals*, pp. 287–90.

31. See, for instance, 'Suppress Rightist Thinking, Continue to Launch Attacks on the Class Enemies, Freely Mobilize the Masses, Carry on this Great Proletarian Cultural Revolution to the Very End', *People's Daily*, 16 April 1968, and 'Factionalism Should be Given a Class Analysis', *People's Daily*, 27 April 1968.

32. Interviews by Jonathan Unger relating to three universities – two in Peking, another in Yunnan – similarly indicated that the issue was absent on campuses. In a classroom at Canton's Jinan University examined by Unger, the students did divide largely along class lines, but this was not an ordinary university. Jinan University was financed by overseas Chinese, and much of the student body was of overseas origins. They had chafed at the bad-class status they had been saddled with, and rose up against the school's activists of better class backgrounds.

33. In this, Bai's own particular experiences support Mao's interpretation of the factionalism.

34. It should be noted that, when made up of high-level cadres' children, this kind of 'minority group', as it came to be called, was not in essence similar to the 'minority groups' set up by Chang and Deng. The latter were taking a rebellious stand at great risk, whereas high-level cadres' children rebelled with the knowledge that rebelling was to be *the* trend

and that their parents could protect them if their predictions turned out wrong.

35. This was probably the incident referred to by Xie Fuzhi, Chairman of the Peking Municipal Revolutionary Committee, in a speech laying out the guidelines for the 1968 Cleansing of Class Ranks campaign. See 'Summary of the Proceedings of the 13th Plenum of the Peking Municipal Revolutionary Committee', *Wenge Tongxun* (Cultural Revolution Bulletin), no. 16 (July 1968) translated in *SCMP*, no. 4225 (25 July 1968) 12–13.

36. Jonathan Unger's interviews on two universities in Peking and Yunnan also indicate such a tendency.

37. These interviews were conducted as part of a collaborative research project on this particular village. See Anita Chan, Richard Madsen and Jonathan Unger, *Chen Village*. In all, twenty-six former residents of the village were interviewed.

38. The formation of this Red Guard group, composed mainly of poor and lower-middle peasant youths, was in accordance with a Central Committee directive: 'Circular of the Central Committee on the Great Proletarian Cultural Revolution in Rural Districts', 15 Dec 1966; in *Current Background*, no. 852 (May 1968) 31. Also see Chan, Madsen and Unger, *Chen Village*, ch. 4.

39. On this campaign, see Chan, Madsen and Unger, ibid., chs 5 and 6.

40. Nationwide, the campaign became so extreme, and the targets of attack widened to include so many people, that the excesses had to be repudiated at the end of the campaign by the central government, which was apparently afraid too many new 'bad elements' would be created. The Party Central Committee ordered that the 'black materials' that had been collected on the campaign's victims be publicly burned.

41. In the concluding chapter, I shall examine in detail how these elements came together with the teenagers' emotional needs to shape the 'authoritarian social character' of that generation.

CHAPTER 5

1. For discussions of the problems of the sent-down youth policy before and after the Cultural Revolution, see Gordon White, 'The Politics of Hsia-hsiang Youth', *China Quarterly*, no. 59 (July 1974) 491–517; Thomas Bernstein, 'Urban Youth in the Countryside: Problems of Adaptation and Remedies', *China Quarterly*, no. 69 (March 1977) 75–108; and Jonathan Unger, 'China's Troubled Down-to-the-Countryside Campaign', *Contemporary China*, vol. III, no. 2 (Summer 1979) 72–92.

2. See Jonathan Unger, *Education Under Mao* (New York: Columbia University Press, 1982) chs 7, 8, 9 and 10. The new recruitment policy specified that the applicants should be recommended by their work units. Since academic qualifications counted for little, this practice opened the door to the use of influence by parents who had power.

3. The recitations were similar to the pre-dinner grace of the Christian

tradition. A standard recitation went like this: 'We respectfully wish a long life to the reddest, reddest red sun in our hearts, the great leader Chairman Mao. And to Vice-Chairman Lin's health: may he forever be healthy. Having been liberated by the land reform we will never forget the Communist Party, and in revolution we will forever follow Chairman Mao.'

4. For a better understanding of the former Cantonese Rebel Red Guard's critique of the policies of the 1970s and their antipathy to the Shanghai radicals (the Gang of Four), readers should refer to the Li Yizhe manifesto, titled 'On Socialist Democracy and the Legal System'. This was widely circulated in Canton in 1974. For a translation of the manifesto and my introduction to it, see *Chinese Law and Government*, vol. x, no. 3 (Autumn 1977).

5. Some former Rebels did temporarily revive their activities in 1974 during the Criticize Lin Biao/Criticize Confucius campaign. They were secretly encouraged by the Guangdong provincial leadership, which belonged to the 'moderate' faction, to launch written attacks against the 'Shanghai faction' (the Gang of Four) in the guise of attacking Lin Biao. Details of these intricate political manoeuvrings are vividly described in a serialized article, 'Li Yizhe and I' (in Chinese), *Bei Dou* (Hong Kong), in the June, July, August, September, November and December 1977 issues.

6. The number of people from China entering Hong Kong illegally each year between 1970 and 1974 is estimated by the Hong Kong government to have risen from 7000 in 1970 to 12 000 in 1971, 20 000 in 1972, 25 000 in 1973 and 30 000 by the end of 1974 (Director of Immigration, *Hong Kong Annual Departmental Report*, 1969 to 1975).

7. Ted Tapper, *Political Education and Stability: Elite Responses to Political Conflict* (London: John Wiley, 1976) p. 35.

8. Barrie Stacey, *Political Socialization in Western Society: An Analysis from a Life-span Perspective* (London: Edward Arnold, 1978) pp. 70–4.

9. Ted Tapper, *Political Education*, p. 23.

10. Ibid., p. 65.

11. The term is used by Ted Tapper, ibid., p. 35.

12. The term 'desocialization experience' is used in David C. Schwartz and Sandra Kenyon Schwartz, 'New Directions in Political Socialization', in Schwartz and Schwartz (eds), *New Directions in Political Socialization* (New York: Free Press, 1975) p. 16.

13. See, e.g. Kazuko Tsurumi, *Social Change and the Individual – Japan Before and After Defeat in World War II* (New Jersey: Princeton University Press, 1970).

14. Tapper also points out how a belief in the legitimacy of a system, once lost, will lead to instability. Tapper, *Political Education*, p. 34.

CHAPTER 6

1. Erich Fromm, *The Fear of Freedom* (London: Kegan Paul, 1942) p. 141.
2. See, e.g. Fred I. Greenstein, 'Personality and Political Socialization:

The Theories of Authoritarian and Democratic Character', *The Annals of the American Academy of Political and Social Sciences*, vol. 360 (Sept 1965) 81–95. One major reason that political scientists have given particular attention to theories of the 'authoritarian personality' is that central to both politics and the 'authoritarian personality' is the notion of power relations, particularly between ruler and ruled.

3. Erich Fromm, *The Fear of Freedom*; Wilhelm Reich, *The Mass Psychology of Fascism*, 3rd edn (New York: Orgone Institute Press, 1946). Reich's theory that the authoritarian personality owes its origin to sexual repression by the family and the state unfortunately comes close to relegating an otherwise stimulating study to the level of crude psychologism.

4. T. W. Adorno, Else Frenkel-Brunswik, Daniel J. Levinson, R. Nevitt Sanford *et al.*, *The Authoritarian Personality* (New York: W. W. Norton, 1969 edn). This book was first published in 1950. For the ideas of the Frankfurt School and Adorno see Russell Jacoby, 'Toward a Critique of Automatic Marxism: The Politics of Philosophy from Lukacs to the Frankfurt School', *Telos*, no. 10 (1971) 119–46; Paul Piccone, 'From Tragedy to Farce: The Return to Critical Theory', *New German Critique*, no. 7 (Winter 1976) 91–104; T. W. Adorno, 'Society', in Robert Boyers (ed), *The Legacy of German Intellectuals* (New York: Schocken Books, 1972) pp. 144–53; and Martin Jay, *The Dialectical Imagination* (Boston: Little, Brown, 1973).

5. It was based on this assumption that the Berkeley project was carried out in the United States and not in postwar Germany, even though a major purpose of the project was to attain a deeper understanding of anti-Semitism and the psychological makeup of Nazism.

6. Adorno's statistical 'F scale' of fascist personality traits suggested, for instance, that people who are aggressive towards inferiors tend to be submissive to superiors, just as Fromm had postulated. However, as yet there is no consensus on the validity of the F scale as an absolute statistical measure of authoritarianism. Indeed Adorno himself, coming from a non-empiricist German sociological tradition, has downplayed the statistical significance of his book and thinks the book's contribution is 'above all in posing the issues, which were motivated by a genuine social concern'. (T. Adorno, 'Scientific Experiences of a European Scholar in America', in Donald Fleming and Bernard Bailyn (eds), *The Intellectual Migration: Europe and America, 1930–1960* (Cambridge, Mass: Harvard University Press, 1969) p. 361.)

7. Erich Fromm, *The Sane Society* (New York: Holt, Rinehart & Winston, 1955) pp. 78–9. Though the Berkeley project was interested in identifying isolated cases of latent authoritarianism in a society which was not at that time promoting an authoritarian 'social character', the study was in agreement with Fromm's thesis in its concluding remarks: 'people are continuously molded from above because they must be molded if the over-all economic pattern is to be maintained' (p. 976).

8. Erich Fromm and Michael Maccoby, *Social Character in a Mexican Village* (New Jersey: Prentice-Hall, 1970) p. 16.

9. For the German authoritarian personality, refer to Zevedi Barbu, *Democracy and Dictatorship* (London: Routledge, 1956); Wilhelm Reich, *Mass Psychology of Facism*; Erich Fromm, *Fear of Freedom*. For an analysis of the prewar Japanese personality see Kazuko Tsurumi, *Social Change and the Individual – Japan Before and After Defeat in World War II* (New Jersey: Princeton University Press, 1970); Douglas C. Haring, 'Japanese National Character: Cultural Anthropology, Psychoanalysis, and History', in Douglas G. Haring (ed), *Personal Character and Cultural Milieu* (Syracuse University Press, 1956) pp. 424–37; and Weston La Barre, 'Some Observations on Character Structure in the Orient: the Japanese', in Bernard S. Silberman (ed), *Japanese Character and Culture* (Tucson: University of Arizona Press, 1962) pp. 325–69; Agnes M. Niyekawa, 'Factors Associated with Authoritarianism in Japan', PhD Dissertation (New York University, 1960). For an analysis of the Soviet personality see Margaret Mead, *Soviet Attitudes Towards Authority* (New York: McGraw-Hill, 1951); Zevedi Barbu, *Democracy and Dictatorship*; and Nikolai K. Novak-Deker (ed), *Soviet Youth: Twelve Komsomol Histories* (Munich: Institute for the Study of the USSR, Series I, no. 51, July 1959). These studies of Soviet political socialization practices and of the nature of the Soviet orientation towards authority provide an idea of how similar the Chinese and Soviet systems used to be in this particular respect. However, from the autobiographies written by the twelve Komsomols of the first generation educated after the October Revolution, one gets the impression that in the 1920s and 1930s the demands on young people to become 'new socialist men' were less intense than in China during the two decades after Liberation.

10. Numerous studies on the authoritarian personality have tried to measure the differential presence of authoritarian traits among the members of different social and political groups. See John Kirscht and Ronald Dillehay, *Dimensions of Authoritarianism: A Review of Research and Theory* (Lexington: University of Kentucky, 1967) pp. 95–126. As an example of this kind of study, also see Leonard Weller, Samuel Levinbok, Rina Maimon and Shaham Asher, 'Religiosity and Authoritarianism', *Journal of Social Psychology*, no. 75 (1975) 11–18.

11. Precisely because of this presumption as to the universality of the authoritarian personality, the Berkeley project took as its task the development of a means to diagnose potential authoritarians so as 'to prevent or reduce the virulence of the next outbreak' of Nazism (T. W. Adorno, *The Authoritarian Personality*, p. v). Wilhelm Reich, however, had a more pessimistic view of human nature: 'Fascism is only the politically organized expression of the average human character structure, a character structure which has nothing to do with this or that race, nation or party but which is general and international' (Reich, *Mass Psychology of Facism*, p. ix).

12. Lucian Pye, *The Spirit of Chinese Politics* (Cambridge, Mass: MIT Press, 1968); Richard Solomon, 'Mao's Efforts to Reintegrate the Chinese Social Process', in A. Doak Barnett (ed), *Chinese Communist*

Politics in Action (Seattle: University of Washington Press, 1969) pp. 271–364; and Richard Solomon, *Mao's Revolution and the Chinese Political Culture* (Berkeley: University of California Press, 1972).

13. The attacks against Solomon were from three angles: he was charged with misinterpreting traditional Chinese thought (F.W. Mote, 'China's Past in the Study of China Today – Some Comments on the Recent Works of Richard Solomon', *Journal of Asian Studies*, vol. XXXII, no. 1 (Nov 1972) 107–20); he was criticized for transforming Freudian psychoanalytic technique into an unconvincing 'diapertology' (Chen Pi-chao, 'In Search of Chinese National Character Via Child-training', *World Politics*, vol. XXV, no. 4 (July 1973) 608–635); and he was accused of adopting an ethnocentric Western vantage point that adjudged differences in Chinese culture as pathological (Richard Kagan and Norma Diamond, 'Father, Son and the Holy Ghost: Pye, Solomon and the "Spirit of Chinese Politics" ', *Bulletin of Concerned Asian Scholars*, vol. V, no. 1 (July 1973) 62–8).

14. See Leo Bramson, *The Political Context of Sociology* (Princeton University Press, 1961) pp. 136–7; the Frankfurt Institute of Social Research, *Aspects of Sociology* (Boston: Beacon Press, 1972) pp. 129–45.

15. Zevedi Barbu, *Democracy and Dictatorship*, p. 254.

16. David Riesman, *The Lonely Crowd: A Study of the Changing American Character* (New York: Anchor Books, 1953).

17. It should be noted here that studies of the effects of social change on social character, especially in societies experiencing extreme social change, suggest that the parents themselves often smooth the way by adopting and transmitting new values and behavioural norms. Parents of my interviewees' generation were aware that their children would have to inhabit a new world, and they had adjusted their own teachings to fit those of the agents of state socialization. On the more general case, with illustrations taken from Russia, see Alex Inkeles, 'Social Change and Social Character: The Role of Parental Mediation', in Amitai Etzioni and Eva Etzioni (eds), *Social Change: Sources, Patterns and Consequences* (New York: Basic Books, 1964) pp. 343–53. See also Martin K. Whyte, 'Child Socialization in the Soviet Union and China', *Studies in Comparative Communism*, vol. X, no. 3 (Autumn 1977) 235–59 and David Raddock, *Political Behavior of Adolescents in China – The Cultural Revolution in Kwangchow* (Tucson: University of Arizona Press, 1977) pp. 174–203. The Chinese urban family's remaining influence on its children lay not so much in formal ideology but rather in underlying values: for instance, children of the former middle-class intelligentsia inherited their parents' achievement orientation and patriotism. But these values, notably, were not at odds with the state's own teachings. In the 1950s, following China's prolonged nationalistic struggle against foreign domination, both agents of socialization, the state and family, were transmitting these same two messages. The result was that the effects of each agent were compounded on the other.

18. Ted Tapper, *Political Education and Stability: Elite Responses to Political Conflict* (London: John Wiley, 1976), ch. 3.

19. The members of the 'wandering faction', who preferred to stay at home

rather than be carried away by the tide, may have been low scorers on an authoritarian scale, but further research would be needed to affirm this.

20. T. B. Bottomore, *Classes in Modern Society* (London: Allen & Unwin, 1965) p. 47.

21. Jonathan Unger, 'The Class System in Rural China: A Case Study', in James Watson (ed), *Class and Social Stratification in Post-Revolution China* (Cambridge University Press, 1984).

22. Mao Zedong admitted, in a Cultural Revolution speech of 24 October 1966, that 'Nobody had thought, and I had not expected, that a single big-character poster, a Red Guard and one big exchange of revolutionary experiences would create such turmoil in various provinces and cities'. *The Thought of Mao Zedong*, translated in *Joint Publications Research Service* (US Govt.), no. 49826 (12 Feb 1970) p. 9.

23. Erich Fromm and Michael Maccoby, *Social Character in a Mexican Village*, p. 22.

24. See 'Learn from Comrade Lei Feng', *Peking Review*, vol. 20, no. 11 (11 March 1977) 3–4.

Select Bibliography

ENGLISH-LANGUAGE SOURCES

Adorno, T. W., 'Scientific Experiences of a European Scholar in America', in *The Intellectual Migration: Europe and America, 1930–1960*, ed. Donald Fleming and Bernard Bailyn (Cambridge, Mass: Belknap Press of Harvard University, 1969).

——— , 'Society', in *The Legacy of German Intellectuals*, ed. Robert Boyers (New York: Shocken Books, 1972) pp. 144–53.

Adorno, T. W., Else Frenkel-Brunswik, Daniel J. Levinson and R. Nevitt Sanford *et al.*, *The Authoritarian Personality*, 1969 edn (New York: W. W. Norton, 1950).

Barbu, Zevedi, *Democracy and Dictatorship* (London: Routledge, 1956).

Bauer, Raymond, *The New Man in Soviet Psychology* (Cambridge, Mass: Harvard University Press, 1952).

Baum, Richard and Frederick Teiwes, *Ssu-Ching: The Socialist Education Movement of 1962–66*, China Research Monograph no. 2 (Berkeley: University of California Center of Chinese Studies, 1968).

Bennett, Gordon and Ronald Montaperto, *Red Guard: The Political Biography of Dai Hsiao-ai* (London: George Allen & Unwin, 1971).

Bernstein, Thomas, 'Urban Youth in the Countryside: Problems of Adaptation and Remedies', *China Quarterly*, no. 69 (March 1977) 75–108.

Bottomore, T. B., *Elites and Society* (Harmondsworth: Penguin Books, 1964).

——— , *Classes in Modern Society* (London: Allen & Unwin, 1965).

Bronfenbrenner, Urie, *Two Worlds of Childhood, US and USSR* (Harmondsworth: Penguin Books, 1970).

Cary, Charles D., 'The Goals of Citizenship Training in American and Soviet Schools', *Studies in Comparative Communism*, x, 3 (Autumn 1977) 281–97.

Chan, Anita, 'Chinese Dissidents Abroad', *Index on Censorship*, 9, 1 (Feb 1980) 32–4.

——— , 'Images of China's Social Structure: The Changing Perspectives of Canton Students', *World Politics*, xxxiv, 3 (April 1982) 295–323.

——— , Stanley Rosen and Jonathan Unger, 'Students and Class Warfare: the Social Roots of the Red Guard Conflict in Canton', *China Quarterly*, no. 83 (Sept 1980) 397–446.

——— , Richard Madsen and Jonathan Unger, *Chen Village: The Recent History of a Peasant Community in Mao's China* (Berkeley: University of California Press, 1984). [See the sections on Ao.]

Chen Pi-chao, 'In Search of Chinese National Character Via Child-training', *World Politics*, xxv, 4 (July 1973) 608–35.

Chin, Robert and Ai-Li S. Chin, *Psychological Research in Communist China, 1949–1966* (Cambridge, Mass: MIT Press, 1969).

Christie, Richard and Marie Jahoda (eds), *Studies in the Scope and Method of 'The Authoritarian Personality'* (Glencoe, Illinois: Free Press, 1954).

Clausen, John A., 'Recent Developments in Socialization Theory and Research', *The Annals of the American Academy of Political and Social Science*, vol. 377 (May 1968) 139–55.

Clopton, Robert W. and Tsuin-Chen Ou (trans. and ed), *John Dewey's Lectures in China, 1919–1920* (Honolulu: University of Hawaii Press, 1972).

Dawson, Richard E. and Kenneth Prewitt, *Political Socialization* (Boston: Little, Brown, 1969).

Dennis, Jack, *Political Socialization Research: A Bibliography* (Beverly Hills: Sage Publications, 1973).

Dennis, Jack and M. Kent Jennings (eds), *Comparative Political Socialization* (Beverly Hills: Sage Publications, 1970).

Dewey, John, *Impressions of Soviet Russia and the Revolutionary World: Mexico – China – Turkey* (New York: New Republic Publisher, 1929).

Dewey, John and Evelyn Dewey, *Schools of Tomorrow* (New York: E. P. Dutton, 1915).

Djilas, Milovan, *The New Class* (New York: Praeger, 1957).

Dreitzel, Hans Peter (ed), *Childhood and Socialization* (New York: Macmillan, 1973).

Dworkin, Martin S., *Dewey on Education: Selections with an Introduction and Notes* (New York: William Byrd Press, 1959).

Dykhuizen, George, *The Life and Mind of John Dewey* (Carbondale, Illinois: Southern Illinois University Press, 1973).

Easton, David and Jack Dennis, 'The Child's Image of Government', in *Political Socialization*, ed. Edward S. Greenberg (New York: Atherton Press, 1970).

Embree, John, *Suye Mura – A Japanese Village* (University of Chicago Press, 1939).

Fiszman, Joseph R., 'Child Socialization: Comments from a Polish Perspective', *Studies in Comparative Communism*, x, 3 (Autumn 1977) 260–80.

Frankfurt Institute of Social Research, *Aspects of Sociology* (Boston: Beacon Press, 1972).

Fromm, Erich, *The Fear of Freedom* (London: Kegan Paul, 1942).

———, *The Sane Society* (New York: Holt, Rinehart & Winston, 1955).

———, *The Crisis of Psychoanalysis* (Harmondsworth: Penguin, 1970).

——— and Michael Maccoby, *Social Character in a Mexican Village* (New Jersey: Prentice-Hall, 1970).

Greenstein, Fred I., 'The Benevolent Leader: Children's Images of Political Authority', *American Political Science Review*, 54, 4 (Dec 1960) 934–43.

———, 'Personality and Political Socialization: The Theories of Authoritarian and Democratic Character', *The Annals of the American Academy of Political and Social Sciences*, vol. 361 (Sept 1965) 81–95.

———, 'The Impact of Personality on Politics: An Attempt to Clear Away

Underbrush', *American Political Science Review*, LXI, 3 (Sept 1967) 629–41.

———, *Personality and Politics: Problems of Evidence, Inference, and Conceptualization* (Chicago: Markham Publishing Company, 1969).

———, 'A Note on the "Ambiguity of Political Socialization": Definitions, Criticisms and Strategies of Inquiry', *Journal of Politics*, no. 32 (1970) 969–78.

———, 'Children and Politics in Britain, France and the United States: Six Examples', *Youth and Society*, 2, 1 (Sept 1970) 111–28.

———, 'The Standing of Social and Psychological Variables: An Addendum to Jackman's Critique', *Journal of Politics*, no. 32 (1970) 989–92.

——— and others, 'Children's Conception of the Queen and Prime Minister', *British Journal of Political Science*, 4, 3 (July 1974) 257–87.

Gregor, A. James, 'On Understanding Fascism: A Review of Some Contemporary Literature', *American Political Science Review*, 67, 4 (Dec 1973) 1332–47.

Handlin, Oscar, *John Dewey's Challenge to Education* (New York: Harper & Row, 1959).

Haring, Douglas G., 'Japanese National Character: Cultural Anthropology, Psychoanalysis, and History', in *Personal Character and Cultural Milieu*, ed. Douglas G. Haring (Syracuse University Press, 1956).

Hinton, William, *Hundred Day War: The Cultural Revolution in Tsinghua University* (New York: Monthly Review Press, 1972).

Hyman, Herbert H., *Political Socialization: A Study in the Psychology of Political Behaviour* (Glencoe, Ill: The Free Press, 1959).

Jacoby, Russell, 'Marxism and the Critical School', *Theory and Society*, vol. 1 (Summer 1974) 231–8.

———, *Social Amnesia: A Critique of Conformist Psychology from Adler to Laing* (Boston: Beacon Press, 1975).

Janis, Irving L., *Personality: Dynamics, Development, and Assessment* (New York: Harcourt, Brace, 1969).

Jay, Martin, *The Dialectical Imagination – A History of the Frankfurt School and the Institute of Social Research, 1923–1950* (Boston: Little, Brown, 1973).

Kagan, Richard and Norma Diamond, 'Father, Son and the Holy Ghost: Pye, Solomon and the "Spirit of Chinese Politics" ', *Bulletin of Concerned Asian Scholars*, 5, 1 (July 1973) 62–8.

Keenan, Barry, *The Dewey Experiment in China* (Cambridge, Mass: Harvard University Press, 1977).

Keniston, Kenneth, *Young Radicals – Notes on Committed Youths* (New York: Harvest Books, 1968).

Kessen, William (ed), *Childhood in China* (New Haven: Yale University Press, 1975).

Kirscht, John P. and Ronald C. Dillehay, *Dimensions of Authoritarianism: A Review of Research and Theory* (Lexington: University of Kentucky Press, 1967).

Krahl, Hans-Jurgen, 'The Political Contradictions in Adorno's Critical Theory', *Telos*, no. 21 (Fall 1974) 164–7.

Kraus, Richard, 'Class Conflict and the Vocabulary of Social Analysis in China', *China Quarterly*, no. 69 (March 1977) 54–74.

_____ , *Class Conflict in Chinese Socialism* (New York: Columbia University Press, 1981).

La Barre, Weston, 'Some Observations on Character Structure in the Orient: the Japanese', in *Japanese Character and Culture*, ed. Bernard S. Silberman (Tucson: University of Arizona Press, 1962).

Langton, Kenneth P., 'Peer Group and School and the Political Socialization Process', *American Political Science Review*, vol. LXI (Sept 1967) 751–8.

Lee, Hong Yung, 'The Radical Students in Kwangtung During The Cultural Revolution', *China Quarterly*, no. 64 (Dec 1975) 645–83.

_____ , *The Politics of the Chinese Cultural Revolution* (Berkeley: University of California Press, 1978).

Lee, Sarel, 'Subterranean Individualism: Contradictions of Politicization', *Telos*, no. 33 (Fall 1977) 5–25.

Li Yizhe, 'Socialist Democracy and the Legal System', trans. and ed. Anita Chan and Jonathan Unger in *Chinese Law and Government*, X, 3 (Autumn 1977).

Lipset, Seymour Martin, *Political Man: The Social Bases of Politics* (New York: Anchor Books, 1963).

Liu Shaoqi, 'How to Be a Good Communist', in *Collected Works of Liu Shao-ch'i: Before 1944* (Hong Kong: Union Research Institute, 1969); a different version, re-edited after Liberation, appears as *How to Be a Good Communist* (Peking: Foreign Language Press, 1951).

Livingston, Jon, Joe Moore and Felicia Oldfather (eds), *Imperial Japan, 1800–1945* (New York: Random House, 1973).

Mao Zedong, 'Analysis of the Classes in Chinese Society' (written in 1926), in *Selected Works of Mao Tse-tung*, vol. I (Peking: Foreign Language Press, 1965) pp. 13–21.

_____ , 'Report on an Investigation of the Peasant Movement in Hunan' (written in 1927), in *Selected Works of Mao Tse-tung*, vol. I (Peking: Foreign Language Press, 1965) pp. 23–39.

_____ , 'Friendship or Aggression' (written in 1949), in *Selected Works of Mao Tse-tung*, vol. 4 (Peking: Foreign Language Press, 1961) pp. 447–9.

Marcuse, Herbert, *Soviet Marxism: A Critical Analysis* (New York: Columbia University Press, 1958).

Maruyama, Masao, *Thought and Behaviour in Modern Japanese Politics* (London: Oxford University Press, 1963).

Mead, Margaret, *Soviet Attitudes Towards Authority* (New York: McGraw-Hill, 1951).

Mehnert, Klaus, *Peking and the New Left: at Home and Abroad*, China Research Monograph No. 4 (Berkeley: Center of Chinese Studies, 1969).

Meisner, Maurice, *Mao's China* (New York: Free Press, 1977).

Montgomery, R. L., S. W. Hinkle and R. F. Enjie, 'Social Change in High- and Low-Authoritarian Society', *Journal of Personality and Social Psychology*, vol. 33 (June 1966) 698–708.

Mote, F. W., 'China's Past in the Study of China Today – Some Comments on the Recent Works of Richard Solomon', *Journal of Asian Studies*, XXXII, 1 (Nov 1972) 107–20.

Munro, Donald J., *The Concept of Man in Contemporary China* (Ann Arbor: University of Michigan Press, 1977).

Nee, Victor, *The Cultural Revolution at Peking University* (New York: Monthly Review Press, 1969).

Nivison, David S., 'Communist Ethics and Chinese Tradition', *Journal of Asian Studies*, 16, 1 (Nov 1956).

Niyekawa, Agnes M., 'Factors Associated With Authoritarianism in Japan', PhD Dissertation (New York University, 1960).

Novak-Deker, Nikolai K. (ed), *Soviet Youth: Twelve Komsomol Histories* (Munich: Institute for the Study of the USSR, Series I, no. 51, July 1959).

Parsons, Talcott, *Social Structure and Personality* (London: Free Press of Glencoe, 1964).

Peking Research Group on the Problem of Family Origin, 'Origin Theory', *Middle School Revolutionary News* (*Zhongxue Wenge Bao*), 2 Feb 1967. Translated by Gordon White, *The Politics of Class and Class Origins: The Case of the Cultural Revolution* (Canberra: Australian National University Press, 1976).

Perry, Arnon and William H. Cunningham, 'A Behavioral Test of Three F Subscales', *Journal of Social Psychology*, no. 96 (1975) 271–5.

Piccone, Paul, 'From Tragedy to Farce: The Return to Critical Theory', *New German Critique*, no. 7 (Winter 1976) 91–104.

Pierce, John C. and Richard A. Pride (eds), *Cross-National Micro-Analysis: Procedures and Problems* (Beverly Hills: Sage Publications, 1972).

Pye, Lucian, *The Spirit of Chinese Politics* (Cambridge, Mass: MIT Press, 1968).

Raddock, David M., *Political Behavior of Adolescents in China – The Cultural Revolution in Kwangchow* (Tucson: University of Arizona Press, 1977).

Raynor, John, *The Middle Class* (London: Longman, 1969).

Reich, Wilhelm, *The Mass Psychology of Fascism*, 3rd edn (New York: Orgone Institute Press, 1946).

Renshon, Stanley Allen, 'The Role of Personality Development in Political Socialization', in *New Directions in Political Socialization*, ed. David C. Schwartz and Sandra Kenyon Schwartz (New York: Free Press, 1975).

Ridley, Charles, Paul Godwin and Dennis Doolin, *The Making of a Model Citizen in China* (Stanford: The Hoover Institute Press, 1971).

Riesman, David, *The Lonely Crowd: A Study of the Changing American Character* (New York: Anchor Books, 1953).

Riester, Robert W. and La Verne Irvine, 'A Methodological Inquiry into the F Scale', *Journal of Social Psychology*, no. 94 (Dec 1974) 287–8.

Rosen, Stanley, 'Comments on "Radical Students in Kwangtung during the Cultural Revolution" ', *China Quarterly*, no. 70 (June 1977) 395–6.

——— , *Red Guard Factionalism and the Cultural Revolution in Guangzhou (Canton)* (Boulder: Westview Press, 1982).

Rush, Michael and Philip Althoff, *An Introduction to Political Sociology* (Bristol: Nelson, 1971).

Samuels, Richard (ed), *Political Generations and Political Development* (Lexington, Mass: D. C. Heath, 1977).

Schwartz, David C. and Sandra Kenyon Schwartz (eds), *New Directions in Political Socialization* (New York: Free Press, 1975).

Sheng-Wu-Lian, 'Whither China?', trans. in *Peking and the New Left: at*

Home and Abroad, China Research Monograph no. 4, ed. Klaus Mehnert (Berkeley: Center of Chinese Studies, 1969).

Sheridan, Mary, 'The Emulation of Heroes', *China Quarterly*, no. 33 (Jan–Mar 1968) 47–72.

Shirk, Susan, *Competitive Comrades: Career Incentives and Student Strategies in China* (Berkeley: University of California Press, 1982).

Solomon, Richard, 'Mao's Efforts to Reintegrate the Chinese Social Process', in *Chinese Communist Politics in Action*, ed. A. Doak Barnett (Seattle: University of Washington Press, 1969).

———, *Mao's Revolution and the Chinese Political Culture* (Berkeley: University of California Press, 1972).

Spiro, Melford E., *Children of the Kibbutz* (Cambridge, Mass: Harvard University Press, 1958).

Stacey, Barrie, *Political Socialization in Western Society: An Analysis from a Life-span Perspective* (London: Edward Arnold, 1978).

Stewart, Don and Thomas Hoult, 'A Social-Psychological Theory of the Authoritarian Personality', *American Journal of Sociology*, 65, 3 (1959) 274–9.

Tapper, Ted, *Political Education and Stability: Elite Responses to Political Conflict* (London: John Wiley, 1976).

Tsurumi, Kazuko, *Social Change and the Individual—Japan Before and After Defeat in World War II* (New Jersey: Princeton University Press, 1970).

Unger, Jonathan, 'Post-Cultural Revolution Primary School Education: Selected Texts', *Chinese Education*, x, 2 (Summer 1977).

———, 'China's Troubled Down-to-the-Countryside Campaign', *Contemporary China*, iii, 2 (Summer 1979) 72–92.

———, *Education Under Mao: Class and Competition in Canton Schools, 1960-1980* (New York: Columbia University Press, 1982).

———, 'The Class System in Rural China: A Case Study', in *Class and Social Stratification in Post-Revolution China*, ed. James Watson (Cambridge University Press, 1984).

Vogel, Ezra, 'Preserving Order in the Cities', in *The City in Communist China*, ed. John Wilson Lewis (Palo Alto: Stanford University Press, 1971).

Weber, Max, *Economy and Society: An Outline of Interpretative Sociology*, ed. Guenther Roth and Claus Wittich (Berkeley: University of California Press, 1978).

Weller, Leonard, Samuel Levinbok, Rina Maimon and Shaham Asher, 'Religiosity and Authoritarianism', *Journal of Social Psychology*, no. 75 (1975) 11–18.

White, Gordon, 'The Politics of Hsia-hsiang Youth', *China Quarterly*, no. 59 (July/Sept 1974) 491–517.

———, *The Politics of Class and Class Origin: The Case of the Cultural Revolution* (Canberra: Australian National University Press, 1976).

Whyte, Martin, *Small Groups and Political Rituals in China* (Berkeley: University of California Press, 1974).

———, 'Child Socialization in the Soviet Union and China', *Studies in Comparative Communism*, x, 3 (Autumn 1977) 235–59.

Wilson, Richard, *Learning to be Chinese: The Political Socialization of Children in Taiwan* (Cambridge, Mass: MIT Press, 1970).

Wirth, Arthur G., *John Dewey as Educator: His Design for Work in Education, 1894–1904* (New York: John Wiley, 1966).

Wrong, Dennis H., 'The Pitfalls of Social Reductionism, the Oversocialized Concept of Man in Modern Society', in *Personality and Social Systems*, ed. Neil J. Smelser and William T. Smelser (New York: John Wiley, 1970).

CHINESE-LANGUAGE SOURCES

'A Brief Account of the Denunciation of Bourgeois Metaphysics by Some Teachers in Schools of Higher Education', *People's Education* (*Remin Jiaoyu*), June 1955, pp. 55–66.

'Abstract of Letters Concerning the Debate Over the Question of All-round Development', *People's Education*, Nov 1956, pp. 19–22.

Chen Yousong, 'Examining the Reactionary Influence of Hu Shi in Education and its Influence on Myself', *People's Education*, Jan 1955, pp. 32–5.

Editorial, ' "Lively Education" and New Democratic Education Are Basically Incompatible', *People's Education*, Feb 1953, p. 19.

Excerpts from Lei Feng's Diary (*Leifeng Riji Xuan*) (Peking, 1964).

Guo Lin, 'This is How We Cultivate Children's Creativity', *People's Education*, vol. 1, no. 2 (1950) pp. 51–2.

Huabei Government Education Department, *Primary School Educational Theory and Practical Reference Materials* (*Xiaoxue Jiaoyu Lilun Yu Shiji Cankao Ziliao*) (Shanghai: Xinhua Bookstore, 1949).

Huang He (Hong Kong), nos. 1–5 (1976–8).

'Lenin's Struggle Against Subjective Metaphysics and Its Meaning to Scientific Psychology and Pedagogy', *People's Education*, May 1975, pp. 9–25.

Li Bingde, 'Cleanse the Influence of "Pragmatic Education" from Our Country's Educational Arena', *People's Education*, Feb 1956, pp. 53–6.

Li Rui, *The Youthful Revolutionary Activities of Comrade Mao Zedong* (*Mao Zedong Tongzhi Shaonian Shiqi de Geming Huodong*) (Peking: China Youth Press, 1952).

'Li Yizhe and I', a 6-part series, *Bei Dou* (Hong Kong), June, July, Aug, Sept, Nov, and Dec 1977.

Liu Songtao, 'Criticize the Reactionary Educational Thoughts of Hu Shi', *People's Education*, May 1955, pp. 31–5.

Mao Zedong, 'Research in Physical Exercise' (written in 1917), in *Mao Zedong's Works* (*Mao Zedong Ji*), vol. I (Tokyo: Hokubosha, 1972) pp. 35–47.

———, *Long Live the Thought of Mao Zedong, 1969* (*Mao Zedong Sixiang Wansui, 1969*) (Taiwan, reprinted by the Institute of International Relations); translated by the US government into English as *Miscellany of Mao Tse-tung's Thought* (1949–68), *JPRS*, 61269 (20 Feb 1974).

Mo Xin, *The Road to New Education* (*Xin Jiaoyu de Daolu*) (Peking: Everybody's Bookstore, 1949).

Psychology Textbook for Teachers Colleges (*Shifan Xinlixue Keben*), 5th edn (Peking: People's Educational Publishing House, 1957).

Ren Yuwen, *How to Teach Children to Love the Country (Zemma Yang Jiaohao Haizimen Ai Guo)* (Peking: Xin Beijing Publishing Co., 1951).

Revelations that Move the Earth to Tears: A Collection of Post Cultural Revolution Poems and Essays by Chinese Youths (Ganyou Geyin Dongdi Ai) (Hong Kong: Seventies Biweekly, 1974).

'Scholar Kairov on the Main Principles in Pedagogy Involving the All-round Development of the Personality', *People's Education*, May 1957, pp. 10–11.

Stories of Young Heroes (Qingnian Yingxiung Gushi), vol. 1 (Peking: Chinese Youth Press, 1964).

Stories of Young Heroes, vol. 2 (Peking: Chinese Youth Press, 1965).

'Teachers Speaking on the Internal Contradictions of Educational Work', *People's Education*, Jan 1957, pp. 6–8.

The Thought Reform of Teachers (Jiaoshimen de Sixiang Gaizao) (Shanghai: Huadong People's Publishing Co., 1952).

Wang Tie, 'Criticizing Dewey's Theory that Education Transcends Economics and Politics', *People's Education*, Aug 1955, pp. 34–5.

'Where Is the Central Point of the Debate?', *People's Education*, Sept 1956, pp. 7–8.

Wu Yanli, 'After Reading Comrade Li Zhengzhong's "Critique on How to Implement the Five-Loves Education" ', *People's Education*, Jan 1952, p. 30.

Wu Yanyin, 'Discussions on the Characteristics of Traditional Primary Education', *People's Education*, vol. I, no. 3 (1950) pp. 22–4.

Xu Han, *An Introduction to the Teaching of Disciplinary Education to Primary School Pupils (Xiaoxue Ertong Jilu Jiaoyu Jingyan Jieshao)* (Canton: Huanan People's Publishing Co., 1953).

Yu Luojin, 'A Fairy Tale in Winter', *Dang Dai*, no. 3 (Sept 1980) pp. 58–107.

Zhang Jian, 'Criticize the Ridiculous Discussions on School Education in Dewey's Theory of Pragmatic Education', *People's Education*, July 1955, pp. 23–5.

Zhang Lingguang, 'A Discussion of the Educational Issues Concerning the Cultivation of Students' All-round Development', *People's Education*, Aug 1956, p. 48.

Zhang Tengxiao, 'Critique of "Understanding Children is an Important Condition for Becoming a Good Teacher" ', *People's Education*, vol. 1, no. 1 (1950) pp. 53–6.

———, 'Where Lies the Reactionary Nature of Pragmatic Pedagogy?', *People's Education*, May 1955, pp. 26–30.

Zhang Yiyuan, 'The Basic Situation and Tasks of New China's Pedagogy', *People's Education*, Feb 1952, pp. 15–18.

Index